Gardening
in the
CARIBBEAN

Iris Bannochie and Marilyn Light

EDITED WITH ASSISTANCE FROM

Barry R. Phillips, Dip Hort Kew, MIHort,
Curator, The Sir Harold Hillier Gardens
and Arboretum, England

CARIBBEAN

First published 1993 by
MACMILLAN EDUCATION LTD
London and Oxford
Companies and representatives throughout the world

www.macmillan-caribbean.com

ISBN 0-333-56573-8

14	13	12	11	10	9	8	7	6	5
10	09	08	07	06	05	04	03	02	01

This book is printed on paper suitable for recycling and
made from fully managed and sustained forest sources.

Printed in Malaysia

A catalogue record for this book is available from the
British Library.

Contents

LIST OF COLOUR ILLUSTRATIONS

Foreword

Iris Bannochie was a friend of mine over many years and a woman whose knowledge and experience I enjoyed tremendously. Her many exhibits of tropical plants were always a joy and gave pleasure to very many people. Her exhibits at Chelsea in particular were an outstanding event for several years and are nowadays sadly missed. One of her more dramatic exhibits was surely in St Vincent where it was assembled with some speed and eventually finished in pitch darkness. However, one could see the next day that the effort was very well worth while.

A woman of tremendous experience and wide knowledge, Iris will be much missed and I think it is unlikely that we shall ever see anyone like her again, but to have known her was a joy in itself.

L. Maurice Mason VMH

Preface and Acknowledgements

When Iris Bannochie passed away suddenly in September 1988, she left this manuscript as an unfinished dream and a legacy of a lifetime of experience growing plants in the Caribbean. I had been fortunate to have known Iris Bannochie since 1968, to have met with her on many occasions in her beloved Andromeda Gardens, St. Joseph, Barbados, and to have had her counsel when confronted with the challenge of gardening in the Caribbean. It was she who aided me to turn that challenge into an opportunity.

If I learned anything from Iris Bannochie, it was to prepare for the unexpected. Essential to her gardening success were knowledge and planning and an essential curiosity to learn something new. Completing this book as she would have liked it was a considerable challenge and was not taken lightly. I am indebted to her husband John Bannochie for his able counsel and many constructive comments during the months of preparation.

This book has been written so that little or no formal knowledge of plants is required. Indexes for both common names and botanical names are provided.

No gardening book is complete without pictures. While the majority of photographs are by the authors, others have been graciously provided by G. W. (Bill) Lennox and by Michael MacConaill. I wish to thank them for their assistance. Each source is acknowledged after the respective caption.

I also wish to acknowledge all those Caribbean gardeners who willingly shared their knowledge with me including Linda Antrobus, Angela and Michael Birkett, Diane Collins, Carmen Redman and Hazel Redman. I would also like to thank horticulturalist Ann Ginns for reading some of the chapters and for her helpful comments. I am indebted to Charles B. Thomas, President, Lilypons Water Gardens, for providing a list of Water-lily varieties suited to tropical culture.

One cannot complete a project such as this without the help and support of family, colleagues and friends. I wish to thank my husband, Michael MacConaill, for his assistance in formatting the manuscript and printing the final manuscript. I also wish to acknowledge the inspiration of my grandfather Thomas A. Light, my uncle Harold A. Light and my father, Gordon W. T. Light, who taught me at an early age to understand nature and to know her many moods; and my mother, Evlyn, who encouraged me to write and share my experience. Sharing plants, knowledge and experience is all part of the joy of gardening.

Marilyn H. S. Light

Introduction

Before the time of Columbus (AD 1492), indigenous peoples of the Caribbean region grew and harvested native plants such as the avocado pear, beans, Barbados Cherry, cassava (manioc), corn (maize), cocoa, guava, red peppers, mammee apples, peanuts, pineapples, squash, tomato and vanilla. Some of these plants are known to have been in cultivation for over 2000 years. Cotton and agaves provided fibre for clothing and hammocks; indigo and annato, pigments with which to dye the fibre. The calabash provided containers for water, bowls for food and bailers for boats. The bulb of the lovely salmon-orange Easter Lily *Hippeastrum puniceum* was used by the Carib and Arawak people as an arrow poison.

Christopher Columbus discovered some valuable spices on his voyages to the 'Indies', including allspice and red pepper. When he returned to the Caribbean in the late 1490s, he brought with him plants from Spain and the Canary Islands. These included useful plants such as oranges and cereals, ornamental plants, and as well, some very undesirable weeds. Some of the introductions spread rapidly aided both by humans and the favourable climate. The fleets of other nations that followed Columbus, the British, Dutch, French and Portuguese, populated the area with explorers, missionaries, adventurers, settlers, indentured servants and slaves. Each culture brought their own favourite plants, some to thrive, some to perish. Some of these introductions included the breadfruit, hibiscus, khus-khus grass, pigeon pea, pomelo, turmeric and rice. Settlers cleared forests to make way for crops, built houses, and around these houses established gardens.

Cottage gardens are a mixture of ornamental and food plants; flowering shrubs and annuals to the front; bananas, pigeon peas, okras, herbs, a lime or coconut tree in the back; with a pumpkin, a christophene (cho cho) or a passion fruit vine on the fence between neighbours. Suburban gardens are aflame with Bougainvilleas, Hibiscus, Mussaendas and Oleander: some may have clipped hedges and manicured lawns. Larger gardens of the old plantations and of the more affluent society may have a traditional formal style and magnificent old trees. In some cases, different levels have been used to take advantage of spectacular views. Botanical gardens, some established in the eighteenth century, contain rare examples of what once was the indigenous flora of the Caribbean.

Informal, natural gardens are now favoured as they allow the tropical living, indoor merging with the outdoor, with an open patio near the swimming pool and the barbeque in a landscaped setting of colourful shrubs, trees and vines. Palm trees provide light shade by day and a wonderful silhouette on cool, moon-lit nights.

This book is about plants for Caribbean gardens. I have written this book because I wanted to tell all gardeners, old and young, my colleagues and friends, what I have learned and thus share my experiences and knowledge of our beloved hobby, gardening. There is still so much more to be learned.

Iris Bannochie

Units, Abbreviations and Conversion Factors for Metric and Imperial Units

METRIC	IMPERIAL
Length	
10 millimetres (mm) = 1 centimetre (cm) =	0.3937 inches (in)
100 cm = 1 metre (m) =	39.4 in
1000 m = 1 kilometre (km) =	0.621 miles (m)
2.54 cm =	1 in
30.48 cm =	1 foot (ft)
Area	
1 metre × 1 metre = 1 square metre (m^2) =	10.8 square feet (ft^2)
100 m × 100 m = 10 000 m^2 = 1 hectare (ha) =	2.47 acres
Volume	
Liquid measure	
5 millilitres (ml) =	1 teaspoon (tsp)
15 ml =	1 Tablespoon (Tbsp)
28.5 ml =	1 fluid ounce (fl oz)
1000 ml = 1 litre (l) =	35 fl oz = 0.88 quart (qt)
4.5 litres =	1 Imperial gallon (gal)
Mass (weight) measures	
1000 milligrams (mg) = 1 gram (g) =	0.035 ounces (oz)
1000 g = 1 kilogram (kg) =	2.205 pounds (lb)
28.35 g =	1 oz
453.6 g =	1 lb
1 mg/kg =	1 part per million (ppm)

METRIC	IMPERIAL

Application rate/Yield

1 kilogram/hectare (kg/ha) =	0.892 lb/acre
1 metric tonne/hectare (t/ha) = 1 kg/10 m² =	0.446 ton/acre
1 kg/10 m² = 0.1 kg/m² = 100 g/m²	

Temperature

Celsius (°C)	Fahrenheit (°F)
[(9/5°C) + 32] =	°F
°C =	5/9 (°F – 32)
20°C =	68°F
100°C =	212°F

CHAPTER 1

Gardening in the Caribbean – challenge and opportunity

'How does an old and experienced gardener transfer knowledge to the young and enthusiastic without being boring? Yet, if I can arouse a little spark of interest in someone who has never gardened before, it will be worth all the effort.'   I.B.

The Caribbean Sea surrounds hundreds of islands and reefs which form a 3200 kilometre long (2000 mile) necklace. This same sea bathes the eastern coasts of Central and South America. The largest islands located east of the Gulf of Mexico are called the Greater Antilles. These are Cuba, Jamaica, Hispaniola and Puerto Rico. There are groups of smaller islands curving south: the Virgin Islands, the Leeward and Windward Islands, Trinidad and Tobago almost touching Venezuela, the Netherlands Antilles and Cayman Islands to the west and Barbados, alone and to the east. The Bahamas and the Bermudas, even though they are located north of the Greater Antilles, are generally included in the Caribbean grouping because of their common history and plants.

CLIMATE

The Caribbean region is the ideal place to grow tropical plants. There is abundant sunshine, warmth and a year-round growing opportunity. However, within the Caribbean there are a great variety of lands and islands, some with forests, lakes, rivers, mountains or volcanoes. There are relatively flat islands with golden sand beaches where the humid trade winds provide a continual breeze. There are

swamplands and arid places with all gradations between. Humidity and rainfall vary with the distance from the coast, the proximity to mountains as well as to the windward or leeward side of such higher parts. Temperature is affected by the contour and form of the surrounding land and its vegetation, average annual rainfall and the strength and direction of the prevailing winds.

Within each country, there can be considerable differences in rainfall. In the small island of Barbados for example, just west of the central ridge at approximately 300 metres (1000 ft) altitude, the annual rainfall is double that of the nearby sea coast. The moisture-laden trade winds blow from an easterly direction nearly year-round. Most of the islands that are mountainous provide sufficient barrier to the winds that the moisture they carry is deposited on the mountain slopes (Figure 1.1). Rainforests in mountainous regions may have up to 5–6 m (200–240 in) annual rainfall. Generally speaking, summers are hotter and rainy, winters cooler and drier.

There may be very definite wet and dry seasons, although these may not adhere to a rigid timetable and may vary from place to place. There can be considerable variation from one year to the next. Visitors often ask, 'When is your wet season?'. The classic reply is 'From

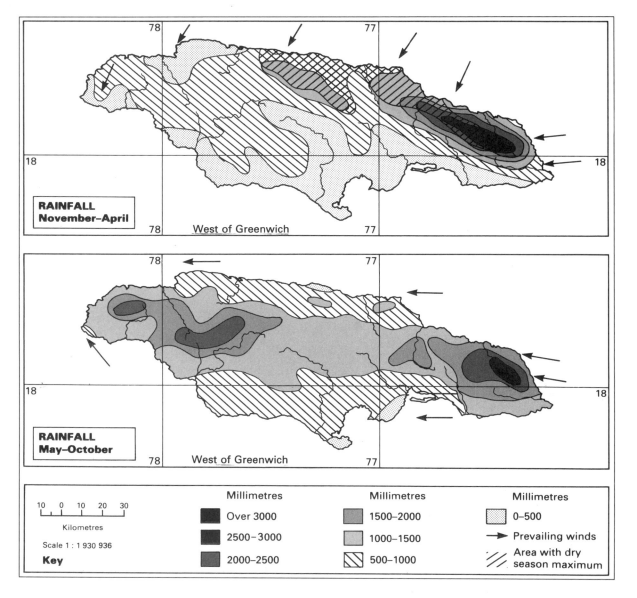

RAINFALL November–April

78 West of Greenwich 77

RAINFALL May–October

78 West of Greenwich 77

10 0 10 20 30
Kilometres
Scale 1 : 1 930 936
Key

Millimetres	Millimetres	Millimetres
Over 3000	1500–2000	0–500
2500–3000	1000–1500	→ Prevailing winds
2000–2500	500–1000	Area with dry season maximum

Figure 1.1 Patterns of rainfall may vary with the season and the direction of prevailing wind. In Jamaica from November to April when the winds are northeasterly, rainfall is concentrated in the Blue Mountains. From May to October, winds are more easterly and rainfall is concentrated on the height of land along the length of the island.

April 15, when the hotels lower their rates, to mid-December when they double them!'. Generally, the bigger or higher the island and the greater the tree cover, the more rain falls. The reciprocal is generally true: the smaller or lower or less forested the island, the less rain falls.

You can refer to seasonal rainfall maps in a Caribbean Atlas for details.

Tropical climate depends mainly upon altitude and latitude. At sea level, it is hotter and more humid near the equator (0° latitude), going cooler farther away from it. Latitude also affects the four seasons which are almost non-existent in equatorial zones but more and more noticeable as we move further away from the equator and the latitude increases.

Altitude also has an appreciable influence on temperature. The higher up, the cooler it is. Even at the equator, altitude changes the climate from distinctly tropical at sea level to sub-tropical and even to temperate. There is no true winter in the Caribbean, at least not winter by temperate zone standards! At sea level, even in December, the night temperature rarely falls below 20°C. Yet above 1500 m (5000 ft) there may be occasional frost. Such elevations are only to be found in Caribbean localities such as the Blue Mountains of Jamaica or the Cordillera Central of the Dominican Republic.

Gardeners should note that there is also a definite gradient of day/night temperature differential with elevation. Many plants respond favourably to a 5°C (9°F) or greater change between day and night. All maps carry a legend giving elevation in metres (or feet) above sea level.

Days are shorter in December. Even in the southern Caribbean, there are approximately 11 hours of daylight in December compared to 13 hours in June. Plants have adapted this subtle daylength variation, the most obvious example being the Poinsettia, blooming as it does with the shortening day.

SOIL

Caribbean lands have been derived from continental movement, volcanic eruptions, coral reefs and from sand bars. The soils found by early settlers were mostly fertile, having been enriched for centuries with decaying vegetation and volcanic ash. The advent of sugar in the Caribbean brought with it the first massive land clearances. Forests were cut down to plant sugar cane. Only the most inaccessible land escaped damage. With the uncontrolled run-off, leaching and erosion that followed, some land never recovered.

Soil, loam, dirt and mould are words used to describe a substance that forms the basis of most conventional gardens. Not all soils are alike. They have been derived from different materials such as limestone, coral, granite and lava. Each parent material has a different mineral composition and a different degree of acidity or alkalinity. Soils derived from lava and granite are acidic whereas soils derived from limestone and coral are neutral to alkaline in reaction. See Appendix 1 pH of soils found in some Caribbean islands.

Soil is often taken for granted, however, it is a valuable resource that can be easily ruined by careless management. Development of soil is not a rapid process yet is on-going. Over thousands of years, exposed rock has been weathered by heat and cold, wind and water, thus fractured into small particles to form the mineral portion of soil. Another source of mineral particles has been ash periodically spewed from volcanoes and carried downwind from the eruptions. Organic matter from plant and animal remains gradually accumulated, blending with the mineral particles to form soil. Just as volcanic eruptions and earthquakes expose new rock to the forces of weathering, so can wind and water erode unprotected soil. Floods and heavy rain can wash soil from a garden and deposit it elsewhere. Likewise winds blowing over dry, exposed garden soil can erode it. Erosion may be gradual but the effects are just as certain. Every effort should be made to reduce erosion, to conserve and to improve soil.

ASSESSING AND MODIFYING SOIL pH AND TEXTURE

Soil acidity and alkalinity

The pH scale is a measure of acidity and alkalinity with a range of 14 units. The nature of the scale is such that each point is ten times greater or lesser than the point below or above. Soils range from pH 3.0 to pH 8.5. An acidic soil has a value below pH 7.0; an alkaline soil has a value above pH 7.0. A soil with pH 6.0 is ten times more acidic than a soil at pH 7.0; a soil with pH 5.0 is ten times more acidic than one at pH 6.0 and one hundred times more acidic than one at pH 7.0.

Where the pH value of a soil is very low, that is below pH 4.7, organic matter rots slowly; the soil is too acidic to support most bacterial growth. Soluble nutrients are then easily washed away by rain. For this reason, acidic soils tend to be deficient in calcium, potassium, magnesium and copper. A gardener can raise the pH of a soil by adding appropriate amounts of lime (calcium carbonate). Lime is sold as limestone dust (a quarry by-product) or as hydrated lime. Lime is spread on the soil surface and left to work its way into the soil. Fertilizers and manures should not be applied for a few weeks after this treatment. Because of the potential serious effects of over-liming, and the narrow pH tolerance of some plants, lime additions should be followed by reassessment of soil pH after 3 months. It is always preferable to apply lime in small quantities over a long period of time rather than a large quantity all at once.

Few plants require a precisely neutral soil; most prefer a soil of pH 6.5. The availability of the most important plant nutrients is optimal at this point (Appendix 2). Soils with a pH value greater than 7.5 may appear to be deficient in minor but important nutrients such as iron and manganese. *Citrus* and *Hibiscus* grown on well-drained, alkaline clay soils (pH 7.5–8.5) will be chlorotic, their leaves pale yellow-green. The apparent deficiency cannot be corrected simply with soil applications of trace minerals. There probably are enough minerals in the soil; one (or more) is simply not available to the plants due to the high pH. It is more difficult to alter the pH of an alkaline soil. Addition of powdered sulphur to-

gether with mulches and compost is the best method although it is a lengthy process.

Modifying soil pH

Soil pH may be determined using a chemical colour indicator or pH meter. Soil test kits contain a colour indicator solution and appropriate instructions. A colour chart is provided for comparison.

TREATMENT OF ACIDIC SOIL (LESS THAN pH 6.0)

1 Raise the pH by adding ground limestone, hydrated lime or coralstone at a rate of 25 kg/100 m² (5 lbs/100 ft²). This application rate will raise the pH by 0.75 of a point on the pH scale. The effect will not be immediately apparent.
2 Re-test the soil after three months and add more lime if required.
3 Do not apply commercial fertilizers, compost or manure at the same time as the lime.

TREATMENT OF ALKALINE SOIL (GREATER THAN pH 7.0)

1 Lower the pH by adding powdered sulphur at a rate of 7.5 kg/100 m² (1.5 lbs/100 ft²). This application rate will lower the pH by 0.75 of a point.
2 Where soil is very alkaline, it is best to gradually lower the pH by making applications three months apart, always testing the soil pH before adding more sulphur.

Where masons have recently been working, newly established garden beds may exhibit problems related not to the soil itself but to cement and mortar left behind. Always watch the leaves: their colour, size and veining will tell if there is trouble with the soil. Chlorosis and other symptoms of distress will persist until the soil is freed of the highly alkaline cement residues. The soil should either be replaced or the contaminated soil should be leached (washed free) of the excess lime.

Soil texture

Soils are classified by the particle size of the mineral component.

Sandy soils are composed primarily of large particles (2.0–0.05 mm diameter) (1 mm = 0.04 in). The particles may be derived from the weathering of lava, basalt, granite, or coral and shells.

Silty soils are derived from coarse muds (0.05 – 0.002 mm diameter) carried by swift-flowing rivers and deposited when the current is no longer sufficient to carry them.

Clay soils are composed of the smallest particles (less than 0.002 mm diameter) and are derived from limestone, coral and shale.

Soil texture assessment – Hand Texturing Test

1 Take a handful of very moist soil and squeeze it firmly. Alternatively take a handful of dry soil, gradually moistening the soil while manipulating it. Avoid adding excess water.
2 Bring the soil to the consistency of putty.
3 Estimate the texture using the guidelines below.

Sand and sandy loams – form a ball that is easily broken; the soil has a gritty feeling.

Loams – form a ball upon squeezing that can be handled without breaking apart; the soil feels gritty.

Silt loams – form a ball that can be handled; the soil has a soapy feeling.

Clay loams – form a ball that is quite malleable, but resistant to breaking.

Clay – forms a ball that is plastic, sticky and highly malleable.

SOIL MANAGEMENT

Knowing the texture of your soil will help you manage it. Sandy soils are granular, the large particles cannot pack too closely; consequently sandy soils are permeable, well aerated and well drained. Coarse-textured sands and sandy loams may be dug and cultivated even when wet. Fine-textured clay soils become sticky and adhesive under similar conditions. The tiny, individual particles of clay are packed closely together; consequently clay soils are impermeable, poorly aerated and easily become waterlogged. Just as the clay forms a plastic mass during the Hand Texturing Test, so will a clay soil become putty if improperly handled. Fine-textured soils should be cultivated only when well-drained and slightly dry.

Despite obvious shortcomings, clays are some of the best soils with which to start gardening. They hold plant nutrients, retain moisture and resist leaching. They can become very fertile when lightened with sand and humus. Loams, with a balance of both sizes of particles, are intermediate in their permeability, aeration and internal drainage.

The physical character of a soil is difficult to change, but the texture can be modified with the addition of organic matter such as compost, manure and mulches. Ideally soil is 45% mineral matter, 50% water and air, and 5% organic matter. The addition of organic matter will improve the permeability, aeration and drainage of clay soil by separating fine mineral particles, making space for water and air to pass between them. The addition of organic matter to sandy soil improves the water-holding capacity of soil, the added particles behaving like tiny sponges within the soil matrix. Gardeners forever search for the perfect soil – deep, dark, rich and perfectly drained. Few find that ideal. However with hard work and conscientious effort, even the poorest soil can be modified to come close to the ideal. Composts and mulches are the most important soil modifiers.

Soil modification using organic matter

Soil organic matter is a complex mixture of material in various stages of decomposition. Plant residues such as roots, stalks, fallen leaves and branches are composed of carbohydrates and proteins that furnish food for soil organisms such as earthworms, bacteria, fungi and protozoa. These organisms assimilate the material into their body tissue giving off energy as heat, nitrogen in the form of ammonia, and also carbon dioxide (and some water). This process gradually eliminates the sugars, starches, proteins and cellulose, leaving the more stable compounds such as waxes, resins and lignins. The end product of organic matter decomposition is humus. This black organic residue has low nutritional value but is a valuable soil conditioner, affecting both the soil structure (aggregation of particles) and the nutrient-holding capacity of the soil.

Organic matter is essential to soil: regular additions are necessary. Nitrogen, phosphorus and potassium are released during the rapid decomposition of green plant material. In the Caribbean, the best times to add organic matter are at the beginning of the rainy season, to assist drainage and prevent tropical downpours from eroding and leaching soil nutrients, and at the beginning of the dry seasons, when mulches are applied to hold the moisture and to keep roots cool.

COMPOSTING

Recycling of plant and animal material is nothing new to gardeners. When we take spent blooms, fallen leaves, clippings and kitchen waste that would otherwise be unsightly litter and turn this into a valuable soil conditioner, that is conservation.

Compost can be made above ground in piles or below ground in trenches. The garden site should be carefully chosen. The composting area should be located in a sunny area that is well-drained but out of sight, screened by shrubs or vines. Water should be close at hand. Never throw away or burn any vegetable matter or kitchen scraps. In a large- or medium-size garden there is always a plentiful supply of garden waste.

Compost pile for a medium to large-size garden

Composting is a process by which organic matter is encouraged to decompose in a fairly rapid, controlled manner. Not only are plant remains essential to the process but also air, water, and micro-organisms assist decomposition. A container is needed such as a pen made of bamboo posts, wooden stakes, pipe, boards or concrete blocks. A wall can form one side. Several small piles are easier to control than one very large one. A good, manageable size is 2 × 3 m (6 × 10 ft) at the base. It should not be more than 2 metres (6 ft) high when the pile has finally settled and been left to decompose.

Before starting to collect material for composting, prepare a coarse platform about 50 cm (20 in) deep from big tree branches, bamboo, and coconut limbs. To this add coconut husks and shells, and other palm debris. The platform is necessary to ensure good aeration and drainage during the composting process. To ensure continued aeration and to reduce the labour of manually aerating the pile by turning it, the gardener should have a few 3-metre (10 ft) lengths of 5 cm (2 in) diameter plastic water pipe, already pierced all along their length with big holes. A drill or a soldering iron can be used to make the holes. Place these pipe horizontally on the heap on top of the coarse material. The ends of the pipe should stick out for 30 cm (12 in) or so at both ends. These pipes allow air into the heap, speeding up the decomposition process and the generation of heat. The same pipes can be used over and over again. This initial investment will be repaid many times when you consider that the alternative is the manual turning of the compost heap using a fork!

The daily collection of fallen leaves, dead flowers and pulled weeds can now be added on top of the pipes. Do not add badly diseased or insect-infested material directly to the heap: such material should be burnt and the ashes added to the heap. The top of the pile should remain flat or slightly concave to encourage better collection and absorption of water. The pile requires adequate moisture throughout the decomposition process. Try to add some dry vegetable matter as well as the softer green pieces. Keep the composting material damp, covering it with black plastic sheeting by night which assists in keeping in the heat generated by the pile and reduces the loss of moisture and gases.

As the material decomposes it will sink. When the pile stands waist-high, sprinkle about 1 kg (2.2 lb) of a nitrogenous fertilizer (ammonium sulphate) on top. Water well and continue adding material until the sinking slows. If you have not used pipes to aerate the pile, use a fork now to turn the material before adding the next layer.

The next layer should be animal manure or seaweed and be about 30 cm (12 in) thick. If these materials are unavailable, use garden soil. Sprinkle this layer with 1 kg (2.2 lb) of a general purpose fertilizer such as 12–12–17. This layer is sometimes called the activator. Activators provide more nutrients to the micro-organisms and so hasten the process. Accelerated decomposition also generates sufficient heat to kill weed seeds and many plant pathogens.

More layering of material can continue until the pile nears 2 m (6 ft) in height. The first layer is always soft garden waste, followed by a second layer of dry garden waste, followed by another layer of organic manure, seaweed or soil and a fertilizer. During the entire composting period, the pile should be kept moist and covered. The compost will be ready to use in three to five months.

Open the pile and remove the decomposed material. Any material not fully broken down should be added to a new pile. A wise gardener maintains two or three piles in different stages of decomposition so that there is always a supply of compost ready for necessary soil amendment.

Trench method for a small garden

The trench method has the disadvantage that the trench can be flooded by torrential rains but for a small garden it has considerable advantages. It is tidier and requires much less material. In dry weather, the composting material will retain its moisture better. If water is in short supply, this will be extremely advantageous. Without moisture, nothing will decompose.

Dig four or five pits 125 × 125 cm (50 × 50 in). The depth should measure 15 cm (6 in). Into one of the pits put green grass clippings and small prunings. Shape the pile to form a depression in the centre and put kitchen waste such as peelings in the hole. Cover this with dry stuff such as leaves and twigs then continue adding garden clippings until the pile measures 50 cm (20 in) above the ground. Add a layer of animal manure, seaweed or soil, and ammonium sulphate or an all-purpose fertilizer as with the heap method. Wet the heap thoroughly and cover with black plastic. At the same time, begin filling the second trench.

When the temperature in trench number one has cooled (about two weeks), open the pile and transfer the contents to trench two. At the same time, begin filling the third trench. Basically, the decomposing pile gets transferred from one trench to another until the compost is well broken down and ready to use.

Plastic bag method for a small garden in a dry climate

Kitchen waste and garden clippings can be

composted using large black plastic garbage bags. This method is probably the most conservative of water and suited to a small garden. Place two bags, one inside the other, in a wooden frame or drum. During the day, keep the bag open and in the sun. As plant debris is added so should 1–2 litres (1–2 quarts) of water. At night, the mouth of the bag should be closed. When the bag is very full, add 250 ml (1 cup) of ammonium sulphate or another nitrogen-rich fertilizer and another 1 litre (1 quart) of water. Close the bag and keep in a sunny location. After one week, open the bag and add another 1 litre (1 quart) of water. The bag can be opened from time to time to check on the results. It will take from three to five months to have useable compost.

MULCHING

Mulches are any material which can be used to cover soil. The most natural mulches are fallen leaves beneath a tree. Other mulches include compost, animal and green manures, seaweed, peanut shells and even newspapers. Adding mulch to cover the soil in all parts of the garden can only be advantageous if it is properly applied and is sufficiently rotted.

Animal wastes are generally mixed with bedding such as bagasse, sawdust or straw. When fresh, animal manures smell, they can burn plant roots and may contain numerous viable weed seeds. When covered and left to compost, the smell disappears, the seeds are killed by the heat of composting and the product no longer burns plants. Composted manure makes an excellent mulch.

Green manures are quick growing plant crops which are grown with the special intent that they will be dug up and returned to the soil while they are still green. In effect, the crop acts both as a living mulch and an economical way to enrich the soil. The process is particu-

larly valuable for improving the texture of light sandy soils. Those plants best suited to green manuring are herbaceous, bushy, rapid growers that can cover a large space in a short period of time. A poor garden bed can be improved by using bush String Beans or bush Soya Beans, reaping the crop before digging the bushes into the soil. Beans and Peas are legumes which can fix atmospheric nitrogen with the aid of special bacteria living with their roots. Once the plants decompose in the soil, the fixed nitrogen and other plant substances are liberated.

Leguminous Rabbit Vine *Teramnus labialis* or *Tephrosia wallichii* can be used as green manures provided they are not permitted to seed before digging under. Likewise the Demerara Primrose *Asystasia gangetica* spreads rapidly, bears pretty flowers and its leaves are rich in protein. These plants are particularly useful on a slope to reduce erosion and surface wash. They can be dug under in strips so that the entire slope is never barren. Shrubs can then be planted in the improved soil and stabilized slope.

Bagasse, the fibrous remnant of sugar cane after grinding, makes an excellent mulch when composted for three years prior to use.

Newspapers are cheap. The paper is biodegradable plant pulp and will rot given time. Wet newspapers can be used to control weed growth around newly planted shrubs and trees. Each plant can have its own newspaper, slit up the centre to fit snuggly about the stem. If weeds persist, a second or third newspaper applied around the tree will hold them in check. Likewise wet newspaper can be used in the vegetable garden to keep roots cool and to control weeds. The paper can be lifted to apply granular fertilizer. The unsightly newspapers can be covered with soil and eventually will degrade to become part of the soil.

All of these fibrous plant remains will assist

in soil improvement. Some may be slow to disintegrate but the eventual benefit is great.

WATER

Rain is a welcomed event in a gardener's life. Gentle soaking rain – there is nothing quite like it for making plants grow. Sometimes there will be too much and you wish it would stop, but do remember that life cannot exist without water and that all water comes from rain.

Water is precious and can be a hoarded, expensive commodity where rains are infrequent. Small flat islands, especially those without trees, are relatively dry. Rain must be collected from roof-tops and stored in cisterns. An expensive alternative is the desalination plant. Even where water is more plentiful, there may be restrictions on garden and home use during extended droughts. We cannot control the weather so we must learn to garden with it.

Drainage, irrigation and watering are part of a gardener's life. Unexpected floods and droughts may upset the routine, however the Caribbean gardener must be prepared for the worst while enjoying the best that the climate has to offer.

Making the garden drought-tolerant

Removal of weeds is a priority: they consume water as much as garden plants. Heavy organic mulches should be applied to the exposed soil surface at the beginning of the dry season to prevent undue evaporation and to keep roots cool. Mulches must be renewed as they eventually decompose. Be certain that the soil surface is not compacted. Forking or tilling will ensure that water enters the soil and does not simply run off the surface. In planning a garden, group together drought-tolerant plants such as cactus, succulents and Bougainvillea. Such beds will not require watering during the average dry season.

DRAINAGE

Drainage whether it be artificial or natural is essential to all cultivated soils. Rainwater or piped water is absorbed by the soil and filters down through it. A problem arises if an excessive amount of water or too little water is retained. The soil should be modified to hold moisture but at the same time be freely draining. Some garden sites are on sloping ground. If the slope is gentle, water drains away naturally. More often the slope is acute or non-existent.

The gardener that has a swampy patch can do some remedial work by observing at the end of the dry season exactly where and how large are the remaining muddy areas. Any drainage system will have to originate there. The next problem is to find a place on the property which is low enough for water to be led away. This could be a pond, a dry well or a drainage ditch or canal. In the Caribbean, open drains should be used whenever possible so that they can be cleaned regularly. A dirty drain is often worse than no drain at all as the dirt and litter choking it will be scattered everywhere when a tropical downpour occurs. Usually open drains are just ditches, dug to about 50 cm (20 in) and with sufficient slope to lead water to a suitable outlet. The fall should be around 10 cm in each 30 m (4 in per 100 ft). To make the drain efficient, the bottom can be lined with tiles which are specially made for the purpose. The tiles must be carefully laid with the correct gradient to carry off the water. Paths can sometimes be used as emergency drains but they have to be properly graded, well constructed and maintained.

Where open drains cross a path, a simple tunnel can be made by digging a trench, pouring in about 10 cm (4 in) of concrete, laying the trunk of Banana on top and covering the whole with more concrete. In a week or two, the Banana tree can be pulled out quite easily, leaving an effective culvert.

In small gardens, an open drain can be unsightly and not at all practical in some areas such as lawns or borders. In these situations, a French drain can be constructed. An open drain is dug about 1 m (3 ft) deep on a gradient of 10 cm in 30 m (4 in per 100 ft). The first 50 cm (20 in) is filled with large stones. Soil and then turf are added to cover the stones. In steep places, a piece of pipe with a minimum diameter 15 cm (6 in) can be used in place of stones. The open ends of such a culvert must be kept free of debris and grass as it cannot function if it is blocked.

On steeper sites, open contoured drains at certain places may be needed to stop torrential tropical rains from causing serious soil erosion. Run the drains and garden beds horizontally along the contour and across the slope gradient. The drains should be about 75 cm (30 in) deep with a gradient of between 10 cm in 2.5 m (4 in per 8 ft) and up to 10 cm in 4 m (4 in per 13 ft) depending upon the dry-ness or the steepness of the land. Remember the steeper the slope, the greater the rate of flow and the greater the need for slowing the rush of run-off. The latter drain is appropriate for the steeper slope. The drains can be augmented with catchment pits at intervals. These pits will trap any soil carried by the water, which can later be recovered and spread on the garden.

On the very steepest sites, terracing is more appropriate. No attempt must be made to stop the flow of water entirely or serious damage may occur. Instead, alternate garden terraces with rows of hedging plants or ground cover planted along the contour (Figure 1.2).

IRRIGATION

There are two ways of applying water to plants: by sprinkling – overhead watering as rain, or by soaking – letting the water seep into the

Figure 1.2 Field showing terracing

Gardening in the Caribbean

soil. Irrigation and watering are really the same thing, differing only in the origin of the two words. Irrigation usually implies some sort of activated system. Watering generally means using a watering can or holding a hose and wetting plants individually. This can be tedious and time-consuming especially if the garden is large and there are many container-grown plants. Hand watering gives the gardener more control. Some form of irrigation is needed in every garden but it is especially important in countries with seasonal rains. The gardener can practise water conservation, cut the water bill, and save time by practising good husbandry and by having efficient irrigation methods and equipment.

Sprinkling – pros and cons

The simplest kind of irrigation is having a few well-spaced faucets (water outlets with a tap) located strategically throughout the garden. A garden hose can then be attached and used for hand watering or for sprinkling (overhead watering). Where water is rich in lime, sprinkler jets may become clogged, requiring regular maintenance. While sprinkling will wash dust and dirt from leaves, it is not a very efficient method of watering garden plants. A gardener may find it necessary to hand water after sprinkling! Sprinkling a garden in the heat of the day wastes more water than sprinkling at night. The only place where daytime sprinkling is to be recommended is in a shadehouse, fernery or orchid growing area. Here the water that evaporates is not wasted but provides beneficial cooling, by evaporation, and necessary high atmospheric humidity.

Drip irrigation

A more highly recommended method of watering is drip irrigation. This method is very economical as little water is wasted by evaporation. Drip irrigation may be used in garden beds, fields and even in pots. The drip system releases small quantities of water at carefully spaced exit points in a network of tubes or pipes. An individual tree, shrub or pot plant can have its own drip outlet, likewise the pipes can be laid along the rows of crops to be irrigated. One must purchase the equipment but where water is not cheap, this is a very good system (Figure 1.3).

Sub-irrigation

Large gardens with substantial plantings of shrubs and trees in shallow soil over bedrock can make use of sub-irrigation, an underground network of pipes to carry water to designated locations (Figure 1.4). The pipes are laid 50–75 cm (20–30 in) deep, small holes being made in the pipe that allow water to emerge where needed. In gardens where the climate is dry year-round, the soil will have to be periodically leached to rid it of dissolved

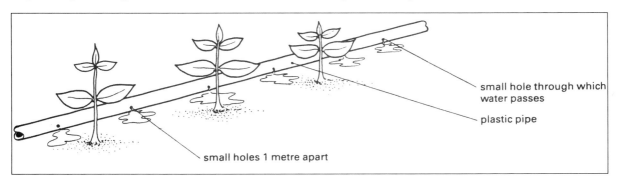

small hole through which water passes

plastic pipe

small holes 1 metre apart

Figure 1.3 Drip irrigation

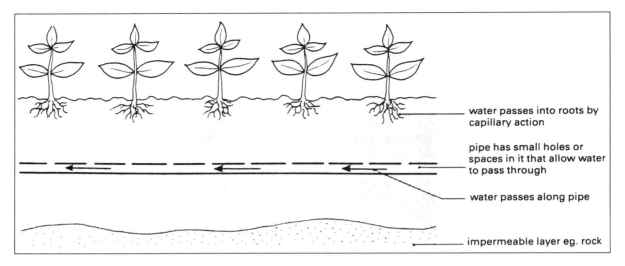

water passes into roots by capillary action

pipe has small holes or spaces in it that allow water to pass through

water passes along pipe

impermeable layer eg. rock

Figure 1.4 Sub-irrigation

salts. Otherwise, seasonal rains will minimize the problem. The major advantage of sub-irrigation is that above ground activities are not impeded by wet soil, pipes, sprinklers or ditches.

Using natural water courses

Most often you may think of water coming from rain, city supply or a well. Water may also be taken from a stream provided that it is sweet and not contaminated with salt, herbicides or other noxious substances. Some water from a stream can be diverted to form a pond or can even be led via channels to irrigate part of the garden. It is most important not to site a pond within the natural stream course as heavy run-off will cause flooding and silting. A pond should always be situated to one side of the stream.

A stream can be used as a source of irrigation water even if it passes through the lower part of the garden. A hydraulic ram (or hydram) can be used to pump water uphill using the stream flow as the sole source of energy to move the water. The stream must have a moderate flow. Water is carried from the stream to the ram using a pipe. Some of the flow is trapped by the ram and sent elsewhere. The remainder flows into the stream further downhill. The hydraulic ram is truly unique and most useful investment if a stream runs near the garden.

SALINITY

The islands of the Caribbean are surrounded by ocean. Land close to sea, especially on a windward coast, is coated with salt-laden sea spray carried by the wind. The soil can contain considerable accumulated salt. Only salt-tolerant plants will thrive close to the shore, above the highwater mark. As one moves inland and the salt content of the soil diminishes, more and more plants can be grown. Salt-tolerant trees include Coconut *Cocos*, Mile Trees *Casuarina*, Button Mangrove *Conocarpus*, Mangroves *Rhizophora*, Sea Grape *Coccoloba* and Whitewood *Tabebuia pallida*. Salt-tolerant shrubs and herbs include the Prickly Pear cactus *Opuntia*, Spanish Bayonet and Adam's Needle *Yucca*, Purslane *Portulaca*, Slipper Flower *Pedilanthus* and *Tamarix*. These plants are also drought-tolerant.

Gardening in the Caribbean

EQUIPMENT

TOOLS

Tools are essential for garden work. Choosing the correct tool to do a particular task will save time and energy. Tools are expensive and should be considered a long term investment. A well-made, expensive trowel that gives many years of excellent service is to be recommended over a cheap one that requires repair or replacement every few months. A regular maintenance schedule will ensure that your investment is secure. Wash, dry and oil your gardening tools after each use. Protect the cutting edges, sharpening them as needed. Store tools in a shed or workshop, not simply propped against a wall but hanging individually on appropriate supports. All this effort will be rewarded by having a tool ready and able to do a job when required.

Tools can range from the historic machete or cutlass to computerized automatic watering systems. Whatever the level of technology, whether a tool be powered by electricity, petrol, wind, solar energy or sheer elbow-grease, it should save time and energy. Beware of 'useless fad implements' which merely clutter up the tool shed!

SOLAR STERILIZER

The same tropical climate that supports the growth of beautiful Hibiscus and Bougainvilleas, unfortunately also encourages the proliferation of pests and diseases. A Solar Sterilizer can be an inexpensive asset in the constant battle against these foes. It can be used to heat-sterilize pots, soil, crocks and pruning tools, and with the aid of abundant free sunshine.

The first solar-powered box built by Iris Bannochie in 1970, was designed to dry and preserve Breadfruit chips and Coconut for use as food for cows, pigs and fish. It was also useful for sterilizing small garden implements and soil. This original model was too shallow for larger articles or big batches of soil. So when it began to disintegrate after ten years of hard work, a new box was designed and built to replace it.

The original model was a shallow double-walled wooden box, 75 cm × 225 cm (2 ft 6 in × 7 ft 6 in) overall, with coconut fibre insulation packed in the wall cavities. (Fibre glass insulation could be used in place of coconut fibre.) The roof was made of a double layer of glass and sloped, the front wall being 20 cm high (8 in), the rear wall 25 cm high (10 in) and hinged at the bottom for access. Air holes were drilled through the bottom of the box and fitted with pieces of hose to prevent loss of insulation. The hinged door at the back was loosely fitted to allow hot air to escape. The temperature could reach over 113°C (235°F)!

The new box has been made to stand on trestles and is easily moved to take full advantage of the sun. It has the front wall as well as the roof made of double glass (3 mm (1/8 in) thick window glass). Temperatures in this one rise to just over 94°C (200°F) on a sunny afternoon.

Sterilizing soil using a Solar Sterilizer

Although the term 'sterilization' is commonly used, the soil is in fact pasteurized with the majority of organisms killed by heat. While 75°C (170°F) is more than sufficient to kill damping-off fungi, insects, mites and nematodes, it may not be enough to kill bacterial spores or to inactivate some plant viruses. Use a thermometer to determine the actual temperature reached in your Solar Sterilizer. Insert the thermometer bulb in the soil. A battery-powered electronic thermometer with a remote probe would be useful. Be certain that the soil reaches 75°C (170°F) and remains at that temperature for at least 45–60 minutes. For best results, lightly dampen the soil before treatment. Let the soil cool for 24 hours before using.

HOUSING FOR FERNS AND FOR ORCHIDS

Fern and orchid houses can be built with wooden laths laid about 8 cm (3 in) apart. The laths should run north–south so as the sun traverses the sky, the ferns will have alternate periods of sun and shade. Polypropylene shade cloth rated 50–90 per cent shade will also provide protection from bright sun. Shade cloth can be supported on a wooden or metal frame. Some gardeners plant vines to help provide shade; this is not entirely satisfactory as the shade easily becomes excessive and the vines may harbour pests.

CHALLENGE AND OPPORTUNITY

Climate and soil are the two most important points to consider when choosing a site for a garden and when choosing plants for a site. Soils can be improved and their composition and characteristics modified but changing the climate is a much more difficult task. Within a garden microclimates can be created. Trees can be planted to provide shade and shelter but they take time to grow.

A gardener must decide if the climate is suitable for favourite plants or whether plants suitable to the climate must be found. Observe the plant species growing well in an existing garden: this will give some clues as to what can be grown. Looking at neighbouring gardens and talking to their owners may also help with decisions about choice of plants.

There are many challenges and openings available to the Caribbean gardener. The opportunities abound for those who plan a garden to harmonize with the nature of the surroundings.

CHAPTER 2

How plants grow and how to grow them well

'There is no end to learning, especially about plants.' I. B.

Gardening is all about plants. If you are to cultivate plants, propagate them and grow them to perfection, you should know something about how they are constructed, how they live, grow, and reproduce.

PLANT STRUCTURES AND FUNCTIONS

HOW PLANTS GROW

For the most part, plant organs are interdependent. During seed germination, first the root develops, then the shoot. The root absorbs water and minerals from the soil, then the shoot draws necessary water and mineral nutrients from the root. Seedlings develop green leaves and are then able to harvest sunlight energy through the process of **photosynthesis**. Sugars manufactured in leaves through photosynthesis are transported to the roots. The rapidly expanding root system takes up more water and mineral nutrients to support the growing shoot; and the plant grows!

Death of the roots means no water can be absorbed: the leaves wither and die. Extensive defoliation because of insect attack means little or no photosynthesis and less energy available for growth and development.

The vigour of a plant is related to its photosynthetic function. Every green plant has its own particular light requirement at which point food production and food utilization are in balance with the available light. Shade-tolerant plants have a lower light requirement to maintain a balance than those requiring a full sun exposure. Plants having a greater light requirement do poorly when grown in the shade. Plants may provide some clues to their light requirements. Those with thin, delicate foliage often require shade while those with rugged, waxy leaves require more light.

Roots can grow both horizontally and vertically in the soil. Delicate, single-celled root hairs are the most important parts of a root. They are produced in a circular band behind the growing point, the root tip. As the root elongates, older root hairs die and new ones are formed to take their place. Root hairs are the principal means by which plants absorb water and mineral nutrients.

Newly transplanted seedlings can wilt, not because of insufficient water but because of massive loss of absorptive root hairs. To avoid such wilting, conserve as much of the root as possible by growing seedlings in individual pots, transplanting the seedlings with the root ball and root hairs intact.

Roots that grow from any part of the plant body other than the root area are called **adventitious roots**. They can arise from the base of the stem as in Indian Corn *Zea mays*, from a node or from stems between nodes as in Banyans *Ficus*, Mangroves, Red Hot Poker *Norantea* or Nutmeg *Myristica*. Some plants develop roots from their leaves: the leaves of African Violet *Saintpaulia*, *Begonia*, *Peperomia* and *Sansevieria* will form roots when cut from the parent plant and placed in moistened sand. Leaves of Mexican Hat *Kalanchoe daigremontianum* go one step further, producing not only roots but also plantlets at notches along their leaf margins.

Shoots differ from roots in many ways. Shoots have leaves especially designed to harvest an optimum amount of sunlight. The stems themselves may also be photosynthetic organs, especially in young plants or where leaves are absent as in the cactus. Shoots have **nodes**, the points where leaves arise. Nestled in the axil of a leaf, are one or more **axillary buds**. Gardeners refer to these buds as eyes. Axillary buds can be vegetative, producing only stems and leaves or they can be reproductive, producing flowers, or they can be both vegetative and reproductive, producing stems, leaves and flowers. Shoots may be erect as in trees and shrubs, or climbing and twining as in Pumpkin *Cucurbita*: they also can be prostrate rhizomes, located at or below the soil surface as in Ginger *Zingiber* and Turmeric *Curcuma*, or they may be specialized food storage organs (tubers) as in English Potato *Solanum tuberosum*.

Woody plants grow from a rapidly dividing tissue (**meristem**) located in stem and root tips and in a cylinder of similar tissue (**cambium**) that extends the length of stems and roots. New tissue is produced both at the growing point in the tip of a root or shoot, and also from the cambium in the stems and roots. In woody plants such as *Bougainvillea*, *Cassia*, *Citrus*, *Hibiscus* and *Rosa*, and in herbaceous plants such as *Coleus*, the growing point is found in both axillary and apical buds. Axillary buds remain dormant under the influence of hormones produced by the growing point. If the growing point (apical bud) is removed by pruning, dormancy of certain axillary buds is broken and their development begins. This is the reason why pruning works.

Bark cambium is found in woody stems just beneath the bark. It produces new bark cells. Very young shoots (**softwood**) are soft, green and without bark. As the woody stem develops, bark begins to form (**semi-softwood**). As the bark development progresses, the shoot is referred to as **hardwood**. These terms take on greater meaning when taking cuttings for propagation.

Gingers, Bananas, Orchids, Palms and Grasses produce shoots from a basal meristem, not from an apical one. New tissue is produced from the base of a shoot, not from its apex. There is no cylinder of meristematic tissue extending along the length of the stem, although there may be nodes having a layer of rapidly dividing tissue. Grasses, Sugar Cane *Saccharum* and Bamboo *Dendrocalamus* have obvious nodes (joints), at which point roots and new shoots can arise. Thus pieces of healthy stem with several nodes are taken for vegetative propagation. Grasses and Bamboos are commonly established using this method.

Some plants do not respond to pruning. Bananas *Musa* and *Heliconia* lack nodes on their upright growths: they grow from nodes of a swollen stem found in the soil. Although the upright shoots may be referred to as 'stems or trunks', they are only pseudostems, little more than an extended furl of leaves. To divide a Banana you must take a division (sucker) including some of the meristem at the base of the mother plant. Cuttings cannot be taken of the upright growth that lacks meristem – it will not grow.

Palms including Caribbean Royal Palm *Roystonea oleracea* have their growing point at the base of the shoot although that point is located high above the ground in the crownstalk near the top of the tree. As you may have observed, the death of the top of a palm results in the death of the whole tree. Without meristematic tissue the length of the stem, no new side branches can develop, no new leaves can form: the plant dies. Some palms such as Golden Palm *Chrysalidocarpus lutescens* form offsets from the base of the principal trunk and may be propagated using rooted suckers.

Buds are compressed stems, having juvenile leaves and sometimes even flower buds waiting for the appropriate cues to begin growth and development. Plant buds may remain dormant for long periods, surrounded by bud scales to ensure their survival. When a bud breaks dormancy, new cells are formed by the meristem, these cells elongating and differentiating to form a new stem, leaves and flowers. A cabbage cut longitudinally gives a good representation of a bud. Central to the bud is a stem from which leaves emerge. There is a growing point at the tip of the stem but in the leaf axils are found axillary buds. Sports (see page 29) can arise from buds.

Leaves vary greatly in shape, size, texture and colour. A leaf may be simple, entire or lobed as in Breadfruit *Artocarpus*, or it can be compound, divided into many segments or leaflets such as in Flamboyant *Delonix regia*. The limb of Coconut Palm *Cocos* is a compound leaf; that of Banana *Musa*, is simple. Whatever its size, colour or shape, the principal function of a leaf is the capture of sunlight energy and photosynthesis. Leaves have special pores that permit gases such as carbon dioxide, oxygen and water vapour to move in and out. Some leaves are specialised to perform tasks such as climbing, floating, catching insects for food, or even protecting a plant from predation. Cactus spines are modified leaves which both effectively reduce leaf surface and water loss (transpiration) and ward off herbivores. An examination of a plant's leaves and more importantly its flowers is a necessary step to its identification.

Some plants are prized for their attractive variegated foliage. Their leaves are variably mottled, blotched or striped with white, cream, pink, red or a myriad of combinations. Such plants include varieties of *Dracaena*, *Acalypha*, *Hibiscus* and *Bougainvillea*. While variegated foliage plants are decorative, they sometimes lack sufficient normal green tissue for sustained growth and development. They will always require more light than their normal green-leaved counterparts and if planted in too much shade, may revert from the variegated to green-leaf state. To maintain variegated plant cultivars, situate them in a bright spot, provide adequate fertilizer and water, and be ready to remove any normal-foliage shoots that may develop (reversion).

PLANT NUTRIENTS AND FERTILIZERS

Plants cannot live and grow without mineral nutrients. Soil, even so-called rich soil, has limited supplies of nutrients. Flooding rains can leach soil of soluble minerals, likewise, continuous cropping of the same plant can leave a soil lacking in certain minerals, especially so if the plant remains are not composted and returned to the ground. Soil acidity or alkalinity can immobilize certain minerals to the extent that even addition of commercial fertilizers may be in vain.

Plants need large quantities of the major nutrients, nitrogen (N), phosphorus (P) and potassium (K); lesser quantities of the minor nutrients, calcium (Ca), magnesium (Mg), sulphur (S) and iron (Fe). They need even smaller quantities of the trace elements, manganese (Mn), copper (Cu), boron (B), zinc (Zn) and molybdenum (Mo). To enrich the soil and to ensure that there is adequate nutrient available for plants, fertilizers are applied by the gardener.

Fertilizers may be divided into two main classes.

1 Organic fertilizers are of animal or plant origin and are applied to the soil in the form of mulches, composts and farm manure. These materials are more beneficial as additives to improve soil texture than as reliable sources of plant nutrient. Fresh animal manure can burn (scorch) plants: organic fertilizers should be well aged before use to avoid this form of damage.

2 Inorganic fertilizers are chemical or mineral in origin and may be applied in solid or liquid form. They can be purchased from garden centres. Most products have little effect on soil texture but provide adequate mineral nutrition depending on individual formulations. Inorganic fertilizers should be applied according to the manufacturers' instructions.

Both organic and inorganic fertilizers are of varying composition. Animal manure composition is less certain and will vary according to the animal species of its origin. For example, poultry manure is richer in nitrogen and phosphorus, and lower in potassium than that from cattle.

Most commercial fertilizers contain the three major plant nutrients, nitrogen (N), phosphorus (P) and potassium (K). The relative proportions of N–P–K in the product is shown as three numbers, for example 7–7–7 or 20–20–20 units of NPK: other nutrients may or may not be present. A fertilizer formulation 2–1–1 contains twice the available nitrogen as phosphorus or potassium. A 20–10–10 formulation has the same relative proportion of nutrients but is more concentrated. If minor nutrients are contained in a product, their proportion will be listed on the package. A commercial product having all major and minor nutrients is called a **balanced fertilizer**. Fertilizers designed for a particular use might be high in nitrogen (for lawns) or high in phosphorus and potassium (for fruit and flowers). Other products might be formulated for particular plants such as *Hibiscus* or *Rosa*.

Major plant nutrients

Nitrogen is used by a plant to make protein and is essential for vigorous growth. Healthy, dark green foliage is a sign of adequate nitrogen. The absence or deficiency of nitrogen is indicated by uniform yellowing of entire leaves including the veins.

Nitrogen fertilizers are easily leached from the soil and therefore should be supplied in small amounts on a regular basis rather than all at once. This is especially true of high rainfall regions.

Sources of nitrogen include manures, ammonium sulphate, potassium nitrate and urea.

Phosphorus is essential for several plant processes including photosynthesis, utilization of food reserves, cell division and reproduction. Plants with adequate supplies of phosphorus have healthy root systems, bountiful flowers and fruit. Plants suffering from phosphorus deficiency have poor rooting systems, inhibited growth and small, reddish bronze leaves.

Phosphorus is commonly present in the soil but unavailable due to the formation of insoluble compounds with iron in acid soil or calcium in alkaline soil. Adjustment of soil pH will help to make some of the phosphorus available to the plants. Additional regular application of phosphorus-containing fertilizer is beneficial.

Fertilizers rich in available phosphorus include superphosphate.

Potassium derives its name from 'pot ashes'. It is essential for plant processes including metabolism of nutrients, synthesis of proteins and promotion of growth, flowering and fruiting. Potassium deficiency causes yellowing and withering of leaf edges and tips; stems become slender and fruit production decreases.

Potassium is very soluble and easily leached from well-drained soils. Palms in particular respond to regular application of potassium in the form of potassium chloride (muriate of potash), potassium nitrate and potassium sulphate (sulphate of potash).

Calcium is essential to the development of cell structure. Without it, fruit production will be limited, roots stunted, leaves will yellow and terminal buds die.

Soils derived from coral or limestone are rich in calcium. Deficiency is only a problem in very acid soils and silts. Guyana imports coralstone dust to improve its coastal silt soils. Calcium-rich products are ground dolomite, gypsum, limestone, coral and shells.

Magnesium is part of the chlorophyll molecule and is therefore essential to photosynthesis and plant growth. A symptom of deficiency is chlorosis or yellowing of the leaf tissue found between the veins. This will be seen first on older leaves. Uptake of magnesium by a plant may be confounded by the high potassium content in a soil.

Dolomitic lime (dolomite) and Epsom Salts (magnesium sulphate) are sources of magnesium.

Sulphur is essential to the synthesis of plant proteins and oils. When sulphur is lacking, young leaves are small, thin and yellow. The veins remain green.

Minor plant nutrients

Iron is required for chlorophyll synthesis. New leaves develop yellowing between the veins. As less and less iron is available, the leaves become golden yellow, not the pale yellow symptomatic of nitrogen deficiency. Iron deficiency is commonly associated with alkaline soil. *Hibiscus* and *Citrus* are particularly susceptible.

Chelated iron is used to correct iron deficiency. The iron contained in this product remains soluble and available for plant absorption.

Manganese is essential for several plant processes including the uptake of nitrogen as nitrate and the maintenance of the chloroplasts (microscopic cell structures containing chlorophyll). Manganese deficiency is characterized by striped or checkered chlorosis on the youngest leaves. Soil alkalinity may lead to manganese deficiency.

As the relative proportion of iron and manganese available to a plant is critical, chelated iron products often also contain appropriate concentrations of manganese. Apply according to manufacturers' instructions.

Molybdenum, copper, boron and zinc are micro-nutrients involved in various plant activities. These nutrients occasionally are lacking because of excessive liming (copper, boron), acid soil (molybdenum, copper), or because too much phosphorus-containing fertilizer has been applied (zinc). Soil pH adjustment and application of a balanced fertilizer containing all micro-nutrients is the most appropriate treatment.

Application of fertilizer

To gain the maximum benefit from any fertilizer, the gardener should know the soil, the plant or plants to be grown and their requirements. Soils that are excessively alkaline or acidic, poorly drained or waterlogged will require more than fertilizer to improve their productivity. Addition of well-rotted compost, manure or mulch will almost always be beneficial. Not only will soil texture, drainage and water-holding capacity be improved but also the humus provided will assist in holding nutrients for uptake by plant roots. With a few exceptions, most plants are quite happy growing in soil of pH 6.0–7.5. Soils more acid or alkaline should be amended several weeks before fertilizer application (see pH adjustment of soil, page 4).

Apply organic fertilizer such as well-rotted manure or compost at the most two weeks before planting seeds or young plants. Spread the material over the soil and dig it in. Alternatively, compost or manure can be applied in bands or strips between rows of plants, or accumulated in mounds. The latter method is especially useful with Pumpkins *Cucurbita*, Cucumbers and Squash *Cucumis*. Well-rotted organic fertilizers can be applied as a mulch on the soil surrounding mature plants.

The choice of inorganic fertilizer will depend upon the age of a plant and the purpose for which it is being grown. Young seedlings will need high nitrogen, high phosphorus and low potassium. As the plants near maturity, they will need high phosphorus and potassium but less nitrogen. Croton *Codiaeum*, *Acalypha* and other plants grown for their beautiful foliage need a high nitrogen fertilizer to promote healthy vegetative growth. *Bougainvillea*, fruiting trees and shrubs, *Hibiscus*, *Ixora* and other plants grown for their flowers or fruit require lower nitrogen and higher phosphorus and potassium once they reach flowering size.

The correct timing and method of fertilizer application are of great importance. The first application should be at the beginning of the rainy season. To reduce loss of soluble nutrients by leaching, split the application into two or three doses at six week intervals. Methods of application will vary according to the product being used and purpose of application. Ideally, fertilizer should be applied as close to the roots as is practicable. This is especially important for phosphorus as it can become immobilized as it passes through the soil.

APPLICATION TO LAWNS

Lawn fertilizers are high in nitrogen and are generally spread evenly (broadcast) over the entire lawn or applied as a top dressing. In either case, the fertilizer should be well watered in to avoid scorching the grass.

APPLICATION TO SHRUBS AND TREES

Apply granular or liquid fertilizer in a band around the plant at a point where the canopy ends (drip line).

APPLICATION TO FLOWER BEDS

Granular fertilizer may be incorporated into the soil before planting and later applied as a side dressing while the plants are growing. The side dressing is spread in between the plants. Care must be taken not to spread fertilizer on wet foliage because this may cause burning (scorch marks).

APPLICATION TO SEEDLINGS

Seeds germinate without need of fertilizer. Once the seedlings have used up their own nutrient store, mineral nutrient will be needed to support vigorous growth. Liquid fertilizer solutions are ideal. Apply dilute fertilizer in place of a regular watering. When seedlings are transplanted, a starter solution of very dilute balanced fertilizer may be applied to help the transplants establish themselves. Some commercial starter solutions contain rooting hormone.

APPLICATION TO PLANTS GROWING IN CONTAINERS

Container-grown plants are mostly at the mercy of their owner for provision of water and mineral nutrients. Additionally, root growth is limited. Unless care is taken, any minerals added to the container are likely to accumulate. Plants suffering from fertilizer accumulation will have yellow foliage with brown leaf tips. The best way to provide adequate nutrients and yet avoid the problem of minerals salts accumulation, is to feed 'weakly weekly': that is, to water the plants with a very dilute solution of balanced fertilizer on a weekly basis. Fertilizer should be withheld during natural dormant periods. The soil should be flushed with rainwater once every five weeks. This is especially important for plants grown indoors or under cover. Sufficient water should be applied as to run freely from the drainage holes.

Foliar fertilizers

Foliar fertilizers are water-soluble preparations that can be sprayed onto and be absorbed by the foliage of certain plants. These products are especially useful with Orchids and Bromeliads. Chelated iron products may also be applied as a foliar spray. These products should not be mixed and applied with pesticides.

HOW PLANTS FUNCTION

Plants do not breathe as animals do. In plants, oxygen, carbon dioxide and water vapour move by simple diffusion. They absorb and transport soil minerals in very dilute solution via the roots, absorbing more water than they require for growth, and allowing the excess to escape as water vapour through pores in the leaves (**transpiration**). Plants such as *Impatiens* can go one step further, producing drops of water along leaf edges (**guttation**). Garden plants need adequate water available to them to make up for water they lose.

Certain plants growing in arid climates have adapted their form and function to periodic water stress. In times of drought, succulent plants open their leaf pores only at night, reducing moisture loss but also allowing the carbon dioxide necessary for photosynthesis to be absorbed and stored in the leaves as an acid. Photosynthesis can thus happen the following day even though the leaf pores are then closed. During extreme water stress, succulent plants can enter a phase whereby pores remain closed both day and night and water loss is minimized. They cannot grow in this condition but they can survive six months or more without water.

PLANT HORMONES

Plants produce chemical messengers called hormones. These substances can affect functions far from their site of production, are effective in extremely low concentrations, and are implicated in the processes of germination, growth, flowering, fruit ripening, seed production, leaf fall and ageing. Gardeners can use commercial plant hormone preparation to control growth and development of garden plants.

Hormones affecting growth – auxins

The best known group of hormones are called auxins. The first hormone that was isolated and identified was an auxin – indole acetic acid (IAA). Auxins are produced in terminal buds and in root tips. Auxins affect cell elongation and also inhibit the development of dormant axillary buds. When the gardener pinches out a growing point of *Coleus* or prunes a Croton *Codiaeum* to induce bushy growth, the growing points, the sources of auxin production, are removed thus allowing axillary buds to break dormancy and develop into side shoots.

Auxins have been found to induce the production of roots from a stem cutting. For cuttings that form roots easily, rooting hormones will speed up the process. Liquid and powdered preparations of the more stable naphthyl acetic acid (NAA) are sold as rooting aids. A lanolin-based preparation of NAA is available for orchid growers to induce root formation on orchid offsets (keikis).

A hormone involved in fruit development – ethylene

Ethylene is the simplest plant hormone. It is produced in ripening fruit and by injured plant tissues. Ethylene gas is also produced during the inefficient burning of wood, oil and petrol: it is a component of automobile exhaust. Smoky fires were once used to induce flowering in glasshouse-grown Pineapples *Ananas* in the Azores. The ethylene component of the smoke was found to be responsible for flower initiation. Farmers in Martinique use ethylene to control the production of small, variegated Pineapples *Ananas comosus* var. *tricolor* for the Paris ornamental horticulture trade. The commercial products containing ethephon, for example, 'Ethrel' C, are now available which breakdown to release ethylene inside plants. Such a product is diluted with water and sprayed on the plants to be artificially controlled. This enables the grower to produce a crop at staged intervals rather than all at once.

Bromeliad enthusiasts can induce a recalcitrant mature Bromeliad to bloom either by using a commercial preparation according to manufacturer's instructions or by enclosing it together with a ripening Avocado Pear *Persea americana*, English Apple *Malus* or Mango *Mangifera* in a large paper or plastic bag for one week. The ripening fruit will release ethylene. Within two or three months, the Bromeliad will flower.

FACTORS CONTROLLING FLOWERING

Plant maturity

A plant must be mature to bloom. Until flower production begins, a seedling is said to be in a juvenile stage of development. Plants grown from seed will make vigorous growth but they will not flower until they are mature. Occasionally one plant in a batch of seedlings will never mature. This is possibly due to a genetic fault.

Plants grow throughout their lifetime. **Annuals** such as *Zinnia* germinate, grow, flower and produce seed in one short growing season. **Perennials** germinate, grow until they reach maturity when they flower for the first time, then continue growing thereafter, flowering and fruiting every year in their particular season. While annuals complete their life span in a few weeks or months, perennials

may survive for tens or even hundreds of years. Trees are mostly long-lived perennials.

Some oddities exist. Talipot Palm *Corypha umbraculifera* grows for 25–75 years then flowers only once, produces seed, then dies. Plants that flower only once then die are called **monocarpic**. Freshly harvested seed must be sown to obtain new Talipot Palms.

Century Plant *Agave* is also monocarpic. Fortunately most Agaves produce offsets, either as suckers from the base of the adult or as offsets formed on the massive inflorescence so that the plant is not entirely lost.

While *Zinnia* seedlings take only nine weeks to flower, Avocado Pear *Persea americana* may begin flowering only 7–9 years after germinating as a seed. Vegetatively propagated, mature plants will flower much sooner than those raised from seed. For this reason, gardeners use budding, grafting, cuttings and other vegetative propagation techniques to increase their stock of flowering plants. A plant grown from a mature flowering stem as an air layer will continue to flower because the stem has already reached maturity.

Cultural conditions

Incorrect culture, lack of appropriate fertilizer, poor soil conditions and insufficient water or sunlight are some of the factors that will result in poor blooms or none at all. *Bougainvillea*, *Hibiscus* and terete-leaved *Vanda* orchids must be grown in full sun to bloom well. Bulbous members of the Amaryllis and Lily families must be permitted to dry out after their growth period after which they will reward the gardener with flowers.

Continuous bloomers

Many tropical plants bloom throughout year. *Hibiscus*, Red Ginger *Alpinia purpurata* and Crown of Thorns *Euphorbia milii* will bloom year-round provided they have adequate light, moisture and nutrients. As *Hibiscus* shrubs flower at the tips of branches, periodic pruning will encourage new shoots and more flowers.

Seasonal bloomers

Seasonal flowering is characteristic of a great many tropical plants including some orchids, fruiting and flowering trees. Avocado Pear *Persea americana*, Mammee Apple *Mammea americana* and Mango *Mangifera indica* are seasonal bloomers, bearing their delicious fruit in the same season each year. Shaving Brush Tree *Bombax ellipticum*, Flamboyant *Delonix regia* and Frangipani *Plumeria* spp. are seasonally deciduous in November–December. Shaving Brush Tree blooms for the next four months then produces wine-red young leaves which gradually change from pink to green. Frangipani and Flamboyant make similar magnificent floral displays before foliage reappears. *Mussaenda* bears its spectacular floral bracts for nine months of the year, becoming dormant towards the end of January at which time it is best to prune and propagate them before the flowering season begins anew.

Heavy watering and rainfall

Heavy rain triggers some plants to bloom. Some of these bloom only once a year after the first heavy rain, others bloom each time there is a real tropical downpour. Yellow Poui trees *Tabebuia serratifolia* make Trinidad hillsides and roadsides a blaze of golden yellow colour soon after the first heavy rains of the year. Golden Shower *Macfadyena unguis-cati* behaves similarly. Clinging to old mill walls or festooned over large trees, this attractive scrambling vine can be seen miles away when in a flush of bloom.

Onion Vine *Pseudocalymma alliaceum*, Queen's Wreath *Petrea volubilis*, Limonia (Mock Orange) *Murraya*, Jamaica Ebony *Brya*, Barbados Cherry *Malpighia glabra*, Barbados

Gooseberry *Pereskia aculeata*, *Crinum* and *Yucca* belong to a second group of plants that are induced to bloom by a dry spell followed by heavy rains. The number of days after the rain to peak display varies with the species. A thorough soaking with a hose can sometimes bring on the same effect. This is useful to know if there is some function or occasion, a special party or a wedding planned to be held during the dry season. Why do plants behave this way? The mystery has not been solved for all but it is known that the sudden drop in temperature that accompanies a heavy downpour is the reason why the Dove Orchid *Dendrobium crumenatum* blooms ten days after a torrential rain. In this case the flower buds are already formed waiting for the temperature shift to signal further development.

Day length

Day length determines the flowering period of many plants, some of them flowering as the days shorten (**Short Day Plants**) such as Poinsettia *Euphorbia pulcherrima*, *Chrysanthemum* and Snow-on-the-Mountain *Euphorbia leucocephala*, and some flowering as the days lengthen (**Long Day Plants**) such as *Cattleya aurantiaca*, *Lagerstroemia*, and *Hylocereus*. This response of plants to the length of day is called photoperiodism. The plants respond to red light found both in sunlight and in certain types of artificial light. If Short Day Plants are illuminated by, for example, an incandescent street light during the night or by light streaming from a bedroom window, the day is artificially lengthened and the plants will not bloom. Commercial growers have long realised that they can force daylength-sensitive plants to bloom at times of peak demand, by using either artificial light to lengthen the day or blackout curtaining to shorten the day. *Stephanotis floribunda* requires 13 hours 5 minutes of daylight to flower. It can thus be forced to bloom in June for use in bridal bouquets or at any other time as required.

Temperature

Night temperature and the day to night temperature differential control flowering in some plants. Even a small drop in temperature experienced at sea level in the Caribbean during December–January will bring *Phalaenopsis* orchids and Jade Vine *Strongylodon macrobotrys* into flower. At cooler, higher elevations these plants can bloom year-round. Peter Pan Lily *Agapanthus africanus*, Day Lilies *Hemerocallis*, and Shasta Daisy *Chrysanthemum maximum* and many other temperate plants bloom with ease in gardens high in the Blue Mountains of Jamaica (much to the envy of gardeners living at sea level).

Knowledge of the flowering cycle and the special needs of each species is most important in planning a garden which will be colourful year-round. The gardener should keep records of when certain plants bloom: these notes will be a useful reference for future planning.

CONTROLLING PLANT GROWTH AND DEVELOPMENT

PRUNING

Pruning involves the removal of unwanted, dead, diseased or damaged branches or shoots to improve the shape of a plant and to make it more productive and vigorous. How to prune the garden plants and when to prune (the techniques of pruning) differ according to the purpose intended.

Pruning awakens dormant buds and forces them into growth. Buds are important to the results of the pruning: their position on the plant must be considered before cutting begins. The same is true of dominant leader stems and secondary branches. Some pruning work is seasonal, especially in the rainy months when overgrowth makes it a necessity. In the Caribbean, maintenance becomes a daily activity as plants grow quickly without much encouragement. Correct pruning will allow you to maintain attractive, healthy shrubs and trees.

Why prune?

The principal reasons for pruning are:

1 to concentrate vigour into certain parts of the plant by cutting away other parts, whether branch, leaf, flower or root, to obtain bigger yields or better quality fruit or flowers;
2 to develop the natural beauty of a plant in an aesthetically pleasing and balanced shape (such training should begin when the plant is young);
3 to encourage side shoots and flowers by forcing dormant buds into action;
4 to train a plant for a special purpose, (for example a shrub or small tree pruned to give a straight trunk without branches so that a view is not hidden but a leafy umbrella forms to give shade);
5 to improve the size or shape of fruit trees for easier maintenance and crop harvesting;
6 to remove damaged or diseased plant material, limbs broken by storm or crowded branches;
7 to remove large surface roots that are damaging garden beds and pathways or threatening foundations; root pruning improves the yield of some fruit trees;
8 to prepare a large tree or shrub for moving by pruning its roots and branches well in advance of the proposed move; and
9 to obtain propagation material. Branches may be removed and cut into suitable pieces for cuttings. The same material can be used for grafting or budding operations. When plants have been grafted or budded it is essential to prune away shoots of the stock plant that arise below the graft, otherwise the graft will be overwhelmed and eventually die.

How to prune

The art of pruning is knowing what branches to remove entirely, what branches should be pruned and at what point along their length, when pruning should be done with certain plants, and what tool to choose for the job. One basic rule of pruning is:

use sharp and clean pruning tools.

SMALLEST BRANCHES

Choose a bud pointing in the direction the new shoot should grow. Cut just above the bud leaving a downward slant on the cut surface. This method is used with Bonsai, Roses *Rosa*, *Plumbago capensis* and Bridal Wreath *Spiraea cantoniensis*.

LARGER BRANCHES

As a branch develops from the central tree trunk, a protective layer of woody tissue develops in the branch crotch. This layer serves to protect the living tree from attack. The layer may be identified externally by a slightly raised bark ridge extending outwards and downwards from the crotch. The **branch bark ridge** (collar) may be darker or rougher than the surrounding bark. If you cut lengthwise through the branch and trunk, you would see that the layer continues within the wood. It is most important that this layer is not damaged when pruning, neither that it is removed by cutting too close to the trunk.

Topping was once an accepted practice for reducing tree size. We now know that this practice leaves large stumps which cannot isolate the wounded tissue. The wounds do not heal properly: weak sucker branches emerge below the cut. Larger branches should always be pruned close to the main trunk just beyond the branch bark ridge.

Heavy or awkward branches should be reduced to several pieces before severing them from the trunk. Prune from the outside in, using secateurs to trim the fine branches that are often intermingled with desirable limbs. As the branch diameter increases, a pruning saw may be needed. Cut the central branch into several manageable sections, removing each piece carefully. Take special care with the final cut. Identify the branch bark ridge as a guide to the correct pruning position. Place the cutting blade outside the ridge. Using a pruning saw, sever the branch from the trunk, at an angle slanting slightly away from the trunk. Take care that the piece being removed does not slump, tearing bark and wood with it. Removal of very large, heavy limbs or those high above ground should be attempted only with professional assistance.

It is not necessary to paint the cut surface. A thin coat of tree pruning paint (bitumastic) may be applied. Do not use house paint or wood preservatives for this purpose.

When to prune

The decision when to prune will depend on the plant and, in many cases, the weather. In the Caribbean, with capricious rainfall and no defined winter rest period, many trees, shrubs and vines keep on growing all through the year. In the wet season things can easily 'get out of hand' in a few weeks. Frequent, systematic pruning is often necessary to keep plants looking the way that the landscaper planned. The task can be made considerably easier by choosing plants appropriate to a particular garden, the seasonal climate, and the availability of labour to keep up the necessary maintenance.

ANYTIME

Plants with colourful leaves or those which flower throughout the year are more flexible, for example Aralia *Polyscias*, Croton *Codiaeum*, *Hibiscus*, *Ixora*, and *Pentas* can be trimmed into shape at almost any time. The only inappropriate time is at the beginning of a long, dry spell and especially when supplementary water is unavailable.

JUST AFTER BLOOMING

The timing of pruning is of great importance to certain ornamental shrubs and trees that flower on wood from the previous season's growth. Pruning of these shrubs should take place soon after blooming is finished to allow time for maturation of new growth resulting from the pruning.

Other plants bear flowers on branches of the current season. These should be pruned to promote new growth whenever the current crop of flowers is finished.

There are trees and shrubs which during the wet summer months, form flower buds for the following year. These same plants become dormant in December–January. Flamboyant *Delonix regia*, some Cassias, Frangipani *Plumeria* and Rose of Sharon *Cochlospermum* drop their leaves and remain leafless for several months. In April–May, the leafless branches come alight with flowers. These plants should be pruned at the end of the flowering season. Large branches of *Plumeria* and *Cochlospermum* can be removed and planted when they are dormant: at this time they will root much better and faster.

AT THE END OF THE RAINY SEASON

Plants which are encouraged to bloom by heavy rains and may have several flowering and fruiting sessions during the year should be pruned towards the end of the rainy season. Examples include Barbados Cherry *Malpighia glabra*, *Macfadyena* (various species), *Murraya* and *Petrea*.

AT THE BEGINNING OF THE RAINY SEASON

At the beginning of the rainy season, *Bougainvillea* and winter-flowering Cassias *C. biflora*, *C. multijuga*, *C. polyphylla* and *C. spectabilis* should be pruned.

FOUR TO SIX WEEKS PRIOR TO DESIRED BLOOMING DATE

Pruning will awaken some flower buds from dormancy. *Plumbago* makes a beautiful show of blue flowers six weeks after it is trimmed into shape. *Ixora*, Canary Bush *Galphimia glauca*, *Pentas*, *Rondeletia*, and Chaste Tree *Vitex agnus-castus* are not truly seasonal but will bloom much more profusely if the dead inflorescences are regularly removed. Bridal Wreath *Spiraea cantoniensis* will be covered in fragrant, white flowers if stripped of all its leaves, 28 days before the blooms are required. Why these plants bloom in response to pruning is a simple question with many possible answers. One possible explanation is a response to the release of apical dominance. Another explanation, and particularly in the case of *Spiraea*, is the effect of hormones released through the stress of defoliation.

SPECIAL CASES

Poinsettia *Euphorbia pulcherrima* and Snow-on-the-Mountain *E. leucocephala* need a special routine. Flower bud formation in these shrubs depends upon day length: over 12 hours of uninterrupted darkness each day for six weeks is required. These shrubs bloom over the Christmas season. By March–April their colourful bracts are faded and the plants look untidy. Prune when the dry season is drawing to an end. Cut back the plants to about 1 m (3 ft) high. Vigorous new green shoots will follow. Nip back (the growing point removed) these shoots every four to six weeks until the end of September by which time the plants should be well shaped and bushy. Flowers and showy bracts will be produced at the ends of branches. The more branches, the more flowers and bracts and a more colourful display.

In the Caribbean, the days shorten as the year draws to a close. To avoid problems with an artificially extended day, grow Poinsettias in full sun but where no artificial light (porch, bedroom, patio, pool or street light) can shine on them by night during the critical weeks of flower bud formation when they require short-day length and uninterrupted, longer nights.

Bougainvillea responds to a pruning and watering routine, especially when grown in pots. Flower bud formation is enhanced by an enforced drought in the early months of the year when there is little rain. Once a year, soon after the beginning of the rainy season, Bougainvilleas should be heavily pruned. After their new growth has matured, these shrubs will flower again and again if there are dry spells during the wet months. Dry spells can be artificially induced by withholding water to pot plants. After each successive flowering the shrubs should be lightly pruned to remove spent blooms. In the garden, place the shrubs in full sunshine on a well-drained site. Use companion plants such as *Agave*, *Aloe*, cactus and other succulents which require little watering. Prune as for pot plants for a glorious display.

BEFORE AND AFTER A STORM

Hurricanes and tropical storms are a fact of life in the Caribbean. Heavy winds topple entire trees and tear the limbs off others. Branches are stripped of their leaves. Objects carried by the wind shred anything in their path. The wise gardener plans for an eventual storm by ensuring that large tree limbs overhanging buildings and power lines are pruned before disaster strikes. Professionals should be consulted to assist in the removal of large limbs.

Storm-damaged, torn and bruised plant tissue is prone to infection by harmful fungi and bacteria. Have pruning tools ready to remove damaged branches after a storm. Severely damaged trees should be removed promptly by a professional having the necessary equipment and expertise.

Root pruning

MOVING A TREE

Root pruning is often overlooked yet is a valuable technique to use when moving large trees or shrubs. Plan to move a tree at the beginning of the rainy season. Prune the roots several weeks before transplanting. Dig a large circular trench about 1 m (3 ft) from the trunk and about 1 m (3 ft) deep. If rain is lacking, water the root ball frequently during the waiting period.

New roots will form in response to the pruning. Top pruning of branches and leaves can also be done simultaneously to compensate for the loss of roots. Given the size and mass of the root ball of a large tree, there is a limit as to the size of tree that can be successfully moved without professional assistance. Even then very large or old trees may never recover from the disturbance. Take special care with palms. They are especially prone to stress when moved.

CONTROLLING A TREE

Some aggressive trees produce large roots that lie just beneath the soil. The root may buckle flagstones or a paved drive, trip a passerby, or take water and nutrients from a lawn or garden bed. Unless the tree is growing on rock with a very shallow soil cover generally it will tolerate reasonable root pruning to keep it in check. Pruning of the top growth should always accompany root pruning. If possible, root prune at the beginning of the rainy season. Use a clean pruning saw or pruning shears. Cut the root at a point between the trunk and the problem spot. Remove as much root as is necessary, then fill the hole and re-plant or re-sod as required.

PLANT PROPAGATION

Propagating plants is the part of a gardener's work that gives the most joy. Not only is there an opportunity to grow new plants from seed but there is also the chance to multiply interesting plants to share with a friend or neighbour. A bonus of the sharing process is that if a cherished plant dies, there will be another somewhere to propagate and share back. Every garden should have a shady sheltered spot where favourite plants can be propagated. The shelter need not be elaborate but provide protection from sun and heavy rain.

The choices of plant propagation

Plants may be propagated by seeds or spores (ferns), divisions, cuttings, layering, marcots or by grafts. The method employed will depend largely upon the ultimate goal (aim) of propagation and the kind of plant to be propagated.

Propagation goal	Recommended methods
1 to have more plants of the same species	seed, division, cuttings
2 to have many new plants from which to choose superior cultivars	seed
3 to have more plants of the same clone or cultivar	division, cuttings, air layers (marcots), grafts
4 to have a more vigorous plant	graft desirable clone on compatible, vigorous rootstock

Plants raised from seeds will be similar to but will not necessarily be exactly the same as the parents. Horticultural varieties that come true from seed include hybrids derived from inbred parents so that variation in the progeny is limited. Thus the seed of hybrid *Zinnia* 'Gold Sun' produces uniform, fully double 10 cm (4 in) diameter blooms on bushy 50 cm (20 in) plants.

Plants breeders choose individual plants with superior characteristics in an attempt to improve the quality and uniformity of flowers, fruit or foliage. In any batch of seedlings from a given pollination, differences will be seen. Superior individuals may display traits such as early flowering, dwarf habit, better colour or vigour. It takes experience to choose the best.

Types of plants to be propagated

CLONES AND CULTIVARS

A clone or cultivar is a plant selected for one or more specific merits or distinctions. The only way to propagate a clone or cultivar and preserve the desirable characteristics is to reproduce it vegetatively by division, cuttings, grafts or by layering. Cultivars of economic importance can also be reproduced by tissue culture.

SEEDLESS PLANTS

Vegetative propagation is absolutely necessary when a plant does not produce seed.

You may know the examples described below. Cavendish Banana *Musa paradisiaca* is a dwarf cultivar resistant to Panama Disease. It also withstands high winds and is more tolerant of drought conditions. Commercial banana cultivars do not produce seeds but rather suckers or vegetative offsets at the base of the plant. Suckers may be divided from the parent to make identical new plants. The herb French Tarragon *Artemisia dracunculus* is valued for its flavourful foliage yet is not known to produce viable seed. The cultivar has been preserved for generations by taking cuttings and divisions. Breadfruit *Artocarpus communis* is a seedless form of Breadnut *Artocarpus communis*. Both trees produce root suckers, particularly if the ground about the trunks is disturbed by forking. Root suckers can be removed and grown separately from the parent plant. Vegetative propagation bypasses a prolonged juvenile phase (ten years for a Breadnut grown from seed): Breadfruit and Breadnut grown from suckers will fruit in just two to three years.

SPORTS

Sporting is a word used by gardeners to describe a sudden spontaneous change (mutation) in leaf, flower or fruit. You may find variegated foliage appearing on a green shrub, different coloured flowers or superior fruit appearing on the same stem. *Bougainvillea* is very prone to sporting. Some of the best modern cultivars have been developed from such mutations. Mrs Helen McLean in San Fernando, Trinidad, discovered a lovely sport in her garden. It had orange bracts fading to shades of pink. The sport cultivar bears her name and is still very popular with horticulturalists. Another famous *Bougainvillea* is 'Mary Palmer', a sport of a severely pruned cultivar 'Mrs H. C. Buck'. Cultivar 'Mary Palmer' sported again giving long sprays of large, pure white bracts ('Mary Palmer's Enchantment'). The observant gardener upon finding an attractive sport can reproduce it through vegetative propagation such as by cuttings taken from the part of the plant that has produced the sport.

Propagation medium

Cuttings may be rooted either in sterilized damp sand or in a mixture of sand and well-rotted compost (2 parts sand to 1 part compost). The medium can be sterilized in a solar sterilizer or in an oven. Resterilize between each use.

Mist propagation

Water continually or intermittently sprayed on cuttings cools them and helps reduce transpiration loss. Under constant misting, cuttings can be rooted even in full sun. The mist is provided by a series of fine nozzles and can be automated. A moisture-sensitive device is used to switch on the water when needed. Two kinds are in general use and both are reliable. One depends upon the interruption of an electric current between two terminals mounted

in plastic, the current being interrupted when the plastic surface dries. The other device relies on weight lost from a flat surface due to evaporation. The equipment is a worthwhile investment if a gardener intends to propagate a large number of cuttings at a time.

VEGETATIVE PROPAGATION BY DIVISION

Simple division

The most basic of all plant propagation techniques is applicable to plants that form clumps.
1 Dig a plant from the garden bed or knock the plant out of its container.
2 Gently pull the clump apart with your hands. The likely points of division will become apparent.
3 Use a sharp sterile knife to sever any rhizomatous or root connections. Make certain that each clump has roots and one or more growing points.
4 Divisions are then re-planted in a prepared garden bed or in new pots with fresh soil.

Plants that can be propagated by division include *Aglaonema*, *Calathea*, *Liriope*, *Asparagus*, various Orchids, Ferns, Gingers and Heliconias.

Root suckers

Some shrubs and trees produce root suckers near the base of the plant or at some distance from it. Root suckers can be induced by forking the soil near the plant. Injury to the roots leads to the development of a flush of suckers. The best time to harvest root suckers is when the plant is not in active growth, just before the rainy season begins.
1 Expose a root sucker using a fork or a trowel.
2a If the sucker has already developed its own root system, sever the parent root,

remove the sucker with its root ball and transplant to a prepared propagation bed or individual container.

2b If the sucker lacks a root system, sever the parent root about 3 cm (1.2 in) from the sucker (between the sucker and the parent), making the cut straight across the root.

3 Cut the parent root again, about 20 cm (8 in) outwards from the sucker.

4 Remove the cutting and insert it into damp propagation medium until the sucker is level with the top.

5 Keep the cutting evenly moist or use an automated misting system until the sucker forms its own roots.

Plants that can be propagated by root suckers include Breadfruit and Breadnut *Artocarpus communis*, *Clerodendron*, *Ixora*, African Tulip Tree *Spathodea campanulata*, and Rangoon Creeper *Quisqualis indica*.

Keikis, bulbils, tubers and corms

Some plants form structures that can be used for vegetative propagation. Orchids produce aerial offsets (**keikis**). *Epidendrum* and *Dendrobium* species and hybrids readily produce keikis. These may be removed when they have developed several roots. *Phalaenopsis* species and hybrids occasionally produce keikis on their inflorescence. These plantlets are sometimes reluctant to produce roots. A lanolin-based rooting hormone paste can be used and the keikis removed when they have two healthy roots.

Red Ginger *Alpinia purpurata* produces **bulbils** in a mature inflorescence. Many Agaves do so as well. Mature bulbils complete with several leaves and roots should be removed to a propagation tray. When the roots have developed more fully, the plants can be transferred to garden beds.

Certain plants form underground storage organs (**tubers**) to carry them through periods of drought. Ornamental plants with resting tubers include Gloriosa Lily *Gloriosa superba* and *Caladium*. To propagate them it is best to wait until the plant enters its dormant period:

1 lift the tuber and cut it into two or more pieces each with an eye (growing point);

2 dust the cut surfaces with powdered sulphur or charcoal to assist drying and to protect from fungal attack;

3 store the cut pieces in an airy spot, watching for signs of sprouting; and

4 plant the tuber when sprouting has begun, in a well-drained sandy soil. Water sparingly until rooting occurs.

CUTTINGS

One of the commonest methods of propagating plants is by cuttings. What gardeners call a cutting (sometimes referred to as a 'slip') is a portion of stem which has nodes or places where leaves and side branches arise. As a general rule, the closer the nodes are together, the easier the cutting forms roots. Examination of the average shrub or tree will show three distinct types of wood:

1 softwood – the tender, green, pliable growing tip without bark or fully developed leaves;

2 semi-hardwood – the stem is still green although bark is beginning to form, leaves fully developed; and

3 hardwood – stem brown with bark (Figure 2.1).

Softwood cuttings

EASY ROOTING

Some plants are very easily and quickly rooted as softwood cuttings. *Alternanthera*, *Begonia*, *Coleus*, *Impatiens*, Marigold *Tagetes*, *Pentas*, *Peperomia* and *Portulaca* are among the easiest, rooting readily in damp sand. Slips of Sweet Potato *Ipomoea batatas* will root di-

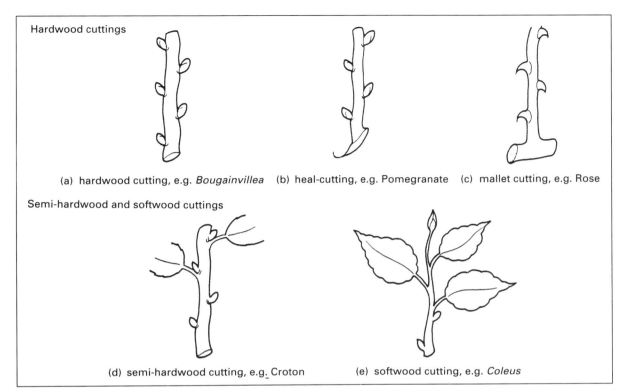

Semi-hardwood and softwood cuttings

(a) hardwood cutting, e.g. *Bougainvillea*   (b) heal-cutting, e.g. Pomegranate   (c) mallet cutting, e.g. Rose

(d) semi-hardwood cutting, e.g. Croton   (e) softwood cutting, e.g. *Coleus*

Figure 2.1 Types of cutting

rectly in the garden provided there is sufficient moisture.

Use a sharp knife or secateurs to cut stems into approximately 20 cm (8 in) pieces. The lower cut should be about 1.5 cm (½ in) below a node; the upper cut about 2 cm (¾ in) above a node.

TRUE SUCCULENTS

Huernia, *Euphorbia* and *Crassula* can also be propagated as cuttings, however, they are very prone to rot if kept too wet.

1 Take a cutting (length of cutting determined by the individual plant) and allow to air dry for a day or two before placing it in damp sand.
2 Keep the propagation tray under cover to control watering.

TIP OR SOFTWOOD CUTTINGS OF SHRUBS AND TREES

1 Dip cuttings into rooting hormone powder before planting to hasten the development of roots.
2 Place in damp medium and use an automated misting system to keep the cuttings evenly moist and to reduce transpiration loss.

Shrubs and trees appropriate for softwood cutting propagation include Oleander *Nerium*, *Jasminum rex* and *Dracaena*.

Stout young branches of Frangipani *Plumeria* can also be propagated as softwood cuttings although care should be taken as too much water can cause the cutting to rot before it forms roots. A cutting of Frangipani can be an entire young branch of 50 cm (20 in) or more.

1 The cutting is best removed at the branching point and left to air dry until the flow of latex has stopped.
2 Insert the cutting base into 5 cm (2 in) of damp sand in a pot and anchor in place by fastening the cutting to an upright prop.

Semi-hardwood cuttings

Cuttings of some shrubs root more easily if they are partly mature. Croton *Codiaeum*, *Lantana* and *Bauhinia* are some examples.
1 Take cuttings as described for softwood.
2 Remove about half of the leaves, especially those near the base.
3 If desired, dip the cutting in rooting hormone powder before planting.

Hardwood cuttings

Young stems with developed bark are recommended as a source of cuttings for the propagation of *Allamanda*, *Beaumontia*, *Bignonia*, *Bougainvillea*, Golden Dewdrop *Duranta*, *Hibiscus*, *Ixora*, *Mussaenda*, Pomegranate *Punica*, and Rose *Rosa*.
1 Take cuttings having a minimum of two nodes and approximately 20–30 cm (8–12 in) long.
2 Remove most of the leaves, especially those near the base, to reduce transpiration loss.
3 If desired, dip the cutting in hormone rooting powder before planting.
4 Plant about one-third of the cutting in damp sandy propagation medium. The lowermost node should be in the soil and another one should be above ground.

Heel cuttings are recommended for plants that are sometimes difficult to root such as Pomegranate *Punica* and Juniper *Juniperus*. Remove a branch from the parent plant when it is not in active growth. Pull side branches from it so that each breaks away with a piece of the main stem and mature wood attached. This manoeuvre is best achieved by pulling a side branch down and away from the main branch in a swift continuous motion. Although this procedure may seem crude, the branch does break at the most appropriate place. Alternatively, the cutting can be made using a sharp knife. Plant the heel in damp medium, keeping it evenly moist. An alternative to the heel cutting is the **mallet cutting** where the branch is cut into a number of sections, each with a mallet-shaped piece of mature stem and side branch. In both instances, rooting will take place at the juncture of immature and mature wood.

UNFAMILIAR PLANTS

When working with an unfamiliar plant, make different kinds of cuttings to see which works best. Keep records as to when the cuttings were taken and the time taken to root. Written information is often more reliable than memory.

HOW TO RECOGNIZE IF A CUTTING HAS ROOTED

If a cutting develops leaf buds and appears healthy and vigorous, chances are that it has formed roots. Carefully tip the container of rooting medium and cuttings. If roots are formed, they will be apparent. If not, re-plant carefully and keep moist. Cuttings have very delicate roots. Take care not to damage them when the rooted cutting is transplanted.

Leaf cuttings

Just a few plants are commonly propagated by leaf cuttings.

Sansevieria – cut leaves into 5 cm (2 in) lengths and place upright in damp sand.

African Violet *Saintpaulia* and *Kalanchoe* – sever leaves from the parent and root the petiole or leaf base in damp sand. Plantlets can be removed when they develop adequate roots.

BEGONIA

1 Sever mature leaves from the parent with as long a petiole (leaf-stalk) portion remaining as is possible.
2 On the underside of the leaf cut the main leaf veins using a clean razor blade.
3 Then pin the leaf with the cut veins touch-

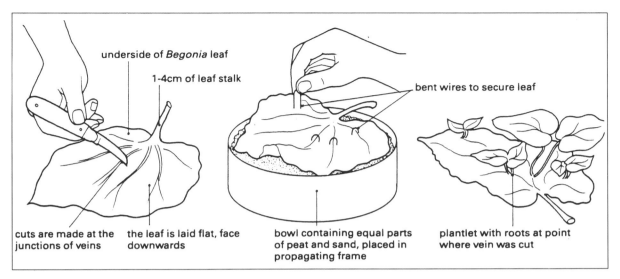

underside of *Begonia* leaf

1-4cm of leaf stalk

bent wires to secure leaf

cuts are made at the junctions of veins

the leaf is laid flat, face downwards

bowl containing equal parts of peat and sand, placed in propagating frame

plantlet with roots at point where vein was cut

Figure 2.2 Preparing a leaf cutting

ing a tray of damp sand (Figure 2.2). (Old-fashioned hairpins work well.)

4 Buds and later plantlets should develop at each place that a vein was cut. Roots will emerge below the plantlet. Plantlets can be separated once they have several leaves and substantial roots.

GRAFTING AND BUDDING

Grafting techniques are used to propagate valuable cultivars that either will not propagate by other means or have been found to be more vigorous when grown on another plant. Some of the most interesting examples are seen with cactus where cultivars lacking photosynthetic pigment, yet very attractively coloured red or golden yellow, are grafted onto a vigorous photosynthetic stock plant. *Gymnocalycium mihanovichii* var *friedrichiae* forma *variegata* 'Hibotan' is such a plant. Despite the long name, the cultivar 'Hibotan' will not live unless grafted to a another cactus. The most common stock used for cactus grafting is *Hylocereus*.

Whether grafting cactus plants or fruit trees,

the principles are the same. Two different plants are cut, united by tissue regeneration and come to grow as a single plant. The tissue joins most actively in the meristematic cambium layer found within the stem. By convention, the plant providing the rooting system is called the **stock** (or rootstock) while the grafted shoot is called the **scion**. The stock and the scion are always closely related.

CHOOSING THE STOCK

Choice of rootstock will depend largely upon the plant to be grafted and the pest and disease problems of a particular region. Sour Orange *Citrus aurantium* being resistant to Gummosis Disease and Nematodes, two serious problems particular to the Caribbean region, is an excellent choice for *Citrus* stock. Likewise, rooted cuttings of a strong nematode-resistant *Hibiscus* cultivar should be used for budding stock.

Inverted T-budding method

In budding, a bud of the scion is attached to stem of a vigorous-growing stock. It is best to take a healthy bud from a portion of stem that

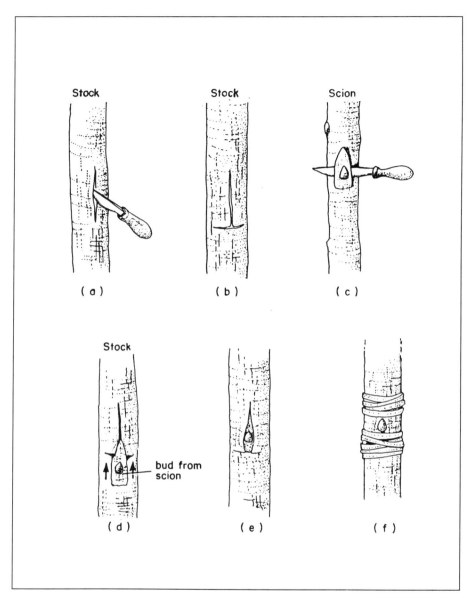

Figure 2.3 The steps for inverted T-budding

is mature and that has lost its leaves. You will need a sharp budding knife and some raffia or plastic budding tape to hold the stock and scion close together and exclude water and air. While an experienced gardener should expect an 80 per cent success rate using the T-budding method, a beginner should not be discouraged. Practice makes perfect. Practise budding citrus on seedling rootstocks until you achieve success. You will then see that the whole process is quite easy (Figure 2.3). This method is especially recommended for high rainfall areas.

1 Exposure of the cambium layer on the stock plant

Make an inverted T-shaped cut in the bark

Gardening in the Caribbean

of the stock plant. The cuts should penetrate through the bark but not into the wood. The bark above the horizontal cut is gently prised upwards and away from the wood to expose the cambium. If the stock is actively growing the bark should separate readily.

2 **Preparation of the bud**
Cut and remove the bud from the scion with an area of bark about equal to that of the area exposed on the stock. If a bit of wood has been removed with the bud this should be carefully removed with the tip of the knife. Nothing should prevent the cambial layer of the bud from touching that of the stock.

3 **Joining the scion bud and the stock**
Slide the prepared bud into the T-shaped cut so that the flaps of bark overlap the edges of the bud. Tie the bud in position with raffia by wrapping it around the stock both above and below the bud.

4 **Checking to see if the bud has taken**
Examine the bud about two weeks after the procedure. If the bud is developing a shoot the union has been successful, in which case cut the stock about 2–3 cm (about 1 in) above the bud union.

Wedge grafting method

Avocado *Persea* and *Citrus* can be wedge grafted. The technique consists of three main steps (see Figure 2.4).
1 Make a longitudinal slice into the stock stem.
2 Cut and prepare the scion stem so that it forms a wedge that will fit in the stock cut.
3 Tie the two parts together with raffia.

When the scion shows signs of new growth the graft can be considered successful.

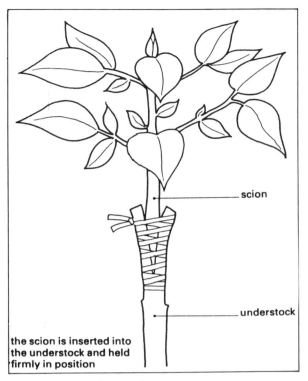

the scion is inserted into the understock and held firmly in position

Figure 2.4 Wedge graft

Cactus grafting

1 Remove the top of an actively growing stock plant with a sharp knife.
2 Also cut the plant to be grafted.
3 Match as closely as possible the two central rings of tissue. The two stems are held closely together with an elastic band.
4 Keep the newly grafted plant in a shaded location for a week.

Air layering (Marcotting)

Air layering or marcotting is a procedure used to root a stem while it is still attached to the parent plant.
1 Choose a mature stem. Make a 1 cm ($1/2$ in) deep cut into the stem just above a node, about 30 cm (12 in) away from the growing point.
2 Insert a tiny wedge of wood to keep the cut surfaces apart.

3 Wrap moist Sphagnum Moss around the cut surface including the node.
4 Wrap the moss with plastic sheeting and fasten in place with raffia.
5 When roots form (within 8 weeks), sever the stem below the roots and pot the propagated plant.

Plants that can be propagated by air layering include *Dieffenbachia*, *Ficus*, Croton *Codiaeum*, Flamboyant *Delonix*, Queen of Flowers *Lagerstroemia*, *Casuarina*, Oleander *Nerium* and *Ixora*.

RAISING PLANTS FROM SEED

Seeds are dormant embryonic plants. Packed inside a resilient seed coat together with the embryo is a food store of starch, fat, and protein. The largest seed that a Caribbean gardener will probably encounter is that of the coconut. Like most palm seeds, the coconut embryo is supplied with a fatty food store and may take two or more months to germinate. Among the smallest seeds are those of the orchids: these seeds have a limited food store that they are unable to use without help. For this reason, orchid seeds require very special techniques for their successful germination.

Most seeds have three requirements for germination: moisture, air and warmth. Some seeds also require either total darkness or light to germinate.

Seed supplies

Seeds of most vegetables and flowers may be purchased from a local supplier or can be imported. When purchasing vegetable seeds, choose varieties suited to the Caribbean climate. Rare seeds may be obtained from specialist growers and societies. You can also collect seed from your own plants and exchange it with neighbours and friends.

However the seed is obtained, it must be fresh. Some seed rapidly loses the ability to germinate if it is not properly stored. Commercial packets are usually dated to assure freshness. Seed of most plants with the exception of the Aroids, Heliconias and Palms, should be kept dry and cool in a sealed jar or tin. A packet of silica gel or other dessicant should be put with the labelled packets. Seeds of Aroids such as *Anthurium*, Palms and *Heliconia* should never be allowed to dry out and should be sown as soon as possible after collection. Palm seeds are best stored in plastic bags with a few strands of barely dampened Sphagnum Moss: this prevents the seeds from becoming fully dried and can extend their viability.

Occasionally a gardener has to keep seed such as Sorrel *Hibiscus sabdariffa*, until the appropriate planting time. The seeds are collected in December when the crop is reaped, cleaned, dried, and then stored until the rains come in May–June. Sorrel seeds can be planted directly into a prepared garden bed using Method II (see page 38).

Germination media

Some seeds are sown directly in the garden, for example Butter Beans, while others are started in trays of soil, bags of damp moss or individual pots. There are considerable advantages to be had when germinating seeds in trays or pots: complete control over sterility of the mix, watering and screening from slugs and insects (pests that could make short work of the seedlings!).

If using soil, sieve it to remove stones and large lumps. Because soil will contain weed seeds and fungi that could harm seedlings, it should be sterilized before use. Soil or any other material used as a germination medium can be sterilized in a Solar Sterilizer (see page 13) or in an oven at 121–149°C (250–300°F) for about 30 minutes. Allow the soil to cool before using.

Ready-to-use blends of peat, vermiculite and perlite (soil-less mix) may be purchased from your garden centre or you can prepare your own recipe.

MIX RECOMMENDED FOR GERMINATING MOST SEEDS

one part* garden loam (sieved and sterilized)
one part leaf mould, well-rotted compost or peat moss (sieved and sterilized)
one part sharp sand or perlite (rinsed free of dust)
* all parts by volume

Use a plastic pot or large tin as a measure. Blend the ingredients well and moisten before use.

Preparing to sow seed

CONTAINERS

Use plastic trays by preference over wooden ones: the latter are difficult to clean and may harbour injurious fungi. Clean the trays with soap and hot water. Be certain that there are drainage holes. Fill each tray with moist, sterile germination mix.

LABELS

Prepare labels for each kind of seed to be planted. Use a wax or indelible pencil/pen and plastic markers. Inexpensive labels can be cut from discarded plastic food tubs.

SPECIAL INSTRUCTIONS

Read any instructions provided with the seed. The depth of planting should be about twice the diameter of the seed but there are exceptions. Check if light or complete darkness is required for germination. Seeds of the African Violet *Saintpaulia*, *Begonia*, *Coleus*, *Crossandra*, *Cuphea*, *Gerbera*, *Impatiens*, Snapdragon *Antirrhinum*, *Portulaca*, *Petunia* and *Pentas* need light to germinate. Seeds of *Tithonia* require total darkness.

Seeds requiring light must be sown on top of the soil while those requiring total darkness should be covered by soil and light further excluded by covering the tray with a black cloth.

WATERING

Success or failure in producing plants from seeds depends on keeping the soil evenly moist at all times but never having it soaking wet. Make it a habit to check the trays every morning. Use a watering can with a fine nozzle or a sprayer. Do not use a hose: the vigorous stream of water can dislodge seeds and seedlings, ruining all your efforts.

LIGHT

Light is necessary for germinating some seeds and is essential for the growth of all seedlings. Even seeds that require total darkness to germinate produce seedlings requiring light to grow. As soon as seedlings appear, expose them to more light but not direct sun. If the seed tray has been covered with glass or plastic, be certain to prop it open during the day allowing air to circulate. Seedlings without adequate light will be weak, spindly, and susceptible to disease. The amount of sun the seedlings can take can be judged by the requirements of the mature plant. Observe the seedlings: if they bend towards the light or if they appear spindly, they require more light. It is worth remembering that even sun-tolerant cactus seedlings grow best in filtered sunlight rather than direct sun.

PROTECTION FROM HEAVY RAIN

Seed trays should be placed under shelter or they can be individually covered with glass. Prop the glass open a little to ensure air circulation. Be vigilant for Rots and Damping-off as seedlings are most susceptible during the rainy season.

For additional information refer to Appendix 3 Germination Guide.

METHODS I, II, III AND SPECIAL CASES

Three basic methods are recommended for sowing seed. In addition different procedures should be followed for special cases – Cactus, Crotons, Heliconias, Palms, Water Plants, Ferns and Orchids.

Sowing seed – Method I: for very fine, dust-like seeds or for seeds that need light (L) to germinate

Examples: *Begonia* (L), *Coleus* (L), *Crossandra* (L), *Cuphea* (L), *Achimenes*, African Violet *Saintpaulia* (L), *Episcia*, other African Violet relatives Gesneriads, *Petunia* (L), *Portulaca* (L), *Pentas* (L) and *Antirrhinum* (L).

Use a table indoors and out of the wind. Have ready, clean labelled containers filled with moist sterile mix. Sometimes ants carry away seeds. If this problem exists, dust the soil lightly with a powdered insecticide such as carbaryl.

1 Empty the contents of the packet onto a folded greeting card, using it as a sower. This way you can see what you are doing.
2 Gently sprinkle the seeds over the soil being careful not to crowd them.
3 Do not cover the seeds with additional mix.
4 Mist the seeds with water.
5 Cover the tray with glass or plastic wrap, placing it in a bright spot but out of direct sun. Keep the glass in place until the seedlings have two pairs of true leaves.
6 When watering, use only a fine mist.

Sowing seed – Method II: for small to medium-size seeds or for seeds requiring darkness to germinate

Examples: Alyssum *Lobularia*, Chili Peppers *Capsicum*, Carnation *Dianthus*, *Celosia*, Marigold *Tagetes*, Parsley *Petroselinium*, *Salvia*, Periwinkle *Catharanthus* and Zinnias.

1 Prepare a tray of moist, sterile soil.

2 Make grooves (rows) of appropriate depth using a straight edge tool.
3 Waggle the ruler back and forth to widen the top of the groove.
4 Sow the seeds in the groove as thinly as possible. This makes transplanting much easier.
5 Label the tray or individual rows.
6 Using a coarse plastic household sieve, sift soil over the seeds. Pat down firmly.
7 Water the tray using a sprayer or the fine rose of a watering can.
8 Cover the trays with screening, glass or plastic wrap. Place in a bright location but out of direct sun and observe daily. When seedlings appear provide more light.

Note If the seed requires total darkness to germinate, cover the tray with black cloth or foil. Observe every two or three days. When seedlings appear, remove the cover and provide filtered sunlight.

Sowing seed – Method III: for larger seeds

Examples include Flamboyant *Delonix*, *Canna*, *Cassia* and *Hibiscus*.

1 Pre-soak the seeds in water: most of the larger ones will benefit from this treatment; (be certain to label the cups or jars as things can easily get mixed up!)
2 The seeds should sink to the bottom of the water then swell. After 24 hours, remove any floaters.
3 Sow any seeds that have begun to swell. Very large seeds should be planted individually into pots or plastic plant bags (liners).

HARD SEED COATS

Some seeds such as those of *Delonix*, *Cassia* and *Albizia* have very hard seed coats. To encourage these seeds to take up water and to swell, pour very hot water, about 88°C (190°F), over them, let the water cool and continue to soak for an additional 24 hours. Sow any seeds that begin to swell. If some seeds are still recalcitrant, give them another hot water treatment. If the seeds still do not take in water and swell, use a file or sandpaper to break the seed coat then soak for two or three days, changing the water daily until the seed swells.

Transplanting seedlings

There comes a time when seedlings are ready to be transplanted. They should be still actively growing and not yet slowed because of competition for space.

1 Choose seedlings with two to six leaves depending upon their size, rate of growth and the degree of crowding.
2 Water seedling trays to loosen the soil about roots before removing plants.
3 Hold the leaves gently with the fingers and using a small fork (or similar tool), lever a seedling out of the soil. Be certain to conserve as many intact roots as possible.
4 Transplant the seedling to a tray or pot of fresh moist soil. Make a hole large enough to take the roots, hold the seedling at the same depth as it was growing previously and press soil around the roots. Water the transplants right away.
5 Keep the tray or pots in a shady place and well misted for a few days until the plants have recovered.

Seedlings can also be transplanted directly into a garden location. Transplanting is best done in the afternoon. Water the transplants well and provide extra shade for a few days until they are **hardened off** or accustomed to the extra wind and sun. Use shade cloth, leafy branches or coconut limbs to provide the supplementary shade.

FERTILIZER

Dilute liquid fertilizer can be applied to transplants about one week after moving them. Make a solution of 1 ml ($^1/_4$ tsp) 7–7–7 in 5 litres (1 gal) water or use a liquid product according to manufacturer's instructions.

Germinating Cactus seed

Cactus seeds are relatively easy to germinate provided some care is taken. For some rare species, seed may be the only way to obtain new plants for your collection. Cactus seed must be soaked or kept moist enough to remove germination inhibitors that may be in the seed coat. Unfortunately the warm, moist environment necessary for germination is also ideal for the growth of Damping-off fungi. To eliminate fungal spores that may be on the seeds before planting, they should be soaked for 10 minutes in a solution of liquid bleach and water before sowing (1 part bleach and 9 parts water). Pots and trays should also be washed and sterilized with the bleach solution. The soil should be heat-sterilized and all water boiled and cooled before using.

1 Prepare shallow seed trays by filling them with a porous soil mix of 2 parts sand and 1 part sieved compost, leaf mould or garden loam.
2 Moisten the soil with boiling water and allow it to cool.
3 Sow the treated seeds on the soil surface. Only the seeds of *Opuntia* need to be buried to approximately four times their diameter.
4 Cover the tray with transparent plastic wrap or a piece of glass. Place the tray in a shaded location where there is no direct sun exposure.
5 Examine the trays daily. Germination may begin as soon as three days after sowing and continue thereafter for several weeks. Greatest variation will occur with mixed packets of seed.
6 Once substantial germination has occurred, the plastic or glass should be raised daily to allow air to circulate.
7 If watering is needed, be careful not to disturb the tiny seedlings.

8 Feeding will not be needed until the plants have established a root system, then apply dilute liquid fertilizer prepared according to manufacturer's instructions.

9 Give the seedlings more and more light but never expose them to direct sunlight for extended periods. Seedlings respond positively to light feedings and increased light, sometimes attaining substantial size in the first year.

10 Seedlings can be transplanted to individual clay pots once they are at least 1 cm ($^1/_2$ in) in diameter or 2.5 cm (1 in) tall. Use the same soil as recommended for sowing. Larger seedlings can be transplanted directly to the garden however it is wise to provide some shading until they become accustomed to their new location.

Germinating Croton seed

Croton seeds resemble small peas and are really quite easy to germinate.
1 Fill a shallow box with moist, sterilized potting mix.
2 Press seeds about 1 cm ($^1/_2$ in) deep into the soil.
3 Cover the soil with damp newspaper, placing the container in a warm, shady place.
4 Keep the paper moist, lifting it every week to check for germination.
5 Once seedlings appear, give them filtered sunlight and their first feed of dilute liquid fertilizer.
6 When they have five or six leaves, pot them individually.

Remember that the foliage character will develop only as the plants mature. When choosing plants, look for Crotons with closely packed, brightly coloured leaves with short stalks. Keep the plants exhibiting the characteristics that you like. These can be grown on in larger pots or transferred directly to the garden. It can take up to two years to determine the value of a particular plant.

Germinating Heliconia seed

Heliconias are humming-bird pollinated plants. Of course the gardener can play the 'bird' in which case the fruit will mature in two to three months. The fruit turns blue and protrudes the day it ripens and can be easily detached. If the flesh surrounding the seed is soft, rub it away to expose the seed. Otherwise let the fruit rest several days in plastic bag or a film container. Do not allow the fruit to decay! Seeds that might eventually germinate should sink when placed in water. As fungi may attack the seed during its long dormancy, pre-treat the cleaned seed in a solution of 1 part liquid bleach and 9 parts water. The seed is not ready to germinate even though the fruit is ripe. It will take a further six or seven months for the embryo to mature and for germination to begin.
1 Sow freshly harvested seeds in sterilized compost, covering them with about 1 cm ($^1/_2$ in) of fine soil.
2 Water well. Keep the seeds moist; do not allow the pots to dry out.
3 Keep the pots in a shady place. Label each pot as to its contents. Six months is a long time to remember just what you did and when.
4 Once tiny shoots appear, provide filtered sunlight and feed with dilute liquid fertilizer.

Germinating Palm seed

It is not possible to propagate a desirable Palm by taking cuttings. Apart from the few Palms that cluster, allowing the removal of offsets, Palms must be propagated from seed. The fresher the seed the better. Palm seeds take two months or more to germinate.
1 Place the seed on top of either moist vermiculite or moist, squeezed Sphagnum Moss in a clear plastic bag.
2 Close the bag and hang it in a warm shaded place.

Gardening in the Caribbean

3 Observe weekly. When the seed coat splits, allow the seed root to develop to the depth of the bag.
4 At this stage, remove the germinating seed and plant it in a pot deep enough to contain the root. Half fill the pot with sandy loam or compost mixed with sand. Holding the seed upright, add a layer of coarse sand and a top dressing of peanut shells or chopped coconut husk. The seed should rest within the uppermost layer.
5 Water well. Keep the pot in a semi-shaded location.
6 Apply a dilute liquid fertilizer when the leaves appear.

Germinating seeds of Water Plants

The seed capsules of Water-lilies mature beneath the water. When the capsules are ripe they rise to the surface, split and release seeds each enveloped in a gelatinous membrane (**aril**). The seeds float for a day or two then sink. Where they come to rest is the place they will germinate unless the gardener intervenes.

Intervention can begin at the pollination stage if you want to hand-pollinate flowers to make hybrids. Bear in mind that the stigmas will accept pollen the first day (or night) of opening and that the anthers mature the second day (or night) of opening.
1 Enclose pollinated flowers in a lightweight net bag. The capsules will take three weeks (*Nymphaea*) to five weeks (*Victoria*) to mature. Seeds will be released into the bag and thus saved.
2 Prepare a propagation area such as a shallow pool adjacent to the growing area, once seeds are seen floating in the bag.
3 Fill shallow clay pots with sand; place these in the pool with the top of the pot at the water surface.

Water-lily seeds should be planted within one week of the floating stage. The aril should be completely disintegrated by this time.

4 Press the seeds into the wet sand. Germination takes one to three weeks.
5 Pot the plants individually in soil mix recommended for adult Water-lilies, only after the first floating leaves have developed.

Victoria **seeds** must be ripened before sowing, otherwise the treatment is the same.
1 Allow the seeds to remain in the net bag until the fruit and arils are completely disintegrated.
2 The seed coats will gradually darken, becoming dark brown to almost black. Then, and only then should they be sown.

Raising Ferns from spores

Fern spores require continual moisture to germinate and develop young fern plants.
1 Sow the spores as soon as possible after you obtain them on the surface of moist, sterilized compost in a clay or plastic pot. The compost should be a sieved mixture of soil, sand and leaf mould.
2 Stand the pot in a saucer of water, covering the pot with a pane of glass or transparent plastic wrap.
3 Keep the soil continuously moist and the relative humidity near 100 per cent until young fern plants are formed.
4 Place the pots in a shaded location out of direct sun.
5 Observe the pale green heart-shaped discs (prothalli) which appear first: the first true leaves will only appear several weeks or months later.
6 Transplant young leafy ferns to individual pots only after roots have developed.

Germinating Orchid seeds

Orchid seeds are very simple. Unlike Bean or Coconut seed with large stores of food for a developing seedling, the orchid embryo has little if any available nutrient for germination and growth. In their natural habitat, orchid seeds need a fungal partner (mycorrhiza) to initiate germination. Very few orchid seeds ever find naturally the right partner and the correct conditions to germinate. Perhaps to compensate for this, orchids produce large numbers of seeds, up to several million per capsule.

Orchids can be germinated in the absence of the otherwise necessary fungal associate by supplying nutrients (simple sugars, amino acids and minerals) provided the seeds are surface-sterilized to remove any unwanted micro-organisms and the nutrient medium is sterilized before sowing. This procedure ensures that no fungi, bacteria or yeasts survive to compete with the orchid seedlings for nutrients. Each orchid species and hybrid seems to have its own particular nutrient requirements although a few commercial preparations will satisfy most of the commonly grown types.

Germination media are sold as pre-mixed powders (Mother Flask Media) ready to be added to water, sterilized and used. There are separate formulations, called Replate Media for transplanting seedlings. Refer to articles or advertisements in *The Orchid Review*, the *American Orchid Society Bulletin* or other horticultural publications. Complete instruction are included with each packet of medium.

REMOVING ORCHID SEEDLINGS FROM STERILE CULTURE FLASK

An inexpensive way to purchase orchids is to obtain a flask of 10 or 25 seedlings. There is generally less problem with importation because the plants are sterile. Plantlets can be transplanted when they are more than 5 cm (2 in) tall or wide and have two or more roots.

1 Open the flask and add a quantity of lukewarm (not hot) tapwater. Swirl gently. If the seedlings do not come out easily the flask will have to be broken to safely remove them. Wrap the flask in several layers of newspaper and hit it with a hammer on the curve of the base. The blow (a sharp tap) should be sufficient to break the glass but not too hard to crush the plants within.

2 Remove the seedlings carefully, separating and washing them free of clinging medium.

3 Plant the seedlings together in a large pot or flat containing moist New Zealand Sphagnum Moss, tree fern fibre or clay shards. *Phalaenopsis* does best in the moss while *Vanda* thrives in the more porous clay shards.

4 Start the plants off well by watering with Transplant Starter Solution containing rooting hormone. There are several commercial products on the market.

5 Feed the seedlings weekly with a dilute, balanced fertilizer solution.

6 Grow the seedlings in a lightly shaded place, making certain that they do not dry out excessively between waterings. After several months the seedlings will be acclimatized to their new surroundings.

7 Remove to individual pots when they become crowded.

TROUBLESHOOTING (GERMINATION AND SEEDLINGS)

COMMONEST CAUSES OF GERMINATION FAILURE

1 The soil mix is too heavy or has been kept too wet.
   REMEDY: use recommended soil mix; protect trays from rain.

2 Too little light
   REMEDY: sow light-requiring seeds on soil surface.

3 Seeds dry out from lack of water.
   REMEDY: check seed trays daily and mist as necessary.

4 Seeds kept too long before sowing.
REMEDY: sow only fresh seed.

5 Seeds have been eaten or carried away by ants.
REMEDY: dust soil with an insecticide such as carbaryl.

6 Seed trays discarded before germination has occurred.
REMEDY: be patient; some seeds take several months or even a year or more to germinate.

COMMONEST CAUSES OF SEEDLING LOSS

1 Overwatering
REMEDY: once seedlings have germinated they need not be kept as moist. Cover seedlings with glass or plastic during rainy weather.

2 Damping-off and other fungus infections
REMEDY: protect seedlings from rain; use an appropriate fungicide.

3 Inadequate air circulation
REMEDY: do not crowd seedlings; keep them well ventilated.

4 Stem biting insects (Cockroaches, Cutworms), Snails or Slugs
REMEDY: dig around the base of freshly cut seedlings to find the large, grey caterpillar (Cutworm) and kill it. Control Slugs and Snails with metaldehyde. Place seedlings trays on layer of wood ashes to discourage pests.

5 Too little sunshine
REMEDY: weak, spindly seedlings need more sunlight to become vigorous. Provide more light gradually so as not to damage weak plants.

6 Too much sun
REMEDY: seedlings unaccustomed to direct sun will suffer bleached or burned foliage; gradually introduce seedlings to sunlight; dappled sunlight (sunshine broken by overhead foliage) is best.

COMMONEST CAUSES OF LOSS AT TRANSPLANTING

1 Root loss or damage during transplantation
REMEDY: take a large mass of soil with the roots; raise delicate plants in individual pots.

2 Failure to partially defoliate the larger seedlings to compensate for root disturbance
REMEDY: Pinch back shoots or remove some of the leaves before transplanting large seedlings.

3 Sunscald
REMEDY: cover transplants with netting or shade with cut leafy boughs for a few days.

4 Lack of water
REMEDY: water seedlings thoroughly before transplanting; minimize root damage; water the plants well after transplanting and daily thereafter until the plants are established.

CHAPTER 3

Landscaping – what to grow where

'Some claim that they love gardens and flowers but not the hard work involved. They do not know the sheer joy of digging, mowing, weeding, sowing, witnessing flowering and fruiting. They do not know what they are missing.'
I.B.

WHERE TO GROW

ELEMENTS OF PLANNING

Designing a garden from scratch can be a gardener's dream: adapting an existing one without adequate planning can become a nightmare. Without design and planning, a garden becomes a confused jumble of unsuitable plants put in wrong places. Some plants will die, some plants will survive; others will get bigger and more intrusive. The only way to salvage such a disaster is redesign and plan again.

It is said that a garden is best planned on the ground. While this method may suffice for the experienced person, a rough paper sketch together with some measurements is essential for inexperienced gardeners (Figure 3.1). Such a simple sketch is not at all intimidating and yet is invaluable in alloting correct placement and space and in determining the number of plants required for the garden. Essential information will include:

1 dimensions of the garden lot;
2 location of slopes, hills, depressions and gullies;
3 size and location of buildings, roads, paths, walls, streams and ponds;

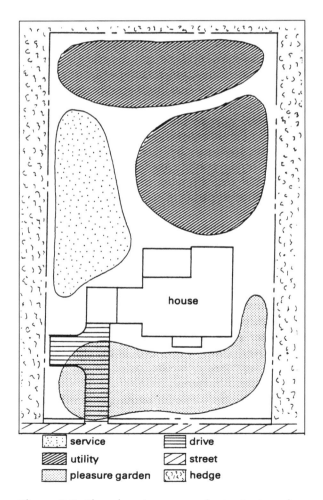

service   drive
utility   street
pleasure garden   hedge

Figure 3.1 Plan showing areas of a typical garden

4 position of existing trees and hedges; and
5 direction of the prevailing wind.

Some consideration should also be given to plans for additional buildings, a swimming pool, an orchid house or fernery.

With this initial sketch, decide upon the function of various parts of the property including views from within the garden and for passers-by; provision of a vegetable, fruit or cut flower area; and the need for screening. As wind, sun, shade, slope, natural features and family needs will all affect your ultimate plan, consider these points individually before preparing the design (Figure 3.2).

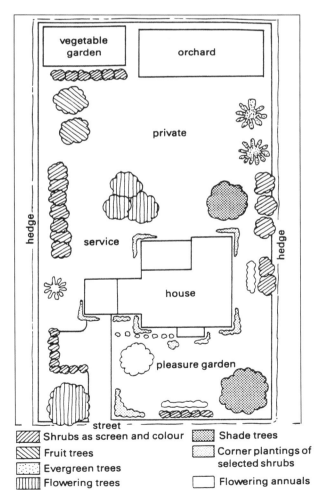

Pattern	Description	Pattern	Description
▨	Shrubs as screen and colour	▦	Shade trees
◩	Fruit trees	▦	Corner plantings of selected shrubs
▨	Evergreen trees		
▥	Flowering trees	☐	Flowering annuals

Figure 3.2 Plan showing types of plants grown in a typical garden

Soil

Soil excavated during building construction is often subsoil and of poor quality. After the builders have finished, even good soil needs treatment to remove the cement debris, paint, tar and other rubbish. The site may have a lovely view but perhaps the lot was sold for housing because the soil was unsuitable for agriculture. On a large property, soil quality and drainage may vary considerably from place to place. Soil assessment is an important part of the planning process. Soil can be improved (see Chapter 1, Soil pages 3–8).

Water

Drainage is of vital importance to a garden. Water running from a roof, bath or kitchen is a problem that can plague an unplanned garden. Areas around taps tend to be wet so they should be placed not only where they are needed but also where adequate drainage exists. Careful planning can turn waste water into a dry season bonanza.

Link the planning of a watering system and a drainage network. Where natural water supplies are lacking and where water use may be restricted during a drought, provide a reservoir for rainwater. Water can be stored in a cistern or in a decorative pond. A pond reservoir may need a liner to conserve the precious resource. Site the pond in full sun, stock it with Water-lilies, Lotus or other decorative water plants, and fish to control mosquito larvae. Water collected from the roof can be directed to the pond. Be sure to install a diversion mechanism in case of torrential rains.

Slope

Banks, hillsides and cliffy slopes offer interesting challenges to the adventurous gardener. The soil may be shallow, well-drained, prone to dryness and erosion. It must be protected from erosion especially during heavy rains.

One way to do this is to establish spreading plants that protect the soil surface from direct impact of rain drops, and deeply rooted or rhizomatous plants which hold the soil in place. Short, gentle banks are the least prone to serious erosion.

Steep hillsides will require more intensive erosion-control planning. Try establishing stepwise terraces across the slope. Plant some of the terraces with a variety of decorative shrubs. Alternate shrubby terraces with those of bedding plants or *Vanda* orchids. If a path network is desired, have it meander along and between terraces rather than straight up and down the slope.

Wherever excessive water movement becomes a problem, interrupt the flow by establishing a rock-filled basin. To stabilise the rocks, enclose them in a wire net basket. Place additional rocks on top to hide the wire.

Wind

While wind can damage a garden (for example breaking stems, tearing leaves or moving soil), a cooling breeze is always an advantage. The house can provide shelter from wind as can hedges of *Hibiscus* and Oleander *Nerium*. Plantings of *Casuarina* trees and Sea Grape *Coccoloba* can be used to diminish the wind effect in a seaside garden. Always try to take advantage of the cooling trade winds and of any existing view, all the while ensuring that your garden is not buffeted by steady winds.

Rocks and cliffs

Rock features are interesting garden elements. Whether of sandstone, limestone, coral or volcanic origin, rocks are found throughout the Caribbean. Where they do not naturally exist in a garden, they may be collected or purchased. A rock garden is a useful addition to a garden having shallow soil. The rocks will provide pockets for placing soil and plants. Drought-tolerant plants such as *Agave*, *Aloe*,

Kalanchoe and *Euphorbia* can be used to create an interesting focal point.

Rocks can also be used to build walls. A decorative vine allowed to grow on the wall will soften the rough surface.

Patterns of light and shadow

Buildings cast morning and afternoon shadows. Some plants cannot tolerate full sun, others are intolerant to total shade. Placing plants correctly according to their light requirements will make them all happy. Walls and fences which cast shadows also afford shelter from heavy winds and driving rain. Study structures and their effect on lighting and air circulation carefully before finalizing your plans. Note that during a year, the sun moves daily a little to the north or to the south. Shade patterns will likewise be affected.

Deciduous trees such as Frangipani *Plumeria* and Flamboyant *Delonix* shed their leaves on a seasonal basis. With foliage, such trees offer shade. Orchids such as 'The Virgin' *Caularthron bicornutum* and 'Cow Horn' *Schomburgkia*, can be established on deciduous trees. As the leaves fall, the orchids will receive more light and will flower.

Light produces attractive shadows such as sunlight passing through a palm hedge and casting patterns of the feathery foliage on the driveway. Likewise moonlight forms magnificent silhouettes of palm foliage overhead.

People

Think of family needs when planning your garden. In the Caribbean, the garden can be an extension of the living room. Merging the indoors with the out-of-doors is necessary and easy to achieve. Consider the daily living routine which may include children at play, pets, parking, delivery of goods, necessary privacy, leisure and entertainment including a barbecue and perhaps a swimming pool. Also consider screening from the road and neighbours, all without necessarily blocking the view. A colourful bed of Crotons *Codiaeum* can be planted inside a boundary wall effectively hiding it. Siting the home appropriately on the lot will take care of some of the privacy and shelter problems before they occur.

DESIGNING A GARDEN

Laying out the garden is rarely accomplished all at once. Usually a garden develops with time, never quite reaching the finishing point. This is one of the delights of gardening. There is always an opportunity for change.

Colour, texture and fragrance

Colourful plants are great favourites with gardeners. Used with skill and artistry they can be blended to create beautiful pictures throughout the year. Imagine a living painted picture, changing between the dry and wet seasons, differing according to the flowering times of each component plant. Careful planning can produce a colourful garden year-round.

The gardener has a veritable palette of colour with which to paint the garden. Green is the most common colour seen in a tropical garden yet there is such a variety of green shades available to a gardener that even the seemingly mundane is no longer so. There are the dark glossy greens of Mahogany *Swietenia*, matt greens of *Cordia*, pale green Bamboos *Dendrocalamus* and *Bambusa*, chartreuse-leaved Aralias *Polyscias* and bronze-green *Acalypha*.

Other colours can be provided by foliage or flowers. *Dracaena* foliage can be green, red, white, pink, all the shades possible in between, and all on the same plant. Variegated foliage plants have foliage with contrasting white stripes, blotches, spots or margins offering an interesting contrast to their all-green counterparts. Variegated *Hibiscus*, *Bougainvillea* and Oleander *Nerium* can be planted as individual specimens or in groups for effect. Multi-coloured Croton *Codiaeum*, *Acalypha*, and *Coleus* are also variegated although with colours other than white. Variegated plants have the most attractive foliage when given sufficient light.

Some plants are hairy or woolly while others may be resplendent with prickles or thorns. Many succulent plants have silvery blue, glaucous foliage which reflects light. Whatever the type of textural element provided by a plant, it can become an interesting focal point if well sited in a garden. Palms are particularly exciting examples with varying colour, spination, hairiness or patterns of petiole remnants on the trunk.

Many plants are fragrant, particularly at night when their flowers attract pollinating moths. Locate scented plants close to the patio or sleeping quarters where they will be appreciated. Flowering trees such as Frangipani *Plumeria* and Ylang Ylang *Cananga odorata* are favourites as is the shrub Lady-of-the-Night *Brunfelsia americana* and vines such as Moon Vine *Calonyction*, Rangoon Creeper *Quisqualis indica*, and Night-blooming Cactus *Epiphyllum oxypetalum*. Moon Vine flowers pop open at dusk adding another element of delight to the entertainment area.

Views

Good views are precious. They can easily be lost to overgrown trees or from lack of planning. Views should be a surprise but never a shock. Allow the garden to create its own atmosphere of peace and quiet.

Caribbean gardens rarely follow formal patterns. Controlling rapid growth such as occurs in the humid tropics can involve a great deal of maintenance. It is better to have plantings that look natural, remembering to take into account the growth rate and ultimate size of shrubs and trees at the planning stage. The aim should always be that of a planting that 'just happened', avoiding the impression of it being artificial and each plant seeming to grow in a place of its own choice. Slow-growing plants such as Rondeletia *Rondeletia odorata* can be included, however they should always be placed with an eye to not being overwhelmed by their quicker growing neighbours.

A good tree in the wrong place is a dangerous nuisance. Roots can heave paving stones and even small buildings. Overhanging limbs can break in a storm. Before deciding what trees you wish to grow and where you want to place them, visit a public park or a private garden where mature trees can be seen. This book gives you guidelines to the height at maturity of trees, but nothing replaces the impact of actually seeing the living tree.

Paths

An important goal in garden design is the harmonious relationship between the garden and its buildings. Paths form an important link between buildings and the environment. Let paths follow strong simple lines: they should allow for natural traffic movement otherwise some ugly short-cuts may develop. Paths should lead somewhere. They might lead to the vegetable patch, to the hidden compost heap or to a bower of orchids naturalized in the trees. Make the paths wide enough to accommodate a lawnmower, a wheelbarrow or a group of friends walking side by side. Paths should be well constructed to ensure safety under all conditions. Plants should not be permitted to overgrow and obstruct a path unless the boughs are well above head height. While low ground covers can be planted right to the edge, most other plants should not be located closer to a path than their height at maturity. For example, a 3–4 m (10–13 ft) tall *Heliconia mariae* should be planted at least 4 m (13 ft) from a path; the shorter *Heliconia stricta* just 1 m (3 ft) distant. Single-stem Palms are a possible exception but even they will be displayed to greater advantage if they are set well back from a path.

Putting it all together

If you have acquired an established garden there may not be much need for drastic change. More often than not, the garden will be overgrown and neglected. It is better to clear and prune sufficiently to take stock of what is growing there rather than to move in with land-clearing equipment only to regret it later. After the initial assessment of garden components and layout, make a sketch map, showing the location and identity of major trees, shrubs and vines, the location of boulders, walls, and existing paths. Prune trees or large shrubs that may be blocking a view or an essential path. It is better to transform difficult objects than to move or remove them. Tree removal is final, costly and potentially dangerous: undertake only after careful consideration and in consultation with a professional trained to execute the work safely. Large boulders and existing stone walls may prove a boon in the new design.

Harmony

The eventual success of a garden will depend upon its relationship to you, your home, the sky, soil, water and natural objects like rocks and cliffs. Rarely can any garden offer perfect conditions for all plants. Although it will be the gardener who will decide what to grow, the garden environment you create will determine what will thrive. Growing some of your favourite plants in containers and moving them about is a possible compromise. Consideration for where container plants will be placed should then become part of the garden plan. Never be shy about trying something new.

USING PLANTS

LAWNS

There is no substitute for a beautifully kept lawn. It forms the framework against which flower beds, shrubs, trees, and arches show to perfection. It also can serve to control erosion and as a surface for recreation. A good lawn should be level, trim and of a uniform texture so that no uneven patches distract the eye from the beauty of the garden.

Grass needs as much attention as any other plant. Soil aeration, good drainage, freedom from weeds and competing tree roots, as well as an adequate nutrient supply, help keep grass healthy and vigorous. Use of the lawn will have a bearing on its condition. Those lawns receiving little traffic will be free of surface compaction whereas high traffic areas may be so compacted to impede the passage of water and air to the grass roots. The appearance of lawn weeds or denuded spots more often than not indicates poor grass-growing conditions that must be corrected.

Soil aeration

While the soil around shrubs can be loosened with ease, cultivating grass plants is more challenging. A spiking tool can be used to aerate the soil. Whether you use a hand held tool with one or two spikes or a large spiked drum pulled by a tractor, the process is the same. The spikes penetrate the soil to a depth of about 8 cm (3 in), breaking the surface crust which allows air and water to gain access to the grass roots. Where the soil has caked sufficiently to kill grass or where a shortcut path has worn and compacted the lawn, the turf is best rehabilitated with a fork. Press the fork into the soil at close intervals, to a depth of 10 cm (4 in), flexing the fork back and forth to loosen the turf and soil. Do not lift the sod, just loosen it. If replanting is necessary, use small pieces of grass with roots (turf) taken from the lawn edges. Discourage passage across the replanted area by closing it off with a temporary fence.

Drainage

Water settling on the lawn indicates poor drainage. A French drain can be installed to draw off excess water. Dig a trench, up to 1 m (3 ft) deep through the poorly drained area. Grade the channel so that the water can run off to the lowest point. Fill the trench with medium-sized stones to a depth of 30 cm (12 in) then fill in the rest with soil. The denuded areas will need to be replanted with small pieces of rooted grass taken from the trench edges.

Other potential problems

Tree roots invading a grass area will rob it of water and nutrients. Tree roots must be dug out. This manoeuvre will not usually harm the tree as new roots are formed quickly, however note that the problem may recur.

Denuded areas of lawn can also be caused by Armyworms, Cutworms or the lawn Webworm. These caterpillars feed on grass leaves and stems. Attacks may be sporadic but the results can be devastating. A clue to an impending problem will be the appearance of the adult moths hovering low over the lawn, laying eggs. Treat the lawn 10 days later (when the eggs hatch) with a drench of appropriate insecticide. Since these pests often have built up resistance to commonly used pesticides, contact your Department of Agriculture (or other Advisory Service) for advice on the most appropriate insecticide for your region.

Fertilizers

Lawns should be fertilized according to fertilizer manufacturer's instructions. Spread the product thinly and water it in immediately to avoid burning the grass. Alternatively, you can prepare your own mixture: to each 15 litre bucket (3 gal) of <u>dry</u> land sand, add 15 ml (1 Tbsp) sulphate of ammonia ($(NH_4)_2SO_4$) and 15 ml (1 Tbsp) of a general fertilizer (18–18–18). Mix well and spread thinly over the lawn. Water well. This procedure can be repeated again one month later, if necessary.

Establishing a new lawn

When starting a lawn from scratch, it is wise to use fresh soil, level the surface and rake it well to remove stones. Water the bare soil. As weed seeds sprout, they will be easy to see and to remove. After several weeks of weeding you can begin planting. In the Caribbean, grass is generally planted from material dug from pastures or purchased by the truckload from nurseries. The sod (turf) is divided into rooted pieces or plugs, using a cutlass. Because of Plant Quarantine restrictions, importation of grass seed may be controlled or prohibited. Check with your local authorities to ensure that what you want to import does not contravene any laws. Treat grass seed with a dry insecticidal powder such as carbaryl before planting (otherwise the ants may feast on your seed!).

Mowing lawns

Grasses adapt well to mowing. Their growing point lies partially buried in the soil, the leaves arising from the base. Mowing cuts off part of the leaf but growth can be renewed. The height of cut is important and dependent upon the type of grass and its growth characteristics. Generally speaking, lawns should be cut to maintain a 2.5–5.0 cm (1–2 in) high turf. Because growth renewal is important to maintain lawn appearance, watering and fertilization must follow mowing.

The size and type of lawn mower will depend upon the area of lawn to be cut and the smoothness of finish required. Hand-powered mowers are suited to lawns of 100 m² (approximately 1000 ft²) whereas power mowers (including those with a seat) are a real labour saver for larger lawns. Electric mowers are reliable however the nuisance of a long cable must be considered. By far the most popular mower for use on large lawns is one powered by a petrol engine. The blade rotates parallel to the ground, thus the common name

'rotary mower'. Mowers with a swath width of 60 cm (2 ft) can be hand-propelled and are suitable for flat areas.

Watering lawns

The need for watering will depend upon rainfall. Those lawns having year-round precipitation need watering only when fertilizers and pesticides are being applied or when new grass is being established. In those regions having seasonal drought, careful consideration must be given to the reasons for watering. Keeping the grass green is one reason. A more important reason is to replenish soil moisture so that the grass will grow faster after use and be more resilient to pest and disease attack. Encourage deep rooting by heavy less frequent waterings. Light sprinklings encourage shallow root growth and increase the probability of damage during dry weather. Dig down in the lawn area to determine the penetration of water. The best time to water is in the early morning or during the evening so that water has a chance to enter the soil before being lost to surface evaporation.

Recommended lawn grasses

See Chapter 4, page 96.

GROUND COVERS

Covering the ground with living plants is one of the most important elements of landscaping. Not only do they keep the garden attractive but they also control erosion by wind and rain, control the growth of opportunistic weeds, protect the roots of permanent plants from excessive heat, and improve the soil aeration and tilth. Even if the ground cover is temporary such as a crop of short term bedding plants such as Marigold *Tagetes*, followed by digging or ploughing under, there will be an immediate benefit to the soil. Marigold plants also produce a nematicide thus rendering yet a second benefit to the process known as green manuring.

Grass lawns are the most popular and widely used of all ground covers but grass may be difficult to maintain or completely unsuitable on rocky outcrops, steep slopes, windy ridges or in deep shade. In place of grass, there are many other plants which can be used to cover the ground effectively. These 'ground covers' include plants for sun or shade, moist or dry areas, and those that are tolerant of wind and salt.

Choosing a ground cover for your garden

Choice of ground cover will be determined by many factors including availability and suitability to the site. Plants recommended for sunny or shady locations are given below and more details on some of these plants will be found in Chapter 4 Favourite Plants.

LAWN LEAF, EVERGREEN LAWN
Dichondra micrantha and D. repens

A creeping low-growing plant which roots freely as it spreads by underground runners. The leaves are kidney-shaped, smooth and lime green. Lawn Leaf can be mowed like grass. In sun, it keeps low 8 cm (3 in) but in damp shade it can reach 16 cm (6 in) in height. It needs extra watering and fertilizer to maintain a rich, velvety appearance.

LILYTURF *Liriope muscari*

An evergreen, clustering plant with long, narrow leathery leaves, Lilyturf spreads by suckering, the clumps gradually enlarging to cover the ground. The inflorescence is upright and crowded with pale mauve flowers followed by attractive polished black fruits. Every two or three years, the plants should be cut with a sickle (or shears) to encourage production of new foliage. At the same time some plants can be dug to harvest suckers for re-

planting elsewhere if need be. Grow in semi-shade. They grow to 20–60 cm (8–24 in) in height.

PURPLE HEART *Setcreasea purpurea*

A fleshy, purple-leaved plant coming from Mexico, Purple Heart is popular for window-box planting and as an edging. It is also useful as a bedding plant and as a ground cover for sunny gravelly locations. The hairy stems are semi-erect and capable of rooting at every node. Reddish-mauve flowers are borne at the tip of a stem.

WHITE LILYTURF, MUNDO GRASS
Ophiopogon jaburan

Often confused with *Liriope*, White Lilyturf is very similar in appearance and behaviour except that the flower spikes are borne amongst the leaves rather than above the leaves. The plants can reach 1 m (3 ft) and bear white to lilac flowers. The variety, 'Variegata' has striped foliage. Grow in semi-shade.

Further ground covers – their details are given in Chapter 4 Favourite Plants.
Aglaonema, Ctenanthe, Calathea: 10–60 cm (4–24 in); shade to semi-shade
Aloe, Crassula, Kalanchoe, Sedum: 15–60 cm (6–24 in); full sun
Bromeliads including *Cryptanthus*: 15–30 cm (6–12 in); semi-shade
Ferns: 30–60 cm (12–24 in); shade to semi-shade to sun
Wild Sage *Lantana*: prostrate to 60 cm (24 in); sun

HEDGES

A hedge is a row of living plants, often trimmed into conventional sizes or shapes. Hedges can vary in size from low borders (edges) of 15–30 cm (6–12 in) to barriers and wind-breaks of 10 m (30 ft) or more in height. Hedges can be used to create discrete spaces and boundaries, to keep out intruders, to provide privacy from neighbours, to screen ugly buildings or views, to give shelter from storms or to act as a windbreak. Hedges can also be used to reduce soil erosion on a slope and to reduce noise pollution from busy roadways. Your choice of hedging plant will depend upon the intended use.

TYPES OF HEDGING

Hedging plants can be trees, shrubs, vines, Agaves, Bromeliads, Cactus, Euphorbias or Yuccas. They can be floriferous such as the ever-blooming *Hibiscus* and Oleander *Nerium* or the dry season bloomer, *Bougainvillea*. They can be chosen for their ornamental foliage. Foliage hedges can be of *Acalypha*, Cordyline *Dracaena*, Croton *Codiaeum*, Aralia *Polyscias*, *Eranthemum* and *Pseuderanthemum*, and variegated-leaved *Hibiscus*. Especially dense and/or prickly plants such as Sweet Lime (Lime Berry) *Triphasia trifolia*, *Bougainvillea*, Cactus Hedge *Euphorbia lactea*, and various cactus including *Opuntia dillenii* and *Cereus* can be used to provide security barriers. On steep hillsides, low hedges can be planted across the slope at intervals as a means of controlling soil erosion. Khus Khus Grass *Vetiveria zizanoides*, or even crop plants such as Tea *Camellia sinensis* and Pigeon Pea *Cajanus cajan* may reduce soil erosion.

Formal hedges

Durable slow-growing plants with dense growth and small leaves are used for formal hedging and topiary work. Sweet Lime is a popular choice for Caribbean gardens. Decorative, relatively drought-resistant and salt-tolerant, it can be used to create the box-type hedge of temperate countries. Bread and Cheese *Pithecellobium unguis-cati* makes a taller, more robust hedge. It can stand neglect but lacks the rich green colour and texture of Sweet Lime. Both plants deter intruders with

their sharp prickles. Bastard Cherry *Ehretia tinifolia*, Philippine Tea *E. microphylla*, and West Indian Holly *Malpighia coccigera* are examples of other small-leaved plants that make compact green hedges.

The dwarf forms of *Ixora coccinea*, *Plumbago capensis* and *Rondeletia odorata* all make colourful formal hedges as they bloom in response to pruning. Pruning can be done three or four times a year and timed, if desired, for special occasions such as family gatherings, parties or receptions.

Clipped hedges should be kept narrower at the top than at the bottom to encourage dense growth near the ground. A 60 cm (2 ft) high hedge should be about 10 cm (4 in) more narrow at the top than at the base. This primary shape should be started with the first trimming, about four months after planting.

Formal hedges need regular maintenance. In order to retain a neat appearance, they will need trimming several times a year. Growth is rapid in the tropics, even more so during the rainy season. If trimming is neglected, plants will lose their lower leaves and become straggly. Special clippers and shears are used for shaping fine-leaved hedges such as China Box *Murraya exotica*, Privet *Ligustrum japonicum*, Sweet Lime *Triphasia trifolia* and West Indian Holly *Malpighia coccigera*.

Semi-formal and informal hedges

Informal hedges are common in the tropics and some quite unusual plants can be used to create them. Gardeners avoid the tedious, hard work at hedge-trimming by planting selections that cannot be trimmed into shape. *Pandanus* and columnar cactus such as *Cereus peruvianus* or *Pilosocereus nobilis* are examples of informal hedging plants. Each needs different treatment to make a useful hedge. Keep the plants tidy by removing dead or damaged foliage or the occasional wayward branch. Palms and *Dracaena* are useful in semi-shaded locations while *Agave americana* makes a very attractive, low maintenance barrier along an exposed cliff edge.

Semi-formal hedges are trimmed but not so frequently. A good pruning once or twice a year will encourage new shoots and fill out bare patches. *Bougainvillea* is a good example of a plant ill-suited as a formal hedge (unless flowers are unimportant) but appropriate to semi-formal management. Choice of *Bougainvillea* variety is important, as is a sunny location. Use *Bougainvillea glabra* and its hybrids as they bear flowers all along the stem. Some regular trimming of errant canes will be required to maintain a neat appearance.

Establishing a hedge

A hedge should be established in a prepared bed and given enough space to grow. Allow as wide an area as the eventual height of the hedge, i.e. 2 m (6 ft) width for an eventual 2 m (6 ft) high hedge. Mark out the area using a line and stakes. A trench should be dug 50 cm (20 in) deep and wide. Any existing plants or turf should be removed and replanted elsewhere. Roots, stones and weeds should be cleared out and clods of earth broken up. The soil must be enriched with plenty of humus, well-rotted compost or manure, and blended with appropriate amounts of all-purpose fertilizer. Generally speaking, 125 ml ($^1/_2$ cup) of 7–7–7 fertilizer is appropriate for each cubic metre (35 ft^3) of soil. Be certain that the soil and amendments are well mixed.

Decide how far apart you wish to position the hedging plants and whether you need to plant a single or a double row. Spacing between plants will depend upon their growth rate and eventual size and shape. Slow-growing or slow-to-establish shrubs such as *Rondeletia odorata* are best planted closer together; fast-growing, spreading plants, for example Christmas Candles *Cassia alata* should be more widely spaced. Allow 50–100 cm (20–40 in) between plants. Closer spacing may be required for small or dwarf plants used for decorative edgings such as *Alternanthera ficoidea* or Periwinkle *Catharanthus roseus*. A hedge may establish more quickly if two rows are planted, the plants in one row being opposite the spaces in the other. This makes a wider hedge and insures the filling in of gaps made by a dead plant. *Bougainvillea* and Poinsettia *Euphorbia pulcherrima* can be planted as a single row whereas the slower growing variegated *Hibiscus* should be established as a double row. Double row planting is also recommended when establishing a windbreak. Plant rooted cuttings or individual plants, but first mark, by inserting small sticks, the place where each plant should go.

Hedging plants may be established as either cuttings rooted by the gardener, or plants purchased from a garden centre. Some plants such as Barbados Pride (Flower Fence) *Caesalpinia pulcherrima* can be started from seed in individual pots. Make a hole in the prepared soil, remove the plant from its container, place it into the hole spreading the roots and covering them with soil, firming well after each soil addition. Water each plant thoroughly to further settle the soil about the roots. If the plants are set lower than the surrounding grade, watering will be more easily accomplished. Water will flow towards the plants not away from them. As with any new plants, extra care has to be taken for them to get established and to build up a good rooting system. Watering must be regular and frequent, starting with a heavy application on the planting day. In sunny, warm or windy weather, two or three waterings a day may be necessary. While the hedge is getting established, you can plant some annuals to act as a temporary and showy groundcover to control weeds. Extra fertilization may be required. Small nematode-deterrent French Marigold *Tagetes* is one choice, others are Balsam *Impatiens* and Forget-me-not *Myosotis*. Wilting annuals will show you that the hedgerow needs water.

Pruning and trimming

The ideal hedge will have dense branching from the base to the top. Rooted cuttings used for hedge planting are often single stems with few side branches. To encourage dense branching, cut off the tops of newly planted hedge plants at 15–30 cm (6–12 in) from the ground. The first shaping should be done about four months after planting. Maintain the desired shape with regular trimming at least twice a year.

Renovating old hedges

Most neglected hedges can be cut back severely at the beginning of the rainy season and can be expected to revive within a year. This is especially true of quick growers as in *Acalypha*, *Aralia*, *Hibiscus*, Oleander and *Plumbago*. Using a sharp pair of secateurs, remove all dead wood and cut back any thick living stems at least 50 cm (20 in) below the desired hedge height. Then using hedge shears, trim finer stems remaining on the top and sides of the hedge to about 25 cm (10 in) below the desired height. Using a garden fork, loosen the soil around the hedge. Mulch the hedge with compost or well-rotted manure. Top dress with a fertilizer such as 14–7–14. For each 15 m (50 ft) length of hedge allow 1 m³ (35 ft³) mulch and 1 kg (2.2 lb) fertilizer. Water thoroughly. Maintain the desired shape with regular trimming beginning about four months after renovation.

Neglected semi-formal and informal hedges generally will not respond to severe pruning. It is usually wiser to remove the old hedge and plant a new one.

TREES AND PALMS

The number of trees and palms planted in a garden and where they will be planted should be determined by the size of the garden, the size of the plants at maturity and the desired effect. Trees and palms can be used to provide a background or to frame a view. They can also be used to provide light or heavy shade, to form a windbreak or screen, or to line a long entry way. Because trees and palms are a major investment and because they will become a large, permanent fixture, they should be chosen with care. Figure 3.3 shows the steps to follow when planting trees and palms.

There are many trees and palms which offer a variety of shape, size and colour. Some details are provided here. Additional information is given in Chapter 4 Favourite Plants under the headings of Trees and Palms.

Planting Palms

When choosing the planting site, remember that the roots of large palms will eventually spread quite a distance and are quite capable of competing with nearby bedding plants for water and nutrients. Prepare the chosen planting area, digging a large planting hole at least twice as deep and wide as the size of the root ball. If the soil is inadequate or poorly drained, a much larger area will need to be prepared. Palms require good soil and plenty of room for their roots to grow if they are to thrive. Prepare the soil by mixing it with well-rotted compost.

Palm roots are fragile. Avoid damage to the roots and drying of the root ball. This is especially important when moving large palms from a nursery or if re-locating palms in an established garden. Clustering palms are easier to transplant than single stem species. Great care must be taken to avoid damaging the growing point when moving palms. It is possible with specialist equipment and skill to move 18 m (60 ft) specimens.

When planting container-grown palms, create a mound of loam in the centre of the hole. Place the palm on the mound, gently spread-

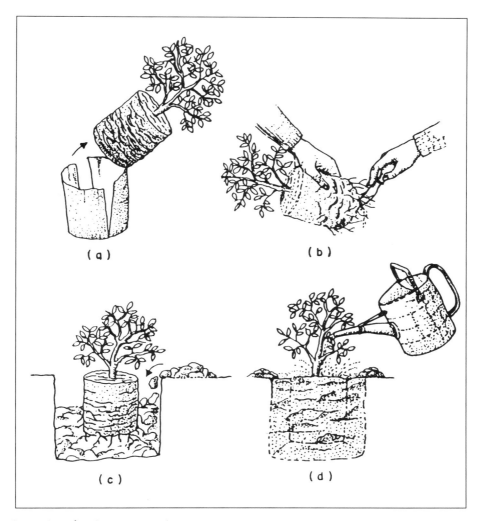

Figure 3.3 Steps in planting a container-grown plant

ing the roots outwards. Holding the palm so that the base of the stem is at the same position relative to the ground level as it was in its container, fill in the hole with prepared soil. When the hole is half-filled, add water to settle the soil about the roots. Add more soil until the hole is filled. Firm gently with your foot ensuring that the soil level is fractionally lower than the surrounds. Water well to avoid stress, especially during the first few months after planting. Transplanted palms should be fertilized for the first time approximately three months after planting, and thereafter twice yearly, using a granular fertilizer (7–7–7) with added trace elements.

Growing Palms in pots

Slow-growing and miniature palms are suited to pot culture. Those that tolerate shade may be grown on a sheltered patio or in bright, indoor locations. Potted palms can be placed individually or grouped for effect.

Pot palms may be started from seed or obtained as seedlings from a nursery. Decorative concrete planters, large clay pots, tubs or large plastic pots may be used as containers. Ensure that there is adequate drainage. Prepare a potting mix of loam and compost. Plant the young palm in the centre of the container and at the level at which it was growing. Fill the pot with soil and press firmly, then water thoroughly. The soil level should be below the edge of the container. If kept in the original container, palms will eventually be restricted in growth although even pot-bound clustering palms will produce new shoots.

To maintain a potted palm, apply dilute liquid fertilizer at monthly intervals according to the growth rate. Ensure that the plants are sheltered from wind and that the soil does not dry out. Water plants thoroughly until water flows freely from the container. If the palms are grown in excessive shade for long periods they may fail to thrive. Such plants should be rotated to a shaded outdoor location on a regular basis. Yellowing foliage is a sign that something is wrong either with the soil, drainage, light or mineral nutrition. There may be an infestation of Spider Mites, Scale Insects or even a disease in progress. Yellow foliage should prompt the grower to examine the plant and take appropriate remedial action.

Favourite Trees and Palms

The colour, height and silhouette (or) of each plant is given in the following selections of favourite trees and palms.

Trees and Palms with attractive foliage and/or fruits

Annatto *Bixa orellana*: 5 m (16 ft); red fruits; wet;

Bearded Fig Tree *Ficus citrifolia*: 18 m (60 ft);

Calabash *Crescentia cujete*: green fruits; 12 m (40 ft); dry;

Caribbean Royal Palm *Roystonea oleracea*: 36 m (120 ft);

Coconut Palm *Cocos nucifera*: green or yellow edible fruits; 12 m (40 ft); dry;

Fishtail Palm *Caryota mitis*: red fruits; 8 m (26 ft);

Mahogany *Swietenia mahagoni*: brown pods; 15 m (50 ft);

Mile Tree *Casuarina equisetifolia*: 25 m (80 ft); dry;

Sea Grape *Coccoloba uvifera*: green to purple fruits; 15 m (50 ft); dry;

Seaside Almond *Terminalia catappa*: green to red fruits; 18 m (60 ft); dry;

Weeping Fig *Ficus benjamina*: 15 m (50 ft);

Trees with beautiful flowers

African Tulip Tree *Spathodea campanulata*: orange scarlet flowers; 20 m (66 ft);

Appleblossom Cassia *Cassia javanica*: pink flowers; 10 m (33 ft);

Bottlebrush *Callistemon lanceolatus*: red flowers; 6 m (20 ft); dry;

Cannonball Tree *Couroupita guianensis*: salmon-red flowers; 20 m (66 ft);

Chaconia *Warszewiczia coccinia*: red flowers; 5 m (16 ft);

Coral Tree *Erythrina* spp.: flame red flowers; 10 m (33 ft); dry;

Cordia *Cordia sebestena*: orange red flowers; 7 m (23 ft); dry; ●

Flamboyant *Delonix regia*: red, yellow, salmon flowers, 7 m (23 ft); ●

Frangipani *Plumeria* spp.: white, yellow, pink or red flowers; 5 m (16 ft); ●

Golden Shower Cassia *Cassia fistula*: yellow flowers; 10 m (33 ft); ●

Horse Cassia *Cassia grandis*: pink flowers; 12 m (40 ft); ●

Lignum Vitae *Guaiacum officinale*: blue flowers; 7 m (23 ft); ●

Mahoe *Thespesia populnea*: yellow flowers; 10 m (33 ft); dry; ●

Orchid Tree *Bauhinia purpurea*: rose-violet flowers; 7 m (23 ft); ●

Pink Poui *Tabebuia pentaphylla* and *T. rosea*: pink flowers; 20 m (66 ft); ●

Pride of India *Peltophorum ferrugineum*: yellow flowers; 20 m (66 ft); ▼

Spanish Ash *Lonchocarpus benthamianus*: mauve flowers; 15 m (50 ft); ●

Yellow Poui *Tabebuia rufescens* and *T. serratifolia*: yellow flowers; 20 m (66 ft); ●

Ylang Ylang *Cananga odorata*: green flowers; 20 m (66 ft); ▼

Trees and Palms suited to smaller gardens (less than 1000 m²)

Bottlebrush *Callistemon lanceolatus*: red flowers; 6 m (20 ft); ●

Chaconia *Warszewiczia coccinia*: red flowers; 5 m (16 ft); ●

Cordia *Cordia sebestena*: orange red flowers; 7 m (23 ft); dry; ●

Frangipani *Plumeria* spp.: white, yellow, pink or red flowers; 5 m (16 ft); ●

Lignum Vitae *Guaiacum officinale*: blue flowers; 7 m (23 ft); ●

Orchid Tree *Bauhinia purpurea*: rose-violet flowers; 7 m (23 ft); ●

Trees and Palms for specimen planting

African Tulip Tree *Spathodea campanulata*: orange scarlet flowers; 20 m (66 ft); ▼

Annatto *Bixa orellana*: 5 m (16 ft); wet; ●

Bearded Fig Tree *Ficus citrifolia*: 18 m (60 ft); ●

Cannonball Tree *Couroupita guianensis*: salmon-red flowers; 20 m (66 ft); ●

Fishtail Palm *Caryota mitis*: 8 m (26 ft); ●

Flamboyant *Delonix regia*: red, yellow, salmon flowers; 7 m (23 ft); ●

Lignum Vitae *Guaiacum officinale*: blue flowers; 7 m (23 ft); ●

Pink Poui *Tabebuia pentaphylla* and *T. rosea*: pink flowers; 20 m (66 ft); ●

Pride of India *Peltophorum ferrugineum*: yellow flowers; 20 m (66 ft); ▼

Shack Shack *Albizzia lebbek*: 7 m (23 ft); dry;

Tamarind *Tamarindus indica*: 20 m (66 ft);

Traveller's Tree *Ravenala madagascariensis*: 12 m (40 ft);

Weeping Fig *Ficus benjamina*: 15 m (50 ft);

Yellow Poui *Tabebuia serratifolia*: yellow flowers; 20 m (66 ft);

Ylang Ylang *Cananga odorata*: green flowers; 20 m (66 ft);

SHRUBS

Shrubs have many uses in the garden including boundary plantings and hedgerows, foundation, background, and specimen plantings. Most shrubs reach maturity in a few years compared to the many years taken for a tree to reach full size. Such quick results appeal to most gardeners.

When designing a garden which will contain shrubs, you need to be familiar with the eventual size of the chosen plants, their texture, colour, and overall habit. The shrubs should harmonize with each other. A few dominant plants can be chosen, the rest being designated as background filler. Filler plants should not clash with dominant or specimen shrubs nearby: for example, glossy, smooth, multi-coloured Crotons *Codiaeum* interplanted with the matt, twisted, coppery foliage of *Acalypha* 'Ceylon' might offer too much contrast to be pleasing. On the other hand, a composite border of different Croton cultivars would offer interest and variety.

Shrubs for boundaries and hedgerows

Vigorous shrubs and other plants can be used to designate the property line as well as to offer privacy. The plant material should harmonize with and be in proportion to the garden. While clipped hedges are a better choice for a small property because they take up less space, tall shrubs (for example Oleander), clustering palms (*Chrysalidocarpus*), bamboos (*Bambusa vulgaris*) and selected small trees (*Bixa*) can be used effectively on larger properties to mark a boundary or to provide a backdrop for a view. Golden Palm *Chrysalidocarpus* and Oleander *Nerium* offer both adequate density and the quick growth needed for boundary or screen plantings. Golden Palm suckers from the base, its arching feathery foliage hiding the trunks. It will require only minimal maintenance such as watering during prolonged drought and removal of dead fronds. Because Golden Palm can reach 6 m (20 ft), tall stems occasionally must be removed to maintain the desired uniformity. Drought- and salt-tolerant Oleander not only produces glossy, goat-proof foliage but it also bears colourful flowers. It can reach 4 m (13 ft) at maturity and will require pruning every 12–18 months to maintain dense vigorous growth. Do not be afraid to prune Oleander: re-growth will be rapid.

Annatto (Lipstick Tree) *Bixa orellana* is a small West Indian tree. It is included in this section because its garden use is primarily as a boundary planting especially where the ground is continually moist such as along a drainage ditch. It can also be used as a specimen on larger properties. Allow a 5 m (16 ft) wide space for this plant.

Plant material suitable for hedging is described in the section on Hedges.

Shrubs with attractive foliage for border plantings and specimens (2 m (6 ft), or more except where noted)

Aralia *Polyscias*: many varieties including those with variegated leaves
Caricature Plant *Graptophyllum pictum*: red-

dish-bronze leaves with creamy yellow splashes; 1 m (3 ft)

Croton *Codiaeum*: many varieties, with green, yellow, red and blended leaves

Dracaena *Dracaena*: narrow-leaf, green or variegated *D. marginata*; broad leaf types in shades of green, red, white and blends

Match-me-not *Acalypha*: many varieties including those with plain and convoluted leaves; green, copper and red foliage

Screw Pine *Pandanus baptistii, P. sanderi*: leaves longitudinally striped cream on green; can be grown as a small plant or into a large specimen of 5 m (16 ft)

West Indian Holly *Malpighia coccigera*: noted for spiny, glossy foliage

Shrubs with beautiful flowers for border plantings and specimens (2 m (6 ft), or more except where noted)

Allamanda *Allamanda cathartica*: yellow flowers

Bougainvillea *Bougainvillea glabra* and hybrids: white, magenta, crimson, orange

Chinese Hat *Holmskioldia sanguinea*: orange red or lime green blooms 1.5 m (5 ft)

Christmas Candles *Cassia alata*: yellow flowers

Coral Hibiscus *Hibiscus schizopetalus*: pink flowers

Golden Dewdrop *Duranta repens*: blue-violet flowers and orange fruits; 5 m (16 ft)

Hibiscus *Hibiscus rosa sinensis* type: various colours

Ixora *Ixora*: red, white, pink, salmon flowers

Mussaenda *Mussaenda*: scarlet, white, pink, yellow flowers

Nasturtium Bauhinia *Bauhinia galpini*: coral-orange flowers

Oleander *Nerium*: pink, white, yellow, red single and double flowers

Pagoda Flower *Clerodendron paniculatum*: orange flowers

Plumbago *Plumbago capensis*: blue or white flowers

Poinsettia *Euphorbia pulcherrima*: red flowers

Pomegranate *Punica granatum*: scarlet flowers; dwarf shrub 50 cm (20 in); standard shrub 4 m (13 ft)

Pride of Barbados *Caesalpinia pulcherrima*: yellow/red flowers

Queen of Flowers *Lagerstroemia indica*: pink, lilac, white flowers

Rose *Rosa*: various colours

Thunbergia *Thunbergia erecta*: dark blue flowers

Turk's Cap (Sleeping Hibiscus) *Malvaviscus grandiflorus*: red flowers

VINES, WALLS AND ARCHES

Vines can be used to advantage when planning a garden. Climbers offer a vertical plane of interest whether they grow up a trellis or cascade down a wall. Vines planted along a chain link fence or a wall will soften otherwise harsh lines, while specimen vines trained over an arch provide an interesting diversion along a garden path. There are many kinds of vines to choose from, most providing a showy display of brilliant blooms, others colourful foliage. Because vines climb in different ways, they must be carefully matched to their intended support. Methods of climbing are categorized as follows:

1 vines that climb by means of tendrils;
2 vines that twine about, scramble or sprawl over a support; and
3 vines that cling by means of hooks, sucker discs or root-like holdfasts.

Support structures suitable for (1) vines with tendrils and (2) those that twine, scramble or sprawl differ from those appropriate for (3) vines with hooks, sucker discs, holdfasts. While vines of category 3 easily adhere to a flat wall surface or climb unaided up a tree, they cannot scale a chain link or wire fence. On the other hand, twiners and vines with tendrils readily climb a fence but cannot adhere to a wall. Consider the ultimate effect of planting a particular vine against a wire fence or modest support. Light-weight vines such as Moon Vine *Calonyction aculeatum*, Blue and White Pea *Clitoria ternatea* or Nightshade *Urechites lutea* are well-matched to a fence or trellis but a heavy vine such as Rangoon Creeper *Quisqualis indica* would soon weigh it down.

Vines that climb by means of tendrils

Corallita *Antigonon leptopus*: flowers year-round, white/pink; woody

Gloriosa Lily *Gloriosa superba*: flowers seasonal, yellow/red; herbaceous perennial

Luffa *Luffa cylindrica*: flowers year-round, yellow; herbaceous annual

Macfadyena corymbosa: flowers seasonal, violet; woody

Passion Flower *Passiflora* sp.: flowers year-round, white, purple, crimson; herbaceous or woody

Vines that twine, scramble or sprawl

Allamanda *Allamanda cathartica*: flowers year-round, yellow; woody

Beacon *Norantea guianensis*: flowers year-round, orange-red; woody

Black Eyed Susan *Thunbergia alata*: flowers year-round, orange or white; herbaceous annual

Bleeding Heart *Clerodendron thomsonae*: flowers year-round, white with red; woody

Blue and White Pea *Clitoria*: flowers year-round, blue; herbaceous annual

Bougainvillea *Bougainvillea*: flowers seasonal, purple, red, orange, white; woody

Chalice Vine *Solandra guttata*: flowers year-round, yellow; woody

Clerodendron splendens: flowers year-round, red; woody

Easter Flower *Securidaca diversifolia*: flowers seasonal, rose-purple; woody

Horsfall Morning Glory *Ipomoea horsfalliae*: flowers year-round, magenta-crimson; herbaceous perennial

Jade Vine *Strongylodon macrobotrys*: flowers seasonal, blue-green; woody

Moon Vine *Calonyction*: flowers year-round, white; herbaceous perennial

Nightshade *Urechites lutea*: flowers year-round, yellow; woody

Purple Allamanda *Cryptostegia grandiflora*: flowers year-round, rose purple; woody

Queen's Wreath *Petrea volubilis*: flowers seasonal, blue or white; woody

Rangoon Creeper *Quisqualis indica*: flowers year-round, changing colour with age; woody

Thunbergia grandiflora: flowers year-round, blue; woody

Thunbergia mysorensis: flowers year-round, yellow/red; woody

Vines that climb by means of hooks, sucker discs or root-like holdfasts

Golden Shower, Cat's Claw Creeper *Macfadyena unguis-cati*: flowers seasonal, golden yellow; woody

Philodendron *Philodendron* spp. waxy green foliage; herbaceous perennial

Wax Plant *Hoya carnosa*: flowers year-round, pink; herbaceous to woody

Jade Vine *Strongylodon macrobotrys*, *Thunbergia grandiflora* and *T. mysorensis* are some good examples of vines best grown over a tall arch. These vines produce pendant racemes of blooms which show to best advantage hanging beneath the foliage where they can be viewed either from beside the support or from beneath it. A strong arch will be needed to support the growth of vigorous woody vines. Locate the arch in an area sheltered from wind.

Some vines are massive and will require considerable support. *Petrea* is one such perennial twiner, Beacon *Norantea guianensis* another. Beacon can reach the tops of forest trees in its South American habitat. These vines are seen to good effect when planted up against or overhanging a steep bank, cliff or wall.

Gloriosa Lily *Gloriosa superba* is a delicate herbaceous climber which thrives best where its tuber-like roots are planted in rich well-drained soil and shaded by the branches of a supporting shrub. It will grow up through the shrub and display its flowers to the sun. The companion shrub must have dark green foliage to form an appropriate foil for the flowers. The vine can also be grown on a standard trellis or arch providing that shallow-rooted annuals are planted as a ground cover.

Luffa (Vegetable Sponge) *Luffa cylindrica* is quick-growing vine that produces large bright yellow flowers followed by 30 cm (12 in) cylindrical fruits that eventually become dry and spongy. Mature fruits are split longitudinally and cleaned to remove the seeds before using them as sponges.

Many flowers are especially fragrant at night. Perennial Moon Vine *Calonyction aculeatum* bears large white blooms that open 'before your very eyes' at dusk. Rangoon Creeper *Quisqualis indica* is also called Lad's Love because the flowers change colour from one day to the next. This vine will establish on a wall in semi-shade or in full sun. Position night-fragrant vines near the home or patio for maximum effect.

If a perennial woody vine must be removed for wall maintenance, cut it back and allow vigorous new growth to re-establish after the work is completed. Vines such as Luffa and Moon Vine can be started again from seeds. Plant woody vines following the steps outlined for trees and shrubs in Figure 3.3.

BEDS AND BORDERS

Annual and perennial herbs, small shrubs and succulent plants can be used very effectively in garden design. Smaller plants are more attractive when planted close together as a group. Imagine a mass planting of velvety red-leaved *Coleus*. As single plants they would be lost against the rest of the garden but as a group, their colour and texture make a statement. Larger shrubs can be grouped for all-round viewing, arranged about a large boulder, or massed along the edge of the house or in a corner of the garden. The shrubs can be all the same cultivar – *Hibiscus* 'Tylene'; different cultivars of the same plant – different *Hibiscus*; or they can be altogether different genera. When mixing cultivars and/or species, the growth habit of each sort should be understood before deciding where to plant it in a bed. Taller specimens should be planted to the back of a bed or towards the centre of an all-round bed. Shorter types are arranged in the foreground. Try grouping flower or foliage colours together in several beds. For instance, establish a group of mauve-flowered *Impatiens* or the green and white-leaved *Caladium candidum* in a shady corner.

Garden beds can be used to provide a natural setting for the house, changing the harsh straight lines of the property into gentle curves. The beds can be arranged to partially obscure the view in the distance. As you pass through the garden there will always be an air of mystery as to what lies beyond. A bench can be placed to allow you to pause and enjoy the view.

Minimal to substantial maintenance is needed for garden beds depending upon the plants chosen. Annuals such as *Cosmos*, Marigold *Tagetes* and *Zinnia* can be planted on a seasonal basis then removed when their blooming season is over. Perennial beds of *Begonia*, Ground Orchid *Spathoglottis*, and *Aglaonema* will last several years before heavy maintenance becomes necessary. Dig, propagate and replant perennial herbs to a freshly prepared bed to avoid possible pest and disease problems. Shrubs require regular seasonal maintenance including removal of spent blooms, pruning, fertilizer application and mulching. A well-managed bed of Croton *Codiaeum* will give many years of pleasure.

CONTAINER PLANTING

Hanging baskets, window boxes, tubs and planters can be used to grow a wide variety of flowers, vines, shrubs and even vegetables. Container gardening presents certain advantages over conventional gardening in beds. Containers save space. Those who have postage stamp-sized patios or simply an apartment verandah will have space to hang a basket or to grow a favourite shrub or annual in a tub. You have complete control over the soil in the container, and the minimal effort and tools required to plant and maintain them. Containers can also be moved and rearranged for optimum results.

Pots can be plastic, pottery, wood or concrete: baskets may be constructed of wire or plastic mesh. Even steel drums cut in half crosswise or lengthwise can serve as containers. Plastic Gro-Bags are ready-to-use containers consisting of a plastic bag enclosing sterilized compost and sometimes with added nutrients.

When starting to plant a container from scratch, follow a few simple rules for best results. The soil mix should be light and porous. Avoid using raw garden soil as it may harbour disease organisms, pests, and weed seeds. You can prepare your own soil mix by blending peat moss, compost, perlite, vermiculite, sterilized potting soil, and crushed dolomitic limestone or marl. To achieve the right consistency, apply the hand texture test. Wet soil mix should just form a mass when squeezed firmly. If the mass is too dense, add more perlite.

Containers will dry out quickly and will require daily or more frequent watering especially during hot, dry, windy weather. Hanging baskets are particularly vulnerable. Line a basket with water-retentive moss, coconut fibre, or black plastic. If you use plastic, be generous: you can always cut off the excess. Make small holes in the plastic to allow for drainage. Large pots, tubs and drums should be lined with insulating styrofoam then filled with potting mix. An alternative way to shelter containers and vulnerable plant roots from excessive heat is to place decorative rocks outside them to shade the exposed surfaces. Sometimes the plants themselves will grow to form a natural foliage shield.

When planting containers, you can either sow seeds directly, use transplants, or rooted cuttings. *Zinnia*, Marigold *Tagetes*, *Cosmos*, Lettuce *Latuca* and culinary herbs should be direct sown whereas Tomato *Lycopersicon* and *Petunia* are best established as transplants, and *Hibiscus*, Croton *Codiaeum* and *Lantana* as rooted cuttings. Choose well-rooted, vigorous plants for containers. Be generous with your planting, especially of flowering plants. Keep pots, tubs and baskets under cover until the plants are established. A heavy rain can easily wash out tiny plants.

Whatever you choose to grow, the plants will need to be fed. A slow-release fertilizer can be added to the soil before planting or you can provide dilute liquid fertilizer solution on a weekly basis using a solution of 20–20–20 at 1 ml/5 litres ($1/4$ tsp/gal). More control can be exercised with weekly feeds. Flowering and fruiting plants will need more phosphorus and potassium in their season.

Dangerous levels of mineral salts can accumulate in container soil. Browning leaf tips will tell you that too much mineral is present. Flushing with rainwater can correct the imbalance. Be certain to water so that the excess flows from the drainage holes. If possible, place the container in the rain for several hours. Flush excess salts from the soil once a month.

Most sun-loving flowers and vegetables will require at least six to eight hours of daily sunshine to thrive. If direct sunlight is lacking or if the sun traverses your growing area, you can place large containers on casters and move them to follow the sun. Alternatively, plant shade-loving annuals, ferns or *Aglaonema*. Palms make excellent subjects for container growing.

WATER GARDENS

Few gardens can compare to those with a water feature included in some aspect of the design. Probably the most important consideration is the location of an ornamental pool. Water plants need sunshine. There must be adequate light to support their growth. The size and shape of the pool are the gardener's choice, however it need not be large nor even conventionally square or round. Small water gardens can be built using anything from a sunken bathtub, to a fibreglass mould, or a lined concrete structure. Whatever container is used, be aware that certain materials contain substances toxic to plants. Concrete pools are best lined with vinyl or butyl rubber.

Concrete pools can be cast in any shape. Prepare a good quality concrete: it has to last! A suggested recipe is 1 part gravel or crushed stone to 2 parts builder's sand to 1 part cement. Contact a local builder if you are not certain about this work. Walls should be a minimum 15 cm (6 in) thick and laid on a 15–20 cm (6–8 in) deep bed of coarse gravel. If you wish to grow Water-lilies *Nymphaea*, you will need a minimum water depth of 60 cm (24 in).

Water circulation and aeration

Spring or stream-fed pools are best located to one side of the natural water course. This is especially important during heavy rains when all can be swept away in a surge, leaving behind a lot of silt and plants somewhere down the hill. Provide an overflow mechanism to control the level in the pool and a bypass to divert heavy flow. Aeration of the pool water is important, especially if you plan to have fish in the pool. A very small pool can be fitted with a recirculation pump and perhaps a small fountain or decorative cascade over poolside rocks. Larger pools generally have sufficient surface area to be self-aerating.

Planting water gardens

Water-lilies *Nymphaea* are unsurpassed for their beauty. Water plants with floating leaves prefer quiet water and should never be planted where the surface is continually disturbed as near a fountain. Large, spreading water plants must also be located with an eye to containing their growth. For each plant allow up to 2 × 2 m² (6 × 6 ft²) of pool surface. Crowded plants will not thrive nor will they be attractive. One of the best ways to control the growth of water plants is to plant them individually in wooden boxes. The boxes need not be large but should be in proportion to the plant root or tuber. For example, a small Water-lily will need a box 30 cm (12 in) square and 30 cm (12 in) deep whereas a Lotus *Nelumbo* will require a box 50 cm (20 in) square and 50 cm (20 in) deep. The boxes should be made of rot-resistant wood such as Greenheart. <u>Do not use wood that has been treated with wood preservatives such as creosote, pentachlorophenol or green salts (copper salts). These substances are harmful to plants and aquatic animals.</u> The box should have solid walls and a base but need not be sealed. Sections of concrete drain pipe, 60 cm (24 in) tall and wide, could be used for Lotus.

Soil mix

Prepare a soil and compost mix of 3 parts garden loam to 1 part composted cow manure or vegetable matter. Granular fertilizer or a slow-release product should be incorporated into the soil before planting. Water plants are heavy feeders. Half fill a box with moist soil mix. Plant the Water-lily or Lotus, growing point up, covering it with more soil but leaving the growing point protruding. Add a layer of coarse sand or gravel to keep the soil from being disturbed when the box is placed in the pool. If necessary, you can use a stone to hold the root in place, especially during the first few weeks after planting.

To provide more fertilizer to water plants as they grow, prepare muslin bags containing about 50 ml (3 Tbsp) of a balanced soluble fertilizer (20–20–20), allowing about three bags per plant. Place these bags in the soil of each box, keeping well away from the growing point. Feed the plants every three months.

One advantage of using boxes as plant containers is that they can be arranged at whatever depth you wish, simply by placing them on stones or bricks of the appropriate height. Lotus roots need a minimum of 10 cm (4 in) of water over their growing point: Water-lilies need 20–30 cm (8–12 in) water cover.

Designing the water garden

The most attractive designs seek to integrate the water garden with its surroundings. As the plants grow and mature, the side of the pool becomes a pond edge, with poolside plantings complementing the floating specimens. Some interesting poolside plants are the 3 m (10 ft) Chinese Goddess Bamboo *Bambusa riviereorum*, the Bromeliad *Aechmea dichlamydea* and Umbrella Sedge *Cyperus alternifolius*. Sunken tubs can be used to accommodate poolside plants that love wet feet. Where the soil surrounding the pool is naturally soggy because of springs, moisture-loving palms such as the colourful Sealing Wax Palm *Cyrtostachys renda* can be grown. Group poolside plants leaving plenty of space to view the Water-lilies. Some water plants are nice on their own without any contrived arrangement, others should be planted deliberately to produce the desired effect. Lotus *Nelumbo lutea* produces leaves 1 m (3 ft) long that stand above the water. These tall plants should be planted in shallow water near the edge of a large pool. Spectacular Water Platter *Victoria amazonica* with up to eight leaves per plant, 2 m (80 in) wide, is perhaps best confined to a pool by itself.

Night-blooming Water-lilies and *Victoria* are best admired if poolside lighting is in-

stalled. Before finalizing the installation, try temporary lighting arrangements at different heights and angles. Observe the lit pool from the patio, the poolside or from a nearby path. Illuminate only one part of the pool, leaving the other part ever mysterious and in shadow. For safety, have the permanent fixtures and fittings installed by a licenced electrician with experience in outdoor lighting.

Gardens for wet places

Another kind of water garden makes use of naturally damp or soggy garden areas to grow moisture-loving plants. The damp area may have developed because of surface drainage or because of a spring. As stagnant pools of water can harbour mosquito larvae, plants that sop up excess moisture are to be encouraged, especially if they are capable of transforming an unsightly wet space into a something of beauty. Choose plants according to light requirements, height and colour.

Tall Aroids such as variegated-leaf forms of *Alocasia macrorrhiza* are an excellent choice. Common salmon-pink and yellow forms of the Shrimp Plant *Beloperone guttata* are recommended for sunny to semi-shaded damp areas. Balsams such as *Impatiens sultanii* prefer semi-shade and offer bright flowers in various shades of pink, mauve and white. They blend particularly well with ferns such as Maidenhair Fern *Adiantum* spp. and will be quite at home when planted in niches of a moist rock surface. Variegated Umbrella Sedge *Cyperus alternifolius variegatus* standing over 1 m (3 ft) tall will thrive in truly wet ground provided there is adequate sunlight. The leaves and stems are striped white, making it most suitable as cutting material for decorative arrangements. The annual grass Job's Tears *Coix lacryma-jobi* 60 cm (2 ft) tall may be grown for its 1 cm (0.25 in) long decorative fruits. Seedlings should be planted about 25 cm (10 in) apart in a sunny damp location. The very spiny, shade-loving Macaw Palm

Aiphanes minima is an interesting choice for a seasonally damp gully while Sealing Wax Palm *Cyrtostachys renda* requires more sun and year-round moisture.

Whatever your choice of **plant material**, always bear in mind the design principle that only a few dominant plants should be used, with other plants harmonizing with the dominant ones. This will ensure that the effect is neither monotonous nor a jumble.

SEASIDE AND OTHER DRY GARDENS

If your garden is located close to the sea or is in a low rainfall region such as Antigua, Aruba or Tortola, it will be subject to stresses which can include salt-laden air and drying winds. How do you go about designing a garden to look attractive and yet withstand these potential adversities? The first adversary of your garden will be the salt-laden wind. No matter how tolerant a plant is to salt, heat or drought, if it cannot withstand the wind, it will be beaten down, bent and deformed, and often die. If shelter belts or fences are erected to deflect hot, drying winds, some garden plants can survive. Adequate supplies of fresh water will be needed to establish those first 'front line' plants.

Creating a temporary wind break

The easiest shelter to build is one of palm fronds woven between upright posts. The wind break should be at least 2 m (6 ft) tall and 3 m (10 ft) wide. Individual units can be built and placed in a staggered fashion or all in a row. The posts must be driven well into the soil to hold the shelters in place. Where only bare rock or coral exists, the structures can be supported by concrete blocks placed on either side of them. Once an effective windbreak is built, drought- and salt-tolerant plants can be planted behind it to form a more attractive,

permanent living shelter. The palm frond fences can be removed once these plants are well established.

Establishing a permanent living windbreak

Choose trees and shrubs that are characteristic of seaside locations. These include Sea Grape *Coccoloba uvifera*, Seaside Almond *Terminalia catappa*, *Casuarina equisetifolia*, Galba *Calophyllum antillanum*, Coconut Palm *Cocos nucifera* and *Cordia sebestena*. Tamarisk *Tamarix* sp. is recommended for seashore locations in Bermuda and in the Bahamas. On sandy beaches and where coconuts are plentiful, sprouting nuts planted almost touching one another will quickly form a windbreak. As soon as a trunk begins forming, they can be thinned. For beach locations where the plants are bathed with salt water at high tide, Manchineel *Hippomane mancinella* and Mangrove *Conocarpus erectus* may prove useful as a windbreak and to stabilize the shoreline.

Note Manchineel contains a POISONOUS MILKY SAP that makes all of its parts dangerous to touch. Use protective clothing then wash with soapy water after planting fruits or saplings.

The living windbreak will develop a characteristic shape dependent upon the wind it is deflecting. Along the East Coast Road of Barbados, Sea Grape trees *Coccoloba* have been established as a windbreak for public gardens and parks. These 'trees' are no more than 3 m (10 ft) tall but have spread out in a wide sloping bank of densely packed branches and foliage. They have been sculptured by the unrelenting wind. Along the sheltered West Coast and without the influence of strong breezes, Sea Grape trees can reach their full 10–15 m (30–50 ft) height.

Designing your seaside garden

While the living windbreak is establishing itself you can experiment with different flowering and foliage plants grown in containers. Some soil improvement will probably be necessary if you wish to establish a lawn, grow shrubs or bedding plants.

If you wish to establish a lawn, try some of the grasses recommended for seashores such as St. Augustine Grass *Stenotaphrum*, *Zoysia*, or for acidic sandy soil, Centipede Grass *Eremochloa*. All of these can be established most easily at the beginning of the rainy season. Plant rooted sprigs about 25 cm (10 in) apart. Given suitable conditions, a well-knit turf will develop in just a few months. Lawn Leaf *Dichondra repens*, a low-growing creeper spreading by underground runners will do well in sandy soil but requires regular watering to become established and to maintain its appearance. Coarse ground covers such as the Seaside Bean *Canavalia maritima* and the Seaside Yam *Ipomoea pes-caprae* are not only attractive when in or out of bloom but also are valuable sand-binding plants. Both will grow to the high water mark. If grass proves difficult to establish, one or both of these plants could be an alternative. Plant rooted cuttings or seeds.

There is a wealth of interesting plant material available to the adventurous gardener. Whether you wish to have a foliage garden, a flower garden, one composed of succulents and cactus or a collection of Caribbean native plants, there are many varieties from which to choose. Among the favourite perennial plants are *Yucca*, Oleander *Nerium*, *Aloe* and *Agave*, *Jatropha*, Slipper Flower *Pedilanthus* and Wild Sage *Lantana*.

Yuccas produce long spikes of creamy-white, bell-shaped flowers. Some plants form stemless rosettes of dark green, sword-like leaves whereas taller growing kinds can resemble small trees. Oleanders can be used to provide both flowers and foliage. The variegated leaf variety is particularly attractive when used as a contrast to darker foliage.

Common Wild Sage *Lantana* spp. are straggly shrubs with flowers of red, yellow, orange, white, purple or rosy lilac. In a moist inland garden they would be considered weeds but in the dry, seaside garden they thrive where others would falter. Plant Wild Sage amongst rocks and in other rough places where soil improvement would be difficult.

There are many cactus and succulent plants to choose from. Entire beds can be devoted to cactus, or inter-planted with the blue-grey *Agave americana*, red-flowered *Aloe* and mat-forming *Crassula*. An interesting effect can be obtained by establishing 'islands' of decorative plants. Link and surround these beds with a path paved with crushed coralstone, coarse sand or gravel.

Periwinkle *Catharanthus roseus* is an attractive flowering plant that can be used in hanging baskets, beds, borders and edgings. New varieties of Periwinkle such as 'Parasol' have 5 cm (2 in) flowers in shades of rosy pink, orchid purple, and snow white, many with a contrasting red eye. Suitable bedding plants include *Portulaca*, *Cosmos* and *Verbena*.

Certain orchids can be grown once the garden is established with trees to provide shelter from wind and sun. These orchids will be those adapted to seaside locations and include the 'Virgin' *Caularthron bicornutum*, *Broughtonia sanguinea* and *B. negrilensis*. Vigorous, flowering size orchid seedlings or divisions of healthy cultivated plants can be attached at eye level to the sheltered side of a living tree trunk or heavy branch. Newly planted orchids should be watered several times daily until roots become established.

Cane-type 'antelope' *Dendrobium* orchids native to the coastal regions of Papua New Guinea and northern Australia are another choice. These orchids present long-lasting sprays of yellow, red, green or purple flowers. They bloom year-round. Hybrids are especially vigorous and recommended. Establish these orchids in pots containing broken crocks. Arrange the pots in a group, surrounding them with coconut husks and enclosing the pots with decorative rocks or bricks to form a bed. When watering, thoroughly wet the husks to provide additional moisture and humidity.

The more plants you successfully establish, the more plant material will be incorporated into the soil. This in turn will improve water retention and nutrient supply. Your seaside garden will improve with time – naturally.

FLOWER ARRANGEMENTS

Now that your garden is brimming with interesting flowers and foliage, choose some to decorate your home. The best time to cut flowers and foliage is early morning or late afternoon. Be certain that the plants are not suffering from lack of water. To extend the vase life of *Heliconia*, Red Ginger *Alpinia*, *Anthurium*, water the plants well two to three hours before harvesting flowers or foliage. Use a sharp clean knife or secateurs to cut stems. Be especially careful when harvesting orchid blooms. Use disposable razor blades or sterilized tools to avoid spreading virus diseases between plants. Have buckets of clean, cool water waiting in a shady place to receive your harvest. Handle delicate blooms with care!

Uncut flowers can last from a few hours to many weeks depending upon the type, its condition and the weather. *Hibiscus* flowers last 12–48 hours depending upon the variety; Carnation *Dianthus*, 10–20 days; Red Ginger *Alpinia*, and *Heliconia*, 3–4 weeks; and Orchids, from 1 day to several months, *Vanda* blooms being among the longest lived. If properly conditioned, a cut flower should last almost as long as if it had remained on the plant. There are many techniques involved in conditioning and hardening freshly cut flowers and foliage to achieve their longest possible vase life.

ROUTINE INITIAL HANDLING OF CUT FLOWERS AND FOLIAGE

1 Remove unwanted or damaged leaves, stems and flowers.
2 Remove prickles and thorns.
3 Dip flower heads in water to freshen them.
4 Remove debris, dirt or ants.
5 Sort the material according to the required conditioning treatments.
6 Before arranging, allow all cut material to have 'a good drink'.

Conditioning treatments

RE-CUTTING UNDER WATER

As soon as a flower or branch is severed from a plant, its supply of water is cut off. The flowers and leaves continue to lose moisture via transpiration, creating a suction that draws air into the water conducting system at the cut ends. As the water remaining in the stem is now limited, the flowers and foliage lose turgidity and droop. Placing the cut stems in water does not remedy the situation because air bubbles now block the passage of water. To resolve this dilemma, simply hold freshly cut stems under water and remove the lower 2.5 cm (1 in) of each stem. The upward flow of water will resume. This simple technique greatly increases vase life.

PARTIAL OR TOTAL SUBMERSION

Most flowers benefit from complete submersion of their stems during the conditioning process. Keep the containers in a cool, shady place. Different plants need different periods of treatment to get maximum benefit. The softer the stem, the less time is needed to fully absorb water. From two to six hours is required for most herbaceous plants. The harder woody stems will require a longer period of up to 24 hours. Aralia *Polyscias*, Croton *Codiaeum*, and Limonia *Murraya* require that the whole branch, leaves and all, must be submerged overnight if the foliage is to last one or two weeks.

Amaryllis *Hippeastrum*, Eucharis Lily *Eucharis grandiflora*, *Gladiolus* and flowers of other bulbous plants require different treatment. Their fleshy hollow stems will buckle and collapse if kept immersed in water. Instead of immersing them, place the cut stems in only a few centimetres of water. It is best to harvest them in the early morning, condition them during the day and arrange them in the late afternoon.

CRUSHING TREATMENT

Flowering branches of trees such as *Bauhinia*, *Cassia*, and *Delonix* can make stunning arrangements but require pre-treatment to prevent drooping. A method used to condition these and other woody stems is to beat the ends of the stems with a hammer and then dip in boiling water. The flowers and foliage should be wrapped in newspaper to protect them from steam. The boiling water treatment can last 30–60 seconds or more, depending upon the size of the stem.

SEALING TREATMENT

Frangipani *Plumeria*, Poinsettia *Euphorbia pulcherrima* and Snow-on-the-Mountain *Euphorbia leucocephala* are plants which exude a milky latex when cut. Boiling water or rubbing alcohol (isopropanol) treatment will help seal their stems and prolong their vase life provided that the blooms are mature. Three or four days before harvesting the stems, remove all leaves that will not be part of the floral arrangement. When harvesting the blooms, first dip the cut ends in sand then into very hot water or alcohol. Every subsequent cut must be similarly treated. Transfer treated material to a bucket containing water and ice cubes. Great care must be taken to avoid bruising or any other accidental cut which can lead to loss of sap. Take particular care not to touch the face while handling plants with a milky latex and always wash hands afterwards: the sap can IRRITATE the eyes.

Arranging flowers

There are many excellent guides on the subject of floral design, however even the best designs will be disappointing if the plant materials are not in the best condition. Harvest mature foliage and flowers. Clean the material and condition it, using the most appropriate method. Choose a container in proportion to and harmonious with the material to be arranged. Use a pinholder or a floral sponge product, for example Oasis, to hold the arrangement in place. For a truly long-lasting arrangement, be certain that the container and holder are clean. Keep the water fresh. If possible, treat the water with a product designed for the purpose, for example Flower Fresh.

One of the simplest arrangements possible is one with *Hibiscus* flowers. The blooms may last but one day but they can be arranged without water. *Hibiscus* blossom pedicels can be impaled upon the thorns of a branch of Natal Plum *Carissa grandiflora*. The shiny dark green leaves form an interesting backdrop for the colourful *Hibiscus*. Blooms of *Hibiscus* may also be tied to thin bamboo sticks or to coconut leaf midribs. Possibly the simplest idea is a lazy daisy chain of *Hibiscus* blooms and glossy *Citrus* leaves laid the length of a luncheon table.

Whether you choose a simple arrangement or a more complex one, you are certain to find a wealth of suitable materials in a Caribbean garden.

CHAPTER 4

Favourite Plants

'This not meant to be a coffee-table book. It is for you to read and refer to. It is for you to learn about gardening and so avoid some of my mistakes. I have tried to pass on as much as possible of the knowledge I have gained in over half a century of appreciating, cherishing, growing, loving, studying, using and working with plants.'   I.B.

INTRODUCTION

Descriptions of some of our favourites are given in this chapter; plants we have grown and plants that have returned our loving care with a fabulous display of foliage, flowers and fruit. While some of these can be difficult to raise, others are decidedly easy. There are suggestions for every garden whether it be wet or dry, sunny or shady, warm or cool. Here you are certain to find some plants that will become your favourites.

This chapter is divided into sections; within each section, plants are arranged in alphabetical order by common name, or if there is no common name, then by botanical name. The Index of Common Names and the Index of Botanical Names are cross-referenced. Refer to the Glossary for definitions of technical terms.

Although some cultural information is provided here, further details about soil mixes, fertilizers, pests, diseases, and propagation techniques are given in the other chapters. Refer to Chapter 2 for seed propagation Methods I, II and III, and Special Cases.

AROIDS

Aroids are grown primarily for their interest-

> **Basic care**
> Light: semi-shade
> Water: high relative humidity; frequent watering during dry periods
> Soil: fibrous peaty soil with good drainage
> Fertilizer: one-quarter strength liquid fertilizer applied every two weeks
> Pests and diseases: Spider Mites can be a problem if plants are kept too dry; Leaf Spot and Soft Rots
> Propagation: cuttings; suckers; fresh seed using Method II

ing foliage, however it is their unusual inflorescence that sets them apart from other plants. Most aroids have a rather inconspicuous inflorescence while a few such as *Anthurium* and Arum Lily *Spathiphyllum* produce a striking 'bloom'. The large white, pink, red or green sheath-like bract is called the **spathe**; the upright flower spike composed of separate male and female flowers is called the **spadix**. Aroids grow best when planted in a rich moist compost and grown in the semi-shade.

AGLAONEMA *Aglaonema*

The best known of these shade-tolerant plants is *A. modestum*, the dark green-leaved Chinese Evergreen. This species and others can be used as ground covers or as bedding plants. More decorative species include

A. commutatum: light green blotches on its dark green foliage

A. costatum: short stem; dark green leaves with white midrib and white spots

A. oblongifolium var *curtisii*: up to. 1 m (3 ft) tall; lovely pale green feathering on dark green leaves

A. roebelinii: pale green blotches on either side of darker green midrib and margin

Propagate by suckers and by rooted cuttings.

ALOCASIA *Alocasia*

Alocasias have very decorative foliage. *A. cuprea* has metallic copper-coloured quilted leaves that are purple beneath. This striking 1 m (3 ft) tall plant grows from a swollen rhizome. *A. sanderiana* is a magnificent plant with metallic dark green, lobed leaves that are veined and edged with white. The petioles are purple-brown. Grow Alocasia in dappled sunlight. Provide a very open soil mix of coconut fibre, coarse sand and leaf mould. Feed every two weeks. Propagate by offsets or from seed.

ANTHURIUM *Anthurium*

Some Anthuriums are grown for their magnificent foliage, others for their beautiful long-lasting blooms. Keep Anthurium lightly shaded. Grow in a very porous mix of compost, leaf mould, or rotted bagasse. Feed the plants every two weeks with a liquid fertilizer diluted to manufacturer's instructions. If the plants fail to thrive, loosen the soil about their roots. Propagate by division and from seed.

ANTHURIUMS GROWN FOR THEIR FOLIAGE

A. aemulum is a climber with glossy compound leaves. It can be grown in a basket.

A. crystallinum has glistening heart-shaped emerald-green leaves with crystalline white veins.

A. warocqueanum is prized as one of the largest Anthuriums, having leaves over 1 m (3 ft) long. The leaves are arrow-shaped, dark green with contrasting white veins.

ANTHURIUMS GROWN FOR THEIR FLOWERS

A. andraeanum and its hybrids are grown for their attractive spathes which can be dark red, salmon, white or pink. The 'Rhodochlorum' hybrids have large irregularly-shaded spathes with colour combinations of green and red. The spathe will gradually change colour as it matures.

A. scherzerianum is characterized by a bright red spathe and a curly spadix.

ARUM LILY *Spathiphyllum*

Dark green foliage and elegant white spathes are the hallmark of the two commonly cultivated species, *S. floribundum* and *S. wallisii*. Propagate by division.

CALADIUM *Caladium*

Caladiums are seasonally-dormant tuberous aroids with very colourful white, red and green foliage. Some choice cultivars are the rose-pink 'Lord Derby', bright red-leaved 'Frieda Hemple', and the miniature 'Miss Muffet'. Plant the tubers in sandy soil enriched with fibrous compost. The soil should just cover the tuber. Caladiums are well suited to pot culture and also to mass planting in semi-shade. After the foliage has lost its appeal, withhold water from pot plants or lift the tubers from the garden. Store in a dry place for three months. Re-plant from February to April. Large tubers can be divided. Treat the cut surfaces with powdered charcoal, a fungicide, or allow the cut surface to air dry for several days before re-planting. Feed these plants more heavily at the beginning of their growing season.

DUMB CANE *Dieffenbachia*

These handsome foliage plants are known as

Dumb Canes because of the IRRITATING JUICE that can cause swelling of the tongue and mouth in anyone unfortunate enough to have bitten into a plant. There are many species, selected named varieties and hybrids. *D. picta* has green leaves irregularly spotted with cream or light green; some varieties have almost entirely white leaves. Grow in semi-shade. Propagate by cuttings and from seed.

MONSTERA *Monstera*

These climbing aroids have juvenile and mature leaf forms which are very different. *M. deliciosa* produces edible banana-like fruits. Root cuttings in a rich compost. Allow the plant to attach to and climb a tree, a wall or a trellis.

ORNAMENTAL TARO *Colocasia*

Purple-stemmed Ornamental Taro *C. esculenta* has light green leaves with contrasting veining. Other ornamental Colocasias have very large arrowhead-shaped leaves either solid green or irregularly blotched white and pale green. These plants can grow to 2 m (6 ft) tall. They grow best in dappled sunlight. Propagate by removal of suckers, by division of the rhizome, or from seed.

PHILODENDRON *Philodendron*

This very large genus has both non-climbing (self-heading) and climbing species. There are a variety of leaf shapes, colours and sizes to choose from.

P. oxycardium (*P. cordatum*) is a rampant, heart shaped-leaved Caribbean climber that can be grown in pots with a small supporting trellis or post, in hanging baskets, or even be established as a ground cover in a semi-shaded garden. Other climbing Philodendrons have shiny dark green leaves, suffused dark reddish purple and reddish petioles. New patented cultivars include the dark red-leaved 'Majesty', yellow orange speckle-leaved 'Painted Lady', and rich green 'Emerald King'.

P. verrucosum is a lovely climber with deep red bristles on the petioles and sparkling green leaves with a salmon-mauve coloration between lateral veins.

P. bipinnatifidum and *P. selloum,* two very popular self-heading Philodendrons, grow into massive specimens that stand 1–2 m (3–6 ft) tall. They are particularly attractive when treated as shade-loving shrubs and interplanted beneath a row of shade trees.

SCINDAPSUS *Scindapsus*

S. aureus is a vigorous climber able to take full sun. Fully mature leaves are large. Smaller marbled juvenile foliage will persist when the plant is confined to a basket or pot. The lovely inequilateral leaves of *S. pictus* are a satiny bluish-green with silvery spots.

BEDDING PLANTS

Basic care
Light: semi-shade to full sun
Water: keep soil moist
Soil: porous mix of loam, compost and sand
Fertilizer: incorporate granular fertilizer into soil twice yearly or apply a liquid fertilizer according to manufacturer's instructions
Pests and diseases: Slugs, various insects; Leaf Spots and Root Rot
Propagation: cuttings; seed

Annuals

ANGELS TRUMPET *Datura*

D. candida, D. meteloides syn. *Wrightii* and other species are sun-loving, drought-tolerant plants with either single or double, white, mauve or cream tubular flowers. They can be used as specimen plants, in beds, as a backdrop (tall varieties) or they can be grown individually in large pots. Daturas will do well in a seaside garden. All parts of the plant are POISONOUS. Propagate from seed using Method II (see page 38) or from cuttings. Seeds may take up to two months to germinate.

CELOSIA *Celosia*

Celosia come in a variety of forms ranging from 15 cm to 50 cm (6–20 in) tall. The flower spikes may be plumed or crested. Plant Celosia as a mass or as an edging to a formal bed. They are dry season plants requiring a sunny spot with well-drained sandy soil. Cultivar 'Pink Castle' is a rose pink plume-type with exceptional tolerance to drought. Propagate from seed using Method II.

COLEUS *Coleus*

The many varieties of *C. blumei* are easy to raise from seed and from cuttings. Coleus is valued for its multi-coloured foliage. Use this plant as an edging, group planting, ground cover, or in individual containers. Best results will be had in semi-shaded locations having about four hours of direct sun daily. Pinch young plants to encourage bushiness. Remove young flower spikes to keep the foliage in top condition. Propagate desirable plants from cuttings. Raise new types from seed using Method I (see page 38). Seed requires light to germinate.

COSMOS *Cosmos*

C. bipinnatus is a pretty annual, 1.0–1.2 m (3–4 ft) tall, with large pink, white or red daisy-like flowers and lacey foliage. It will self-sow in your garden. Use Cosmos as a backdrop or as a mass planting. The tall plants need some protection from the wind. *C. sulphureus* can be used as a backdrop (cultivar 'Diablo') or as a bushy edging (cultivar 'Ladybird'). Flower colours are scarlet, orange and golden yellow. Sow the seed 6 mm (1/4 in) deep in small groups or in rows where you want the plants to grow.

DAHLIA *Dahlia*

Dahlias are not generally recommended for hot humid climates. Heavy rain can ruin the beautiful flowers; soggy soil can lead to injurious rots. If you want to try Dahlias, grow from seed the short, single or semi-double flowered cultivars such as 'Piccolo', treating them as annuals. Dahlias are heavy feeders. They form tubers but these are difficult to store without loss. Propagate from seed using Method II or by cuttings of selected varieties.

FOUR O'CLOCK, MARVEL OF PERU *Mirabilis*

M. jalapa grows to 75 cm (30 in) in height. This bushy plant thrives in full sun or semi-shade, flowering in late afternoon with fragrant blooms in shades of yellow, magenta, or pink. Grow Four O'Clocks in a group or inter-planted with other annuals. It will self-sow. Propagate from seed using Method II.

IMPATIENS *Impatiens*

Balsam (Touch-me-not) *I. balsamina* is an attractive annual for semi-shade to full sun locations. It can also be planted as a background behind shorter, more delicate edging plants or in combination with Cosmos. Balsam grows to 50 cm (20 in) bearing a profusion of single or double flowers close to the stem. Propagate from purchased seed. Another favourite is Patience Plant *I. wallerana* with attractive flat blooms in shades of pink, violet, magenta and white. Both will self-sow in the garden. Propagate Patience Plant from purchased seed or by cuttings. Seed of both species requires light to germinate. Use Method I (see page 38).

LOVE LIES BLEEDING *Amaranthus*

A. caudatus grows quickly from seed reaching more than 1 m (3 ft) in height. Plant it in full sun as a backdrop to smaller plants or grow it as a single specimen. The scarlet pendant blooms resemble those of Chenile Plant

Acalypha hispida. All *Amaranthus* species grow best in a well-drained sandy soil enriched with compost. Provide plenty of water when they begin to grow. Propagate from seed using Method II.

MARIGOLD *Tagetes*

African Marigold *T. erecta* is a sun-loving annual with short and tall varieties. Plant it as a mass, as an edging plant or in a border. Flowers may be lemon yellow, gold or orange, single, double, or crested, and can measure up to 10 cm (4 in) diameter. Favourite cultivars are 'Pineapple Crush' (yellow) and 'Inca Gold' (gold). Overfeeding can cause stems to weaken just below the flower. Remove spent blooms to avoid unsightliness and cessation of bloom. Propagate by seed using Method II or from cuttings of plants with attractive flowers.

PETUNIA *Petunia*

Single small-flowered Petunias are the best varieties to grow in the humid tropics. Sun-loving Petunias are lovely for hanging baskets, window boxes and planters. Avoid large or double bloom varieties as these are more susceptible to water damage and Mildew. Some choice cultivars are 'Comanche' (red), 'Sugar Plum' (orchid pink with purple veins) and 'Mercury' (light blue with a yellow throat). They flower from seed in just four months. Propagate from seed using Method I. Seed requires light to germinate.

SALVIA *Salvia*

The many varieties of *S. splendens* come in short, medium and tall sizes. These sun-loving plants are usually planted as a mass but can also serve as an edging. The scarlet-red spikes of flowers are impressive against the dark green foliage. The cultivar 'Flare' shows remarkable heat-tolerance. Propagate from seed using Method II.

TITHONIA *Tithonia*

The sprawling annual, *T. speciosa*, bears masses of orange red flowers. It blooms best during the dry season. Plant it in a sunny location where the plant can sprawl over and be supported by large rocks or boulders. *T. rotundifolia* cultivar 'Goldfinger' bears 7.5 cm (3 in) diameter orange-red blooms on compact 1 m (3 ft) plants. The cultivar 'Yellow Torch' grows taller, bearing golden yellow flowers. Propagate from seed using Method II. Seed requires darkness to germinate.

TORENIA *Torenia fournieri*

This small attractive annual bears two-lipped flowers in shades of lavender, purple and yellow. Although often recommended for shaded locations, it grows equally well as a ground cover beneath *Vanda* orchids planted in full sun. Torenia readily self-sows. It can be cultivated in pots or lightly shaded garden beds. Propagate from seed using Method II.

VERBENA *Verbena*

Sun-loving Verbena has wonderfully scented foliage and attractive clusters of brightly coloured bloom. Two favourite cultivars are 'Trinidad' which has beautiful bright pink flowers on compact plants, and the crimson-flowered 'Tropic'. Verbenas can be used effectively in a balcony planter or as an edging plant. Certain varieties may be susceptible to Powdery Mildew in the rainy season. Propagate from seed using Method II or from cuttings. Seed requires darkness to germinate.

ZINNIA *Zinnia*

Now that mildew-resistant varieties of *Z. elegans* are available, this sun-loving Mexican annual can grow in almost any Caribbean garden. Mexican Zinnias thrive on heat in full sun but are intolerant of continually wet conditions. The soil must be well-drained. Varieties range in size from 25 cm to 75 cm (10–30 in) tall. Flowers can be single, semi-double or fully double in shades of white, pink, red, yellow and orange. Grow mildew-resistant varieties such as the bicolour 'Chippendale', tangerine-coloured *Z. linearis*, or pink 'Rose Pinwheel'. They are nice for edging or in a mass planting for cut flowers. Propagate from seed using Method II. Transplant with extra care, making certain the plants are at the same depth as they were in the seed tray.

Perennials

ALTERNANTHERA *Alternanthera*

This wonderful multi-coloured edging plant stands just 15 cm (6 in) tall. It is easily propagated by cuttings and by division of mature plants.

ASPARAGUS FERNS *Asparagus*

Asparagus ferns are not ferns at all but are members of the Lily family. Primarily grown for their long-lasting foliage, they also bear small white flowers and red or brown fruits. Some species are massive, their stems growing to more than 3 m (10 ft). Others are miniature, making very attractive pot or basket specimens. They thrive in semi-shade and appreciate regular fertilizer application. Although they can tolerate drought, they are much more attractive if never stressed for water. If the plants are harvested for foliage, give them a chance to recover between harvests. Whether the plants are grown in beds, baskets or pots, the soil mix of loam, compost and sand should offer good drainage.

Propagate by division or from seeds using Method III. The seeds are now commercially available and easy to germinate if they are soaked overnight between pieces of moist paper towel.

A. densiflorus cultivar 'Sprengeri' with yellow-green needle-like leaves on 2 m long (6 ft) stems is one of the most popular ornamental asparagus. Another cultivar of this species 'Meyers', produces shorter plume-like, branched stems. Both of these forms are prized for hanging baskets.

CLIMBING ASPARAGUS *A. plumosus* produces an abundance of emerald-green feathery foliage. The stems elongate and twine about whatever is available. Grow this species together with Anthuriums or orchids in a lath house.

A. cooperi produces long 3–4 m (10–13 ft) long stems bearing fragrant white flowers and bright red fruits.

BROAD LEAF ASPARAGUS *A. falcatus* has dark green flat leaves arranged in groups on its very long stems and clusters of fragrant blooms.

A. myriocladus, shrub-like, grows to more than 1 m (3 ft) tall, with dark green foliage that at first glance resembles that of conifers. This charming species can be cultivated in pots or as specimens planted directly in the garden.

BEGONIA *Begonia*

Begonias are tropical or subtropical plants mostly native to Central and South America, and the Caribbean. Thriving in a lightly shaded location, Begonias prefer a moist, porous organic soil. Protection from strong winds is essential. According to their size, Begonias can be planted at the base of a tree, in window boxes, along borders, or even in hanging baskets. A lath house or fernery provides wind protection and shade for potted specimens. Feed Begonias every two weeks with half strength liquid fertilizer.

Begonias are divided into six groups depending upon their plant habit: cane-like; rhizomatous; fibrous-rooted; tuberous; shrub; and thick-stemmed. The first three groups are easy to grow in most Caribbean gardens. The latter three groups are more difficult to grow, requiring careful watering and a rest: they are not recommended.

CANE-LIKE BEGONIAS are called Angel

Wings because of their attractive, silver-blotched, wedge-shaped leaves. The Brazilian species *B. coccinea* and its many named hybrids are tall 1.0–1.5 m (3–5 ft), having jointed, erect, bamboo-like stems and wedge-shaped leaves. Large trusses of pink to scarlet flowers are borne in the leaf axils. *B. nitida* of Jamaica can grow to more than 1 m (3 ft) tall. This lovely plant has shiny green foliage and fragrant white or pink blooms. Cane Begonias can be grown without shade. They make interesting subjects around a patio or pool, grown in pots or planted in beds. Prune these plants to encourage new branches, leaves and flowers. Cuttings can be easily rooted in damp sand.

RHIZOMATOUS BEGONIAS have creeping fleshy rhizomes and make excellent pot plants. The best known is large ornamental-leaved *B. rex*. The lovely leaf markings are best maintained through careful shading. Another popular rhizomatous type is the Star Begonia, *B. heracleifolia*. Known as the 'Attorney-General' in Trinidad, it has hairy rhizomes, long-stalked and deeply cut leaves, and tall erect stems of white to pink blooms. When planting rhizomatous begonias take care that the rhizome lies on the surface of the soil and is not buried. One suggestion is to cover the potting mix with pebbles, keeping all but the rhizome base in contact with the soil.

FIBROUS-ROOTED WAX BEGONIAS *B. semperflorens* are sun-tolerant bedding Begonias. Available in a wide variety of foliage and flower colours, Wax Begonias are easily raised from seed or propagated with rooted cuttings. Varieties range in height from 15–30 cm (6–12 in). In contrast, *B. ulmifolia* of Columbia and Trinidad is almost shrubby. It has green oval, 10 cm (4 in) long leaves and pure white blooms. Grow these Begonias in a soil composed of leaf mould, sand and loam. Provide light shade.

Begonias are propagated by cuttings and by seed. Male flowers, with anthers and pollen, are often more showy than the adjacent female flowers. The large winged ovary is conspicuous. Pollinate Begonias by brushing ripe anthers over the stigma of a freshly opened female bloom. Both the anthers and the stigma will be bright yellow and conspicuous. Harvest the extremely fine seed with care, removing the mature seed capsule as it begins to yellow. Place the capsule in a paper envelope, letting it air dry for several days. Germinate Begonia seed using Method I.

CANNA LILY *Canna*

The Canna Lily *C. indica* grows to 2–3 m (6–10 ft) in full sun. It can be used as a background plant, as a specimen or in a special centre-piece bed. Incorporate plenty of organic matter into the soil before planting. Feed heavily.

The large showy flowers can be red, orange, yellow; the leaves green, edged maroon or entirely reddish brown. Space the plants at least 45 cm (18 in) apart. Canna Lilies are often damaged by leaf-rolling Caterpillars and Slugs (watch out for these pests!). Re-plant annually at the beginning of the rainy season. Keep like varieties together so that all will be the same height. Rootstock importation may be restricted. Grow Cannas from seed pre-soaked 24 hours in water using Method III, or divide established plants by cutting the rhizome into pieces each with a growing point.

CHRYSANTHEMUM *Chrysanthemum*

Chrysanthemums in general do not thrive in Caribbean gardens, however, there are some pretty varieties of *C. sinense* that have been propagated in the islands for many years. These hardy yellow, white and mauve varieties can be grown in a well-drained sandy loam in full sun. Propagate using softwood cuttings or slips. New varieties can be attempted from seed using Method I. Chrysanthemum seed needs light to germinate.

CROSSANDRA *Crossandra*

This dwarf 30 cm (12 in) shrubby perennial has glossy green foliage and bears heads of apricot flowers over many months. Heads can be removed when finished blooming or left for seed to mature. Grow Crossandra in a sunny border. Propagate by semi-hardwood cuttings or from seed using Method I. Seed requires light to germinate.

GERBERA *Gerbera*

The colourful Gerbera Daisy is prized by flower arrangers and admired by gardeners. Some skill is required to grow the plants well in the hot, humid tropics; they grow best in cooler uplands. *G. jamesonii* is a short-lived perennial that is susceptible to rots. Plant Gerberas in a sunny, well-drained location, about 30 cm (1 ft) apart, taking care that the crowns are not buried in the soil. The foliage forms a rosette to 50 cm (20 in) diameter with the flowers arising from the centre. Mature plants produce side shoots which can be removed for propagation if desired. Flowers may be double or single in shades of orange, yellow, cream, pink and red. Propagate from fresh seed using Method I, or from rooted side shoots. Seed requires light to germinate.

PENTAS *Pentas*

P. carnea is a perennial that forms bushy 60 cm (2 ft) plants if given some judicious pruning and grown in full sun. Clusters of starry flowers can be white, mauve or pink. *P. coccinea* bears red flowers and prefers a semi-shaded bed. Pentas can be grown in narrow edging beds or as a mass for cutting. They grow best in good garden loam. Propagate from cuttings of the best varieties or from seed using Method I. Seed requires light to germinate.

PERIWINKLE *Catharanthus roseus* (*Vinca*)

Great strides have been made in breeding *C. roseus* to give very large-flowered cultivars that are now available from seed. Periwinkles grow best in sunny, dry locations. They will naturalise in cracks of a wall or even in rough, stony ground. Periwinkles are particularly attractive along driveways and paths. Flowers are white or shades of pink, with or without a contrasting red eye. The plants can grow to 50 cm (20 in) although they generally are much shorter and more spreading. Propagate from seed using Method II. Germinate in total darkness.

SHRIMP PLANT *Beloperone guttata*

This shrubby perennial grows to 60 cm (2 ft), bearing reddish or yellowish heads of bracts and flowers that vaguely resemble shrimps. It can be grown in informal borders and responds well to hard pruning. Shrimp Plant does best in a sunny location although it will tolerate semi-shade. Propagate from cuttings or by division of older plants.

BONSAI

Basic care
Light: semi-shade, dappled sunlight, full sun with caution
Water: daily to twice daily watering
Soil: well-drained mix; re-pot annually
Fertilizer: incorporate fertilizer into the soil or provide dilute liquid fertilizer when plants are in active growth
Pests and diseases: as in shrubs and trees
Propagation: seed; rooted cuttings
Special care: prune branches as necessary; prune roots annually

Growing trees in small pots and dwarfing them by pruning their stems and roots, has been practised for over 1000 years. A living art created within an ancient tradition of horticulture and aesthetic values, Bonsai originated in China and was perfected by the Japanese. A translation of the word bonsai is 'to plant a tree in a shallow pot' (bon=pot and sai=tree). Pruning, training and wiring, together with daily loving care, create a Bonsai. Among the attributes that distinguish a potted tree from a Bonsai specimen are personality and character, balanced composition of branches, and an aged, mature appearance.

There is no real mystery to the cultural aspects of Bonsai. Anyone with some horticultural ability can learn how to keep a plant small in an undersized container. It must be watered more often than usual so that the roots do not dry out but at the same time there must be perfect drainage so that the root ball is not at any time waterlogged. It should be fertilized when in active growth, and pruned both above and below ground to keep it in shape. The art of Bonsai emerges when a tree's character is developed over time through the training process.

Choice of specimens

Potential Bonsai specimens exist in most gardens. Remember that the majority of specimens seen in books or at shows began their life as either collected natural material or as seedlings or rooted cuttings. The most important choice lies with the plant material. Traditional Bonsai specimens are hardy shrubs and trees from temperate climates: these are inappropriate for tropical culture. Begin your collection with tropical or subtropical plants. Desirable characteristics include small foliage, pliable branches, no noticeable dormant period, and strong growth of roots and shoots to withstand the necessary heavy pruning. Some of the trees being experimented with locally include:

Aralia *Polyscias* (smaller forms)
Barbados Cherry *Malpighia glabra*
Bougainvillea *Bougainvillea*
Cassia *Cassia* spp. (smaller species)
Flamboyant *Delonix regia*
Fustic *Chlorophora tinctoria*
Mile Tree *Casuarina equisetifolia*

Natal Plum *Carissa grandiflora*
Podocarpus *Podocarpus*
Pomegranate *Punica granatum*
Sea Grape *Coccoloba uvifera*
Spanish Ash *Lonchocarpus benthamianus*
Tamarind *Tamarindus indica*
Weeping Fig *Ficus benjamina*
West Indian Holly *Malpighia coccigera*
Yellow-rim *Serissa foetida variegata*

Training techniques

After choosing your plant, study its form and character before giving the first drastic pruning. Do not be shy: pruning is needed to open up the stems and branches.

The principal technique used in Bonsai culture is the selective pruning of stems, leaves and roots. The branches are pruned to control size, to encourage compact form and to shape the tree. The leaves are removed to reduce surface area for transpiration loss, especially in newly planted specimens. The roots are pruned to encourage the growth of more lateral feeder roots, thereby increasing the potential for absorption of water and nutrients. By pruning both above and below soil level, a necessary balance in growth is maintained.

Branch pruning must be done regularly according to the growth characteristics of a particular specimen. The same techniques that apply to garden shrubs and trees apply to Bonsai specimens. Plan what the final shape should be, prune to attain that shape, and observe the results of your experiment. Use sharp pruning shears.

The other important technique in the training of Bonsai is wiring. The trees are shaped by wrapping brass or Monel wire around the branches and twigs, bending the wired limbs to the desired position. The wire is eventually removed once the desired form is set.

Most Bonsai trees are re-potted every year, at which time root pruning is also completed. Be certain that the roots are not allowed to dry out, that a balance is kept between branches and roots, and that the re-potted tree is given some protection from sun for a few weeks afterwards.

Pots and soil

Good bonsai pots have unglazed bottoms and large drainage holes. The shape and proportion of bonsai containers suggest the type of planting. Shallow trays give the feeling of emptiness and space between weathered trees on a mountain slope. Decorative rock can be arranged with the plant material to develop the theme further. Deeper, earth-tone pots and bowls are suited to group plantings or individual specimens.

SOIL MIX FOR BONSAI

2 parts loam
2 parts peat moss or compost
1 part gravelly sand
1 part horticultural perlite (optional)

Sift all but the perlite through first, a coarse 6 mm ($1/4$ in) mesh to remove large lumps, and secondly, through a fine 1.5 mm ($1/16$ in) mesh screen to remove dust. Retain all that passes through the coarse screen but does not pass through the fine one. This ensures that your mix will have porosity, that it will not compact, and yet at the same time be moisture-retentive.

General care

Prepare your container for planting by covering the large drain holes with a piece of fibreglass cloth. This keeps the soil in while allowing for drainage. Position any large rocks, flat side down so they are stable. Place a thin layer of almost dry soil over the bottom of the pot. Remove the pruned plants from their pots, shaking off clinging soil. Use a potting stick or fingers to spread the roots apart. Prune roots as necessary to fit the container, leaving some fine feeder roots to sustain the plant. Position one or several plants in the container, to the right or left of centre by preference. Add soil, making certain that it penetrates between the roots and that there are no air spaces. Firm the soil gently in place. For the first important watering, set the container in a pan of water, the level of water coming just to but not over the pot rim. When the surface of the soil appears moist, remove the pot and let drain. Use sheet moss or lichens as a ground cover to accentuate forest characteristics or use sand or gravel for a desert effect. Keep newly planted specimens shaded for several weeks or until the roots adapt to their new container.

To maintain your plant, pinch and prune it regularly. Let the natural character of the plant guide you. Fertilize only when the plant is in active growth. Plants in shallow containers require very frequent watering. Do not let the soil and roots dry out! As a rough guide, water Bonsai specimens once a day if no rain fell during the night. In drier months, the plants may be watered again in the early afternoon. Make certain that the Bonsai specimen has adequate light either as dappled sunlight or semi-shade. Your specimen can be moved for display purposes.

Classical Bonsai styles

Chokkan: single straight trunk
Shakkan: single slanting trunk
Kengai: single cascading trunk
Ishitsuki: exposed roots growing over the stone before entering the soil
Yose-ue: several trees planted together giving the appearance of a forest
More information can be obtained from specialist books on the subject.

Applying the guidelines given here is not simple: you will be dealing with living plants. Enjoy the mystery and magic of discovering what your plant prefers. Sit back and meditate on what you and the plant have accomplished: this is part the pleasure of Bonsai.

BOUGAINVILLEAS

Bougainvilleas are woody plants native to South America. They bear masses of large brilliantly coloured bracts and flower during the dry season. Three colourful bracts surround each group of three flowers. All Bougainvilleas produce woody spines, one near each leaf. Three species, *B. glabra*, *B. spectabilis* and *B. peruviana*, have given rise to the several hundred cultivars recorded by the International Registration Authority for Bougainvillea, New Delhi, India. These cultivars developed as seedlings from hybrid crosses, or from bud sports. Some of the most popular cultivars remain so because of their vigour.

Double or multi-bracted forms were first developed in the Philippines. Some popular cultivars are 'Manila Magic Red' (red-purple), 'Doubloon' (apricot), 'Double Pink' and 'Double White'. Double Bougainvilleas may be grown in pots, along low walls or in mounds as specimen plants.

If given space, a sprawling Bougainvillea will fill it with ease. It is up to the gardener to train the plant to form arches, espaliers, standards, hedges or umbrellas. The habits of growth and flowering make some varieties much more desirable for one use than another. For example, naturally compact cultivars that form flowers all along their stems are more suited to pot culture.

Bougainvilleas do well in a variety of soils but prefer a perfectly drained rich loam containing compost or leaf mould. Bougainvilleas are greedy feeders. Use a fertilizer high in potassium, for example 12–12–17 with trace elements. The first fertilizer application should coincide with the first pruning after flowering is finished. A second application should follow four to six weeks later when young shoots have developed. If young foliage appears unusually pale, apply chelated iron according to manufacturer's instructions. Depending upon the rainfall experienced in your garden, further applications of fertilizer may be needed. Heavy watering assists in the uptake of nutrients however torrential rainfall can leach the nutrients from the soil.

Bougainvilleas flower in response to a dry period. Drought sufficient to cause leaf drop and/or cool temperatures will encourage the development of flowers. These shrubs require heavy rains or watering followed by a dry season to bloom well. Some special advice for growing potted Bougainvilleas is to withhold water for two weeks to induce flowers to form on the branches, then reduce watering frequency throughout the blooming period to keep the bracts on the plants.

Propagate Bougainvilleas by softwood or hardwood cuttings, air layers, T-budding or try producing your own hybrids from seed. Vegetative propagation is fairly easy after blooming is finished. Take hardwood cuttings or softwood tips, 15–20 cm (6–8 in) long, remove the leaves and prickles, dip in rooting hormone powder and plant in damp sand. Keep the cuttings shaded and evenly moist. Rooting will take four to six weeks. Do not plant out until the cuttings have a vigorous root system. Prune the tops if necessary to force the production of roots. Once planted the shrubs should be fed with a weak solution of high nitrogen fertilizer every two weeks until they are well established. Variegated forms are particularly difficult to root. These are more easily propagated by air layering.

Varieties of *B. spectabilis* freely produce seed. A very fine artist's paint brush can be used to transfer pollen from flower to flower. Seeds are ready to be harvested in January–March. Sow the seeds in moist, sterile loam using Method II. Transplant the seedlings into individual containers in a shaded nursery. Seedlings can bloom as quickly as one year from the date of sowing.

B. glabra is bushy, clambering, appreciated for its habit of producing flowers the whole length of the stems. Long-lasting purple or pure white varieties prolong the display in a garden. This species does not like to be severely pruned. It can be difficult to propagate from hardwood cuttings: softwood cuttings are more easily rooted. Cultivar 'variegata' is compact with variegated foliage, recommended for pots and for hedging.

B. peruviana is a climbing species with terminal clusters of bloom and has a short blooming season. It shows a poor response to hard pruning.

B. spectabilis is a climbing species that blooms all along the branches. It is often deciduous during the flowering season. Sports are common. Cultivar 'Harrisii' has handsome yellow/green foliage.

B. × buttiana is believed to be a natural hybrid between *B. peruviana* and *B. glabra*, this climber has crimson to mauve blooms in terminal inflorescences.

BOUGAINVILLEA CULTIVARS
'Mary Palmer' (magenta pink with white)
'Snow Queen' (white)
'Formosa' (white)
'Enid Lancaster' (orange to pink)
'Mrs Butt' (cherry red)

'Mrs Helen McClean' (orange aging to cerise)
'Ecuador Pink' (delicate pink)
'Mrs Butt' 'variegata' (young foliage deep pink)
'Golden Glow' (yellow orange)

BROMELIADS

Basic care
Light: semi-shade to full sun
Water: keep soil moist; add water to 'vase' of cup-formers; provide moderate to high relative humidity
Soil: acidic; porous yet water-retentive
Fertilizer: foliar feed at one-quarter strength once a month
Pests and diseases: Scale insects, Slugs
Propagation: offsets (pups), seed using Method I

The best known Bromeliad is Pineapple *Ananas comosus*, a plant which can be cultivated in warm, humid gardens especially those located in the high rainfall areas of the lowland tropics. However it is the other bromeliads, those spectacular plants with brilliantly coloured foliage and long-lasting flower spikes that gardeners love the best. Whether you choose to grow bromeliads for their foliage or for their multi-coloured inflorescences, you will not be disappointed. Bromeliads are easy to grow.

Many of the 2000 bromeliad species are epiphytes, growing in crotches of trees, on branches or even hanging from branches such as Spanish Moss *Tillandsia usneoides*. Others are terrestrial, growing in soil, on moss-covered rocks and logs. Most of the epiphytes will readily adapt to pot culture on condition that the potting medium is open, acidic, moisture-retentive, and does not contain any lime. *Tillandsia* and many of the other epiphytic bromeliads are true succulent plants. Like the cactus, *Agave* and *Aloe*, they have adapted to periodic dry situations. Species with scaly, leathery foliage are the most adaptable to full sun and dryness while those with thin, shiny foliage do best in conditions of semi-shade and high humidity. There are bromeliads for every garden.

Whether you choose to grow tiny *Tillandsia* in pots or very large *Aechmea* in a natural garden setting, the same basic rules apply. Bromeliads need bright light to grow well and to produce their most brilliant colours. Their sparse roots are formed more to anchor the plant than to gather food and water. Moisture and nutrients are absorbed via the foliage. Bromeliads form rosettes of leaves. The leaves of some, for example *Vriesia* and *Neoregelia*, form an urn or cup. This cup should never be allowed to dry out. Very dilute liquid fertilizer (one-quarter recommended strength) can be sprayed or splashed directly on the foliage. Fertilize potted bromeliads at monthly intervals. Bromeliads planted in trees and other garden locations need not be fertilized if you choose not to do so. Bird and frog droppings, decaying insects and other organic matter accumulating in the cup will be an adequate nutrient source.

SOIL MIX FOR BROMELIADS

   2 parts sterilized leaf mould or compost
   2 parts Perlite
   1 part coarse silica sand or charcoal

Bromeliad potting media should provide aeration of the few roots, be acidic in reaction and be moisture retentive. Repotting should be done every two years. Fine or medium grade bark from Redwood *Sequoia*, chopped cork, coarse Perlite and tree fern fibre make a good mix for epiphytes. Tree fern fibre alone is not sufficiently water-retentive, neither is it sufficiently heavy to hold the plants in place. Pebbles or marbles can be placed on top of the medium to weight it down.

Bromeliad rosettes reach maturity, flower, produce seeds, then die although death may not ensue for many months. Certain species become colourful at blooming time, part of the rosette or even the entire structure changing colour to become pink, red or purple. The colours last for many months, in some cases up to a year and long after the flowers are finished. Before a rosette dies, it gives rise to one or more offsets (pups). The offsets grow slowly, establish their own roots, becoming independent of the old rosette. Eventually the old rosette loses its attractiveness and has to be removed. Where more than one offset exists, extras can be cut away from the mother plant, rooted and raised as individuals.

Bromeliads for your garden

AECHMEA *Aechmea*

A. dichlamydea trinitensis, with its red, branched inflorescence and blue floral bracts, will grow quite happily in semi-shade to full sun, nestled in pockets of humus placed in and amongst rocks. Another species, *A. fasciata*, has many foliage variants ranging from banded, grey green leaves to longitudinally striped and white-edged forms. Its magnificent pink inflorescence bears blue flowers. This species makes a lovely pot plant.

AIR PLANT *Tillandsia*

The genus *Tillandsia* contains the largest number of species of all the bromeliads and covers a great variation in size and form. Epiphytic *Tillandsia* is easily grown mounted on a piece of wood or bark, or fastened with fishing line to branches of living trees. Tillandsias require plenty of light so choose a tree with an open canopy. Particularly recommended are
T. baileyi (pink inflorescence and dark blue flowers).
T. seleriana (red inflorescence)
T. ionantha (entire plant reddens during flowering period)

CUP-FORMERS

Epiphytic *Guzmania lingulata*, *Nidularium innocentii* and *Neoregelia carolinae* have a cup formed by the leaf cluster. This cup contains water and can be the home of many animals including tree frogs. When flowering, the leaves surrounding the cup become brilliantly coloured. The colour and the extent of that coloration varies with the species. Cupforming bromeliads require more moisture than others. The cup should never be allowed to dry out. Water them by adding collected rainwater to the cup. Grow them in pots or fastened to tree fern logs or to living tree trunks in a humid garden setting.

EARTH STAR *Cryptanthus*

Cryptanthus species are fondly referred to as Earth Stars: as you might imagine, these bromeliads are terrestrials. Small 15–20 cm (6–8 in) diameter plants, they form flat rosettes of variously coloured leaves. Brown, green, pink, maroon, and some with contrasting bands and stripes, choose any variety you wish to grow in a pot or use it as a ground cover in your garden. Earth Stars reproduce rapidly via offsets so mass planting is a real possibility. Use fast growing cultivars such as 'Black Prince', 'Nancy', or 'Cafe au Lait', planting them 15–20 cm apart (6–8 in).

PINEAPPLE *Ananas*

The commercial pineapple has a number of spectacular relatives including *A. bracteatus* var. *striatus* and *A. comosus* var. *tricolor*. These lovely variegated pineapples have longitudinally-striped cream, red and green foliage. The pineapple fruits are also coloured. They make very attractive and long-lasting additions to floral arrangements. Pineapples are terrestrial and grow best in rich, well-drained humus and bright light.

QUEEN'S TEARS *Billbergia*

Billbergia species, for example *B. nutans* and *B. leptopoda*, are large, upright plants often having mottled or spotted foliage. Their inflorescences are remarkable, tall and drooping. The flowers are not as long-lasting as those of other bromeliads however the attractive foliage is a compensation. Terrestrial *Billbergia* adapts easily to bright garden locations where a pendulous inflorescence can be displayed to best advantage.

CACTUS

Basic care

Light: full sun; light shade for cactus without protective hair or spines

Water: control watering by moving potted plants under cover during rainy season; water only when plants are in active growth

Soil: 2 parts sand or grit plus 1 part sifted leaf mould, humus, or compost; increase humus content of soil for epiphytic cactus

Fertilizer: incorporate slow-release product into soil or use balanced fertilizer at monthly intervals during the growing season; some species require limestone in the soil mix

Pests and diseases: root Mealy Bugs, Scale Insects, Spider Mites; Rots due to overwatering.

Propagation: seed (use method recommended for Cactus, Chapter 2 page 39); division of clumps; top cuttings; grafting

Cactus are plants of the temperate and tropical Americas. They have become especially adapted to a seasonally dry existence. With a few exceptions such as *Pereskia* a cactus having recognizable 'true' leaves, the majority of cactus no longer produce functional leaves. Their leaves have been replaced by spines. Cactus are separated from other flowering plants by distinctive features.

They possess a structure called the **areole** from which arise spines, hairs, and flowers. Their flowers are formed by whorl upon whorl of petal-like segments and have numerous stamens. The ovary is found below the point of attachment of the petals and other flower parts. They come in a variety of shapes and sizes and are valued both for the geometric form and their attractive blooms. Many are easy to grow and flower especially those from the Caribbean region.

It is often believed that cactus plants require a poor soil and must never be watered. This is a false assumption. While they do grow in desert regions and can survive in a variety of inhospitable environments, one never finds them growing in pure sand or where it never rains. More often than not, these plants are found growing in amongst grass, shrubs or succulent plants. The soil is rich in organic debris produced by the companion plants. They also provide shade and protection, especially for seedlings. When the rain wets the soil, a rich blend of nutrients is liberated. The cactus plants begin growing new feeder roots within 48 hours of the first rain and therefore make effective use of the new water and nutrient supply. Knowing this, we can devise a successful scheme to raise cactus in our homes and gardens.

Of the many thousand of cactus species, there are a few that are particularly suited to the Caribbean garden. Miniature species such as Pincushion Cactus *Mammillaria* have attractive flowers. Larger columnar *Cereus* are favourites for landscaping. Cactus species originating from regions with a cold, dry season generally are not suitable; they will be prone to rot. Many will never bloom.

Favourite Cactus

BISHOP'S CAP *Astrophytum*

Tough, attractive *Astrophytum* is ideally suited to tropical culture. The dark green stem is covered with white mealy markings that may serve to reflect light. Of the six species in cultivation, three (see below) are commonly grown. All should be grown in pots, the potting mix being a gritty soil of equal parts humus and crushed limestone or weathered coral. Provide filtered sunlight, with some overhead protection from rain. These plants sometimes develop a brown corky base with age. To avoid such disfigurement place a layer of pebbles about the base of the cactus to protect the stem from touching moist compost. Propagate by seed.

A. capricorne is strongly ribbed, dotted with tiny white flakes and has long, flat, flexible spines that resemble the horns of a goat. The distinctive variety 'Senile' is enveloped in spines. The golden yellow, red-throated flowers are borne annually on new growth. This species is particularly susceptible to overwatering. Keep it under cover where you can control the watering.

A. myriostigma is a spineless species, easily raised from seed. Plants have four or five large ribs that curve in a clockwise or counterclockwise fashion. The stem is usually covered with white flakes. Large, yellow flowers are produced after the dry season.

A. ornatum with ribs edged in golden spines and partially covered in white flakes, is a very attractive species and a desirable addition to the collection. Although easy to grow, it takes a long time to reach flowering size.

CHIN CACTUS *Gymnocalycium*

So named because of the distinctive chin-like protrusions on the ribs, *Gymnocalycium* makes an attractive pot plant both in and out of flower. Most species have white or pink flowers, for example *G. damsii* although a few have lovely red blooms, for example *G. venturianum*. Propagation of Chin Cactus is by seed.

A selected form of *Gymnocalycium* has a plant body completely devoid of chlorophyll, being red, orange or yellow instead of green. Unable to photosynthesize, this oddity is grafted onto a normal green stem of *Hylocereus* and is marketed under the name 'Mr Redcap'. These selected forms do not flower and tend to be short-lived.

COLUMNAR CACTUS *Cereus* and relatives

This group of cactus contains many interesting types suited to planting in seasonally dry gardens. Many are resident in the Caribbean region. Because they can become quite tall, 2 m (6 ft) or more in height, they are better suited to a garden bed than to a pot. All can be grown quite quickly from seed, also propagate by division. Examples include

Myrtillocactus geometrizans: from Mexico; blue-green; ribbed columns with geometric markings

Trichocereus macrogonus: from South America; eventually branching to form thick groups of bluish, ribbed stems

Pilosocereus (*Cephalocereus*) *barbadensis*: from Barbados; densely spined, clustered stems bearing flowers from a hairy cephalium at the top of stems

Cereus variabilis: from Brazil, night-flowering; fragrant; thick green stems up to 15 cm (6 in) in diameter

EPIPHYTIC CACTUS *Hylocereus, Selenicereus, Rhipsalis*

Many examples of epiphytic cactus grow throughout the Caribbean. In Cuba *Hylocereus cubensis*, is a rambling species that flowers continuously for six months or more. Being night-flowering and heavily scented, these plants should be located close to your home but well away from artificial light that could interfere with their blooming cycle. They will easily become established in a small tree such as Calabash *Crescentia cujete*. They can also

be grown in a large pot, their branches trained on a reinforced wooden trellis. Epiphytic cactus produce adventitious roots that hold the stem fast to the tree branches or trellis. The interesting *Rhipsalis* makes a lovely hanging basket. Their flowers are rather insignificant although the white berries are attractive. All epiphytic cactus grow best in a humus-rich soil mix. Feed these plants year-round using a balanced liquid preparation. Propagate from cuttings and from seed.

FLAT HAND CACTUS *Opuntia*

Opuntias are characterized by jointed, cylindrical stems bearing two types of spines. There are larger heavy-bodied spines surrounded by a mass of bristle-like, barbed spines called **glochids**. It is the glochids that make *Opuntia* rather unpleasant to handle, however, the spiny nature of these plants can make them rather formidable deterents to unauthorized entry. Some species are compact and suited to pot culture: these include O. *vestita* with woolly stems and red flowers; O. *microdasys* densely clothed in golden brown or pure white glochids; and the almost spineless O. *argentina* with bright yellow flowers. Other species are massive, able to grow quickly enough to form a living fence or a large specimen plant: good examples are the Caribbean species O. *rubescens*, some forms of which are very spiny and others spineless; O. *dillenii*, another Caribbean cactus with stout spines and yellowish flowers; and O. *santa-rita*, a very colourful reddish plant with few spines. Propagate from seeds and by division.

NOTOCACTUS *Notocactus*

N. leninghausii is often the first cactus grown by Caribbean gardeners. This densely-spined, columnar species comes from the Brazil-Paraguay border region. Adapted to periodic drought, it is also tolerant of high humidity and frequent showers. Lemon yellow flowers do not appear until the plant is at least 20 cm (8 in) tall. Branches form at the base of older specimens. Propagate from seed and cuttings.

PARODIA *Parodia*

The majority of *Parodia* species are solitary plants and rather slow to start from seed, taking two years or more to develop an adequate root system. These plants are densely spined and bear attractive blooms in brilliant yellow, rich orange and scarlet. They flower on new growth, individual blooms lasting several days, opening and closing each day. Parodias will bloom in three to five years from seed. Grow the miniature *Parodia* cactus in filtered sunlight beneath a rain shelter. Use a soil composed of equal parts sand and humus. Fertilize the plants during the rainy season, watering whenever the soil dries out. Withhold water for two months at the beginning of the dry season, allowing the plants to rest and prepare for flowering. Resume watering when the buds appear. Propagate by seed and occasionally by offsets.

PINCUSHION CACTUS *Mammillaria*

The popular Pincushion Cactus are delightful ball-like plants composed of protuberances (tubercles) upon each of which is found an areole complete with radiating spines and sometimes also hairs or wool. Small, brilliantly-coloured flowers in shades of magenta, yellow, and white are produced in a ring about the crown, followed by bright red, finger-like fruits. While some species such as M. *vaupelii* are solitary, growing larger and larger each year but never branching, others such as M. *multiceps* form masses of offsets. When offsets become tightly clustered you must take special care that water does not lie stagnant amongst the stems. Place a layer of coarse gravel or marble chips about the plant base so that damp soil is not in continual contact with the stem. Propagate by seed and offsets.

TURK'S CAP CACTUS *Melocactus*

Melocactus is a tropical American plant found along coastal areas throughout the Caribbean. Upon reaching maturity (5–10 years from seed), these plants develop a cap-like flowering stem, the **cephalium**, hence the name 'Turk's Cap'. The slow-growing cephalium is composed of whorls of areoles bearing tiny pink flowers, bristles, and tufts of white hairs. The cap can become greatly elongated over time, reaching 30–50 cm (12–20 in) in some species. *Melocactus* is a shallow-rooted plant. It should be planted in a clay pot using a very porous soil mix (2 parts sand or grit to 1 part leaf mould). Whatever species is grown, be assured that it will be an attractive addition to a dry, sunny garden or to a pot plant collection.

Seaside gardens may also have a place for this salt-tolerant cactus. Vigorous seedlings can be planted in humus-rich rock niches. Mature *Melocactus* should never be collected from the wild. Not only are they very difficult to re-establish when collected from their natural habitat, but the death of a seed-bearing plant serves no one. Try propagating *Melocactus* from seed – it is really very easy.

M. *caesius*, from the Venezuelan coast, has a blue-green plant body and a wooly cephalium; the spines are reddish.

M. *macranthus* of the southern Caribbean, only growing up to 30 cm (15 in) in diameter is the smallest of this genus. The cephalium is compact, white with very fine spines. Its seedlings are highly variable.

M. *matanzanus*, native to Cuba, has an orange-red cephalium that forms within five years from seed. The ribbed plant body bears rows of stout recurved spines.

Collecting Cactus seed

Cactus produce fleshy, colourful fruits that either dry up and fall off the plant, dehisce by means of a basal pore, or split open, dropping their seeds. Birds and rodents may feed on larger fruits. To harvest cactus seed, you will have to remove mature fruits from the plants. A fully mature fruit should easily separate from the cactus: never tear it loose. Split the fruit open over a dish or tray. If the fruit is dry, the seeds will fall like grains of sand. If the fruit is fleshy, the seeds must be separated from the pulp. Place the pulp and seeds in a bowl of lukewarm water, gently agitating the pulp and separating the seeds with your fingers. According to the size of the seeds, strain the mixture through either a sieve or muslin. Freshly harvested cactus seeds germinate quickly. To store cactus seed for future use, ensure that the seed is thoroughly dried before storing it in a sealed container together with silica gel or an equivalent dessicant. Do not forget to label seed packets with the name and date of harvest.

CROTONS

> **Basic care**
> Light: full sun
> Water: benefit from weekly watering in dry periods
> Soil: well-drained, acidic, humus-rich
> Fertilizer: work a 12–12–17 into the soil twice yearly
> Pests and diseases: neglected plants may suffer from Spider Mites
> Propagation: cuttings; air layers; seed (use method recommended for Crotons, Chapter 2, page 40)

Crotons *Codiaeum* are one of the most popular ornamental shrubs of tropical and subtropical gardens. Their leaves are unrivalled in diversity of shape, size and colour, even on a single plant. Some Croton varieties have leaves of only green and yellow or red and yellow, however there is often a subtle blending of all these colours. Crotons are sunlovers: only with abundant sunshine will they display their spectacular colours to perfec-

tion. Day-long filtered and splashed sunlight, rather than intense mid-day sun, produces the most colourful patterned leaves. These shrubs attain a height of 4 m (13 ft).

Drought-resistant, moderately salt-tolerant plants, Crotons are a boon to the Caribbean gardener who must cope with an annual dry season. Notwithstanding their drought-tolerance, established plants will still benefit from a weekly watering in dry periods: young plants and those in pots will require it daily. When watering, sprinkle the foliage as well as soaking the soil, to wash off accumulated dust and dirt. Crotons will grow in almost any soil but flourish in a well-drained acidic loam containing a good supply of organic matter such as well-rotted animal manure or rotted bagasse and compost. Apply a general purpose granular or liquid fertilizer, for example 12–12–17, at the beginning and again towards the end of the rainy season. Mulch the plants to help conserve moisture.

Crotons are not much troubled by insects or fungus diseases. However Spider Mites and Thrips can become a problem if the plants are neglected. Pesticides can be used to control these pests but perhaps it would be wiser to tackle the reason for the problem: neglect. Grow your plants with adequate sunshine, water and fertilizer, plant them in fertile, well-drained soil and your pest problems will be virtually eliminated.

These shrubs look their best when they are kept bushy. Prune them regularly to avoid a leggy, unattractive appearance. Regular pinching of the young central leaves and terminal buds will encourage two or three new shoots to develop on each branch thus maintaining the shape. Drastic pruning may be necessary to restore neglected plants. Recovery will be slow: it will take several weeks or months for neglected Crotons to regain their splendour.

Crotons are propagated by cuttings, air layers, or by seeds. Cuttings should be taken from stems that are mature but not old. Rooting will occur within six weeks and more

Plate 1 *Ferns and Aroids*

Anthuriums bloom well when grown in a rich moist compost and in light shade. [J. Criswick]

A Staghorn Fern *Platycerium bifurcatum*, hangs suspended from a tree limb. Several leaves have turned over to reveal brown spore-bearing patches. [I. Bannochie]

Philodendron hastatum is a useful plant for the shady garden. [M. Light]

Tree ferns *Cyathea* thrive in high rainfall regions. [J. Criswick]

Plate 2 *Bougainvilleas*

Above: Bougainvillea varieties including from 1 o'clock clockwise 'Double White', 'Scarlett O'Hara', 'Double Pink', 'Lady Mary Baring', and 'Camarillo Fiesta' can all be used as pot plants. [J. Criswick]

Below: *Bougainvillea glabra* blooms the whole length of the stem. [I. Bannochie]

Bougainvilleas make a colourful backdrop for a small water garden. [M. Light]

Grow Bougainvilleas in pots for a mobile feast of colour. [I. Bannochie]

Plate 3 *Bromeliads*

Bromeliad *Nidularium innocentii* produces stemless flowers that rise just above the water level in the cup. [I. Bannochie]

The flame-coloured bracts of *Guzmania lingulata* make this Bromeliad a valuable addition to the garden. [I. Bannochie]

The banded foliage of *Aechmea chantinii* vies for attention with the inflorescence. [J. Criswick]

Aechmea fendleri enjoys a poolside setting. [I. Bannochie]

Aechmea dichlamydea trinitensis. [Dr Sean Carrington]

Plate 4 *Cactus*

Fragrant, night-blooming *Epiphyllum oxypetalum* is a garden treasure. [I. Bannochie]

Barbados Gooseberry *Pereskia aculeata* produces edible fruits and large seeds that are easy to germinate. [I. Bannochie]

Tall columnar *Cereus* and globular *Melocactus* topped with cephaliums share a garden wall with other succulent plants. [M. Light]

Left: *Mammillaria* is the cactus of choice for the beginner. [M. MacConaill]

Plate 5 *Crotons*

A comfortable bench invites us to sit awhile and admire the garden. [M. Light]

Crotons should be grown in full sun. [M. Light]

Regular pruning encourages vigorous growth and pest resistance. [M. Light]

Croton leaves are unrivalled for their diversity of form and brilliance of colour. Here are examples of narrow leaf, broad leaf and semi-oakleaf varieties. [M. Light]

Plate 6 *Bedding plants*

Here a white-flowered *Begonia* is grouped with golden yellow *Pachystachys lutea* and *Opuntia* cactus making an attractive composition for all-round viewing. [I. Bannochie]

Brightly coloured Marigolds *Tagetes* also help to rid the soil of nematodes. [M. Light]

Left: Magificent Canna Lilies grow to more than 2 m (6 ft) tall. [M. Light]

The modern hybrids of *Cosmos sulphureus* make a brilliant display. [M. Light]

Plate 7 *Euphorbias*

Jatropha podagrica is an attractive addition to a small garden. [M. Light]

Top centre: Scarlet inflorescences of Poinsettia grace a terrace. [G.W. Lennox]

The Chenile Plant *Acalypha hispida* makes a colourful addition to the shrub border. [G.W. Lennox]

Left: *Acalypha* 'Ceylon' is valued for its foliage. [M. Light]

Plate 8 *Gingers*

The Hidden Lily *Curcuma Roscoeana* is magnificent in bloom. [I. Bannochie]

The Torch Ginger *Etlingera elatior* provides long-lasting cut flowers. [I. Bannochie]

The Spiral Ginger *Costus speciosus* has both plain and variegated leaf forms. [I. Bannochie]

Left: Plant Red Gingers *Alpinia purpurata* in a bright sheltered location where they will reward you with magnificent blooms. [I. Bannochie]

Plate 9 *Heliconias*

The pendant inflorescence of *Heliconia chartacea* 'Sexy Pink' is shown with three different forms of the *Heliconia bihai* complex. [J. Criswick]

Top centre: *Heliconia psittacorum* is suited to the small garden. [M. Light]

The mahogany red foliage of *Heliconia indica* 'Spectabilis' provides contrast. [I. Bannochie]

Left: A group of *Heliconia caribaea* grows in a Martinique garden. [I. Bannochie]

Plate 10 *Hibiscus*

Hibiscus are available in a wide range of colours. [J. Criswick]

Hibiscus 'Coral Sea Beauty' is very floriferous. [I. Bannochie]

Hibiscus 'Carrie Ann'. [I. Bannochie]

Left: Hibiscus 'Tylene' is a step on the way to breeding a blue flower! [I. Bannochie]

Plate 11 *Ixoras*

Ixora finlaysoniana is very fragrant.
[M. Light]

Ixora coccinea blooms abundantly
throughout the year. [M. Light]

Ixora 'Sunkist' is a miniature cultivar
suited to pot culture. [I. Bannochie]

This pink-flowered *Ixora* hybrid
thrives in a sheltered patio. [M. Light]

Plate 12 *Orchids*

Terete-leaved Vanda hybrids such as
'Miss Joaquim' and 'Amy' are grown
on tree fern posts in full sun.
[M. Light]

Right: Fragrant *Cattleya* orchids are
grown in unglazed clay pots having
additional holes for drainage and
aeration. [G.W. Lennox]

Ground orchids such as *Spathoglottis
unguiculata* make excellent bedding
plants. [M. Light]

Moth Orchids *Phalaenopsis* flourish
beneath shade cloth. [M. Light]

Plate 13 *Palms*

Above: A stately row of Royal Palms (*Roystonea*) lines a driveway. [M. Light]
Right: *Hyophorbe vershaffeltii* and the Sealing Wax Palm *Cyrtostachys renda* syn. *lakka* thrive in the moist soil around a garden pool. [M. Light]
Below: The attractive combination of a prominent green crownshaft and masses of scarlet fruits make the fast-growing *Veitchia merrillii* a lovely garden subject. [I. Bannochie]
Bottom right: The massive costapalmate leaves of *Latania loddigesii* and their woolly covering require space for proper viewing. [M. Light]

Plate 14 *Flowering shrubs*

Christmas Candles *Cassia alata* flowers when quite young. [I. Bannochie]

Queen of Flowers *Lagerstroemia indica* grows well in high rainfall regions. [I. Bannochie]

Right: Some roses especially the old-time varieties do well in a Caribbean garden. [M. Light]

Pagoda Flower *Clerodendron paniculatum* is a magnificent flowering shrub. Prune after flowering to induce branching. [I. Bannochie]

Plate 15 *Succulents*

Kalanchoe gastonis-bonnieri bears masses of bi-coloured blooms. [I. Bannochie]

Edithcolea grandis attracts a fly to its foul-smelling yet exquisitely designed blossom. [I. Bannochie]

Sword-like foliage of *Sansevieria* forms the backdrop to a Pony Tail Plant *Beaucarnea recurvata*. [M. Light]

Aloe arborescens is a magnificent landscape specimen. [G.W. Lennox]

Plate 16 *Flowering trees*

Above: *Cordia sebestena* is a pretty tree for a seaside garden. [G.W. Lennox]

Right: Yellow Poui *Tabebuia serratifolia* makes a fabulous splash of colour during the dry season. [G.W. Lennox]

Top right: The scarlet blooms and lacy foliage of the Flamboyant *Delonix regia* are especially attractive. [M. Light]

Right: The Seaside Mahoe *Thespesia populnea* has handsome glossy foliage and bright yellow flowers. [G.W. Lennox]

Plate 17 *Trees with interesting forms*

The spreading limbs and spirally-arranged foliage of *Pandanus baptistii* make it an interesting focal point for a large garden. [M. Light]

The Bearded Fig Tree *Ficus citrifolia* needs lots of space to grow. [G.W. Lennox]

Pride of India *Peltophorum ferrugineum* bears small reddish pods. Frangipani *Plumeria* blooms in the foreground. Together they form a pleasing combination. [G.W. Lennox]

Right: These seed-grown Traveller's Trees *Ravenala madagascariensis* are 20 years old and stand more than 9 m (30 ft) tall. [M. Light]

Plate 18 *Vines and Scramblers*

Red Hot Poker *Norantea guianensis* is a vigorous climber that can be grown over a wall or allowed to invade a supporting tree. [I. Bannochie]

The Gloriosa Lily *Gloriosa superba* climbs by means of leaf tendrils. [G.W. Lennox]

Jade Vine *Strongylodon macrobotrys* is unrivalled for its beauty and unique colour. [G.W. Lennox]

The two colour forms of *Petrea* can be induced to flower if watered heavily a few weeks beforehand. [I. Bannochie]

Plate 19 *Fruits and Spice*

Various *Citrus* fruits thrive in a Caribbean garden. Grow grafted stock for best results. [M. MacConaill]

Below: Pawpaw *Carica papaya* will grow in a small garden. Protect it from sucking insects that carry Bunchy Top Disease. [G.W. Lennox]

Black peppercorns can be harvested from your own vine of *Piper nigrum* growing on an upright post. [M. Light]

The Jamaican Ackee *Blighia sapida* makes a handsome landscaping specimen as well as providing edible fruits. [G.W. Lennox]

Plate 20 *Water plants and Water gardens*

Floating aquatic plants such as the Snowflake Water-lily *Nymphoides indica* resent having their foliage disturbed by splashing water. [I. Bannochie]

Right: Umbrella Sedge *Cyperus alternifolius* adds another dimension to the water garden. [M. Light]

Some tropical Water-lilies *Nymphaea* bloom by day, others bloom by night. [M. Light]

The magnificent leaves and flowers of the Water Platter *Victoria amazonica* are best displayed in a large pool. [M. Light]

Plate 21 *Plants for the Dry or Seaside garden*

Drought-tolerant *Yucca* plants bear magnificent spikes of creamy white blooms. [G.W. Lennox]

Right: This seaside garden in Tortola features salt-tolerant *Aloe*, *Agave*, *Yucca*, and a silvery grey-leaved *Conocarpus*. [I. Bannochie]

Agaves, such as the almost totally white cultivar 'Andromeda', are useful foliage plants for rocky or dry gardens. [I. Bannochie]

The wide variety of cactus shapes and forms allow us to design an interesting garden even when water is limiting. [I. Bannochie]

Plate 22 *Ground covers and Mulches*

Shade-tolerant *Aglaonema* covers the ground in semi-shade. [M. Light]

For a dry, sunny location, why not try Purple Heart *Setcreasea purpurea* as a ground cover or bedding plant? [G.W. Lennox]

Ctenanthe oppenheimiana tricolor and the Crested Polypody Fern *Polypodium polycarpon* are attractive and novel ground covers. [J. Criswick]

Right: A mulch can be both attractive and beneficial when used with plants such as *Heliconia psittacorum*. [I. Bannochie]

Plate 23 *Hedges and Automated lighting*

The Golden Palm *Chrysalidocarpus lutescens* is prized for informal hedging. [M. Light]

Annatto *Bixa orellana* is a colourful hedging or border shrub for poorly drained land. [M. Light]

Left: *Thunbergia erecta* flowers even in the semi-shade. Here an automated lighting system has been installed at the time of planting. [M. Light]

The interesting foliage of *Pseuderanthemum* brightens a service area. [M. Light]

Plate 24 *Plants for walls and fences*

Poinsettia effectively diverts attention from a cement block wall. Bachelor's Buttons *Gomphrena globosa* provide a light contrast. [M. Light]

A spreading Calabash tree *Crescentia cujete* screens the patio from the road. [G.W. Lennox]

Fast growing Corallita *Antigonon leptopus* quickly hides a chain link fence. Butterflies are attracted to the nectar-laden blooms! [G.W. Lennox]

Right: *Ipomoea horsfalliae* is a magnificent vine for a sunny wall or strong fence. [G.W. Lennox]

Plate 25 *Paths and possibilities*

Paving blocks can be cast using interesting leaves to create the patterns. [M. Light]

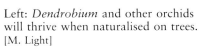

An arbor frames a lovely view. [G.W. Lennox]

Left: *Dendrobium* and other orchids will thrive when naturalised on trees. [M. Light]

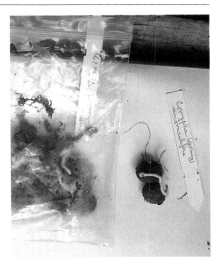

Try germinating palm seeds to gain new varieties. [I. Bannochie]

Plate 26 *Fragrant flowers*

The fragrant blooms of *Crinum moorei*. [M. Light]

Flowers of Ylang Ylang *Cananga odorata* are treasured for their wonderful perfume. [M. Light]

Frangipani *Plumeria* cultivars come in a wide variety of colours. [I. Bannochie]

Angel's Trumpet *Datura candida* forms a lovely specimen plant. [G.W. Lennox]

Plate 27 *Variegated foliage*

Above: Creamy, striped leaves of Variegated Oleander *Nerium* brighten a garden corner. [I. Bannochie]

Above right: Leaves of *Alpinia zerumbet variegata* are useful in floral arrangements. [I. Bannochie]

Right: Flowers of the Coral Tree *Erythrina* compete for attention with the variegated foliage. [G.W. Lennox]

Most variegated Bougainvilleas have developed from bud sports. [I. Bannochie]

Plate 28 *Flower arrangements*

Above: This arrangement of Red Ginger and Anthuriums should last several weeks. [I. Bannochie]

Below: Hibiscus flowers mounted on bamboo stems or coconut leaf midribs form a bright bouquet. [I. Bannochie]

Heliconia psittacorum, Reed-Stem Epidendrum orchids, a sprouting Coconut and *Pandanus* leaves make a pleasing combination. [I. Bannochie]

Create an interesting arrangement with Red Ginger, a variegated Pineapple and a hand of green Bananas. [I. Bannochie]

Plate 29 *Signs and signals of deficiency and disease*

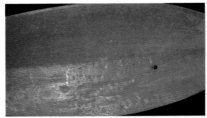

Above: Hibiscus leaves show between-vein chlorosis symptomatic of iron deficiency. [M. Light]

Above right: Suspect a Virus Disease if sunken streaks appear on orchid leaves. [M. Light]

Right: Black Rot *Phytophthora* affects many plants including orchids. [M. Light]

Bacterial rots often begin when water lies in the plant crown. [M. Light]

Plate 30 *Pests and the characteristic damage they cause*

Above: Caterpillars eat jagged holes in foliage. Note the disguised resting stage (chrysalis) attached nearby. [M. MacConaill]

Above right: Speckled foliage of these Sorrel plants *Hibiscus sabdariffa* indicates a Spider Mite infestation. [M. Light]

Above: Blossom Thrips damage orchids and other flowers. [M. Light]

Left: Scale insects on *Citrus* produce honeydew which in turn supports the growth of Sooty Mold fungus. [M. MacConaill]

readily during the wet season. Air layers should be made at the juncture of two fully grown branches. Choose one branch which might have to be removed anyway by pruning.

There are hundreds of Croton cultivars, some of which arose spontaneously as sports, others which are the result of hybridization. Hybrids such as 'Confucius', 'Miami Beauty', 'Sunburst', and 'Tapestry' have larger, more colourful leaves and compact habit. You can try developing your own Croton hybrids.

Crotons are monoecious. The flowers look quite different, the male flowers having conspicuous anthers. The best time to pollinate Croton flowers is early morning when the female flowers are fully open. Remove the pollen from the male flowers of the desired pollen parent with an artist's soft paint brush. Transfer the pollen to the sticky stigma of the female flower. Remove all other male flowers, bag the inflorescence with cheesecloth to keep out insect pollinators. Leave the bag in place to catch the seeds. When a fruit is ripe, it will shatter explosively, yielding one to three seeds. For details of germinating Croton seeds refer to Chapter 2, page 40.

EUPHORBIAS AND RELATIVES

Basic care
Light: full sun
Water: drought-tolerant; no special requirement for water except during severe drought
Soil: porous sandy soil
Fertilizer: all purpose fertilizer applied twice yearly
Pests and diseases: no special problems
Propagation: seed using Method II; cuttings

CROWN OF THORNS *Euphorbia milii*

The shrubby Crown of Thorns plant comes from Madagascar. There are many forms and varieties, the most common having red flower bracts, others bearing yellow, cream or orange blooms. Drought-tolerant and compact, this plant can make a nice low decorative hedge in a sunny dry garden. Propagate by cuttings.

EXCOECARIA *Excoecaria*

A medium-sized ornamental shrub, *E. bicolor* sports interesting two-toned, green and purple foliage and saffron-coloured new growth – quite a startling effect. The flowers are inconspicuous. Propagate from semi-hardwood cuttings.

JATROPHA *Jatropha*

Central American in origin, both *J. podagrica* and *J. multifida* make wonderful additions to the Caribbean garden. These succulent plants grow quickly from seed, reaching 1.5 m (5 ft) in height. They prefer a porous soil mix of compost and sand, and a sunny location. Flower stalks 15 cm (6 in) tall, are topped with a cluster of scarlet blooms. *Jatropha* is easy to raise from seed. Groups of young plants are an attractive addition to the smaller garden.

POINSETTIA *Euphorbia pulcherrima*

Native to Mexico, Poinsettia was cultivated by the Aztecs of Central Mexico before being introduced to the United States by Joel Poinsett. Shrubby Poinsettias grow to 3 m (10 ft) and flower in response to shortening daylength. The actual flowers are inconspicuous, however, the large coloured leaves (bracts) surrounding the flowers become bright red as the flowers mature. Poinsettias are ideal for hedging, as specimen plants or massed together with Snow-on-the-Mountain *Euphorbia leucocephala*. The brilliant colour of Poinsettia floral bracts lasts for three or more months. Light from security or street lamps, even the light spilling from a bedroom window, artificially lengthens the day. Poinsettias will not flower unless they have 12 or more hours of uninterrupted darkness in the weeks prior to blooming. Plantings should be located well away from artificial lights.

Poinsettias are available in a variety of colours and forms including single and double red, white, pink, cream and flecked. The shrubs should be pruned after flowering (March), removing two-thirds of the branch length. Pinch or remove the top 5 cm (2 in) of growing stems several times again until August/September. This will encourage branching, bushiness and more floral bracts. Propagation of selected clones is by rooted cuttings.

SLIPPER FLOWER *Pedilanthus*

Native to the Caribbean, shrubby *P. tithymaloides* stands 1 m (3 ft) high with stems bearing deciduous, succulent leaves and topped with groupings of bright red floral bracts resembling slippers, hence the name. While the most common forms are dark green, there are some beautiful variegated kinds having leaves and stems streaked white, green and even pink. This plant thrives in full sun to semi-shade, is salt-tolerant and can be used for hedging in dry or seaside gardens. Propagate by cuttings.

SNOW BUSH, FOLIAGE FLOWER
Breynia nivosa

A shrub 1–2 m (3–6 ft) tall with roundish leaves variegated green and white, Snow Bush, is sometimes almost completely white, tinged pink (var. *rosea picta*) or even darker (var. *purpurea*). The flowers are not obvious. Snow Bush can be used for hedging but can be invasive. Propagate by suckers.

SNOW-ON-THE-MOUNTAIN
Euphorbia leucocephala

This 2–3 m (6–10 ft) tall shrub bears masses of white bracts surrounding rather insignificant flowers. The entire shrub becomes snow white. Snow-on-the-Mountain can be effectively inter-planted with red Poinsettia *E. pulcherrima* in a border or on a slope. Like

Poinsettia, Snow-on-the-Mountain is sensitive to daylength. Propagate by cuttings.

SYNADENIUM *Synadenium*

Native to East Africa, this succulent shrub has large, thin leaves and a fleshy stem. The whole is blotched reddish-brown and green. Rather insignificant flowers are borne in the leaf axils. The shrub may become completely deciduous in the dry season yet remains attractive. This handsome genus is a valuable addition to a dry, sunny garden, providing both colour and height. Grow the plant in a well-drained location, enriching the soil with leaf mould. Propagation is by cuttings.

FERNS

Basic care

Light: semi-shade; some ferns need complete shade, some tolerate full sun

Water: moderate to high relative humidity (30–50 per cent or more); protect from drying winds, water frequently to keep compost moist

Soil: porous yet water-retentive

Fertilizer: one-half to one-quarter strength solution every two weeks

Pests and diseases: Mealy Bugs, Scale Insects, Spider Mites, Slugs; **NOTE** – ferns are intolerant of many pesticides!

Propagation: spores; division of rhizome; removal of offsets or bulbils

Ferns are the plant of choice for shady gardens or patios. Although some ferns can withstand direct sun and tolerate some dryness, the majority require both shade, moisture and high humidity. Many beautiful ferns can be grown in pots or baskets on protected patios and verandas. Tree ferns are magnificent subjects for tropical gardens located in high rainfall areas. In drier gardens, it is necessary to provide shade, wind protection and conserve moisture by means of a fern house; such a fernery should be kept moist at all times.

Coral stone blocks form excellent benches for pots. They are long-lasting, retaining moisture far better than concrete blocks. Ferns love to grow in coral stone pots, spores germinating readily even on the moist pot exterior. The growth is lush!

Pests such as Mealy Bugs and Scale Insects can be troublesome, especially if the ferns are being kept just a little too dry. Many ferns are intolerant of pesticides. Quarantine of new ferns and regular inspection of the collection for intruders will go a long way in keeping pests at bay. Diseases are rarely a problem with ferns.

Whether you choose to grow ferns in pots or in baskets, potting must be done with care. Pots may be clay or plastic: ferns do equally well in either. If using plastic or glazed clay pots, less watering will be necessary. Hanging baskets made of wire or plastic are appropriate, as are hollowed tree fern stumps. Baskets can be lined with coconut 'cloth' or burlap then filled with potting mix. Black polyethylene (plastic) sheeting can be used as an alternative liner but holes must be made to ensure adequate drainage. Pot drainage holes should be covered with a piece of screening to keep out unwanted 'guests'. A layer of small stones or charcoal pieces in the bottom of the pot prevents potting media from clogging the hole. Some growers crush dried Breadfruit leaves to place in a layer over the stones. When ready to pot, place some moistened mix in the container, position the plant, adding more mix as required to hold the plant in position. Make certain that the growing point is not covered. Water the plant, adding more soil if settling occurs. Favourite soil mixes are porous and moisture-retentive. Soil, charcoal, leaf mould, silica sand, peat moss, coconut fibre, compost, Perlite and vermiculite are some components of fern mixes. Whatever component or blend of components is used, the mix should be loose even if wet. You should not be able to form a ball of mix even when squeezing hard.

Propagation of ferns

Ferns can be propagated in various ways according to the characteristics of a given species. Propagation techniques include division of a rhizome, removal of runners and plantlets found growing on fronds of certain species, as well as by spores. Ferns produce their spores in dots or rows beneath leaves or occasionally an entire leaf is dedicated to spore production. If conditions in a fernery are suitable, numerous young plants will grow spontaneously from spores.

Polypodium and other ferns having extensive rhizomes are easily propagated by division. Choose a portion of rhizome with a growing point and with roots, cutting the rhizome with a sharp sterile knife. Rambling ferns are best potted in baskets. When potting divisions, anchor them in place until they become self-supporting. Wire or cord may be used for this purpose.

Clumping ferns such as *Adiantum* and *Nephrolepis* can be divided by pulling or cutting the clumps into two or more pieces. Each division must have one or more growing points and roots.

Raising Ferns from spores

Collect your own fern spores by cutting a spore-bearing frond and placing it in a paper bag. As the frond dries, the powdery spores will be released into the bag. Alternatively, you can obtain spores from specialist growers and seed companies. For details of germinating spores, refer to Chapter 2, page 41.

Ferns for your garden

BIRD'S NEST FERN *Asplenium*
An epiphytic fern of Malaya, *A. nidus* has

long, broad, bright green fronds which grow out almost horizontally from the base, the whole forming a wide cup or nest. In the wild, the nest serves to trap dead leaves and other debris which when it decays, holds moisture and provides nutrients. These ferns respond favourably to bright light and high humidity. Variety *crispafolium* has deeply ruffled leaves. This fern is propagated from spores.

BLECHNUM *Blechnum*

B. occidentale has orange-red young fronds making it a very attractive addition to a fern collection. Easy to grow in pots or in a sheltered garden, this fern may be propagated by division of a mature clump or by spores.

BOSTON FERN *Nephrolepis*

N. biserrata is large fern, over 1 m (3 ft) tall, tolerant of dry conditions and sun. It is sometimes cultivated as a bedding plant. The Fishtail Fern *N. biserrata* var. *furcata* has attractive leaf tips resembling tails of small fish. This fern forms an attractive hedge against a stone or cement wall, thriving even in full sun as long as it is watered and fertilized regularly.

N. cordifolia has long drooping fronds making it an ideal subject for hanging baskets. Variety *duffii* is smaller with deeply divided leaflets. These ferns have tubers making it both easy to identify and to propagate. Propagation is also by division of creeping rhizome.

N. exaltata is one of the best known ferns cultivated in gardens. The popular cultivars 'Baby's Breath' and 'Fluffy Ruffles' come by their names from the very finely divided foliage.

N. hirsutula is the largest *Nephrolepis* in cultivation. It is most suitable for planting under trees and in garden beds as it is tolerant to sun and drought.

BREADFRUIT FERN *Polypodium aureum*

Native to the tropical Americas, now common to cultivation, this fern has shiny dark green foliage in the shape of breadfruit leaves. It can be grown in baskets or large pots. Propagation is by division of the scaly, creeping rhizomes.

CRESTED POLYPODY FERN *Polypodium polycarpon*

With leaves the colour and texture of the Bird's Nest Fern *Asplenium*, but with each leaf tip being made up of numerous lobes, the Crested Polypody is an attractive fern. It stands about 1 m (3 ft) tall at maturity. This fern spreads by means of a creeping rhizome and may be used as a bedding plant in semi-shaded gardens. Propagate by division.

MAIDENHAIR FERN *Adiantum*

Popular and easy to grow, Maidenhair Ferns are moisture-lovers. When potted, they need plenty of limestone or coral stone in the mix. Leaf petioles are shiny black contrasting with the delicate light green wedge-shaped leaflets.

COMMON MAIDENHAIR *A. tenerum* will readily naturalize in moist, shaded gardens especially if there is a stream or lily pond nearby. It can be cultivated in pots. The cultivar 'Farleyense' originated at Farley Hill, Barbados. No longer found at that location, this fern can only be obtained by division: the cultivar does not produce spores. The dark green arching fronds have a layered effect.

GIANT MAIDENHAIR *A. trapeziforme* grows to a height of 1 m (3 ft). The broad angular leaf segments are impressive.

VENUS' HAIR A. Capillus-Veneris can be found growing in the wild on wet limestone cliffs. This creeping fern will naturalize on the walls of a fernery.

RABBIT'S FOOT FERN *Davallia*

D. fejeensis, from the Fiji Islands, has hairy creeping rhizomes, hence its name. Because of its creeping habit and its finely divided, dark green foliage arises at intervals along the rhizome and not all from one central growing point, this fern must be grown in a basket or even in a hollowed tree fern stump. The fern will grow all over the basket or stump making a veritable ball of lacy foliage. When potting a division of this fern, simply fasten the cutting to the surface of the potting mix.

SILVER AND GOLD FERNS *Pityrogramma*

GOLD FERN *P. chrysophylla* is native to Tobago. The leaf undersurface is coated with golden-yellow dust. This fern is not easy to grow. As with the Silver Fern, an open potting mix, bright light and judicious feeding may yield success. Try raising this fern from spores.

SILVER FERN *P. calomelanos* is common to dry limestone grottos, cave entrances and gullies. It takes its name from the silvery matter adherent to the undersurface of the fronds. Knowing about its native habitat helps to determine the best cultural techniques. Provide a very open potting mix with at least one-third coral stone or limestone chunks. These ferns need plenty of light but not necessarily direct sun. Growing them from spores may be the easiest way to establish them.

STAGHORN FERN *Platycerium*

Staghorn ferns have two types of leaves: curious, disc-shaped leaves which clasp the bark on which they are growing; and large branched fertile leaves resembling a stag's antlers. Spores are produced from brown felted areas on the leaf undersurface. The most commonly seen species is *P. bifurcatum* which may be grown in the cooler uplands where the night temperature could drop as low as 10°C (50°F). Propagate Staghorn ferns from spores or remove offsets from mature specimens. Raise

P. grande from spores; it does not produce plantlets.

TREE FERN *Cyathea*

Tree ferns are found throughout the tropics growing in gullies, ravines and high in mountain cloud-forests. Some species require cool nights to flourish. *C. tenerum* can grow to 20 m (65 ft) although it will take some years to do so. *C. caribaea* is a smaller, stouter plant. Tree ferns are so named because their vertical rhizome resembles the trunk of a tree. The black, wiry roots form a coarse outer layer that is slow to decay. This material can be used for potting orchids or bromeliads. Plant small tree ferns in pots of humus-rich soil or use them to landscape semi-shaded areas of humid gardens in high rainfall regions.

UPSIDEDOWN FERN *Asplenium cristatum*

An attractive Trinidadian species, the name Upsidedown describes the apparent reversed placement of spores on the 30 cm (12 in) arching leaves. This fern prefers limestone in the potting mix.

GINGERS

Basic care
Light: dappled sunlight except where otherwise noted
Water: compost evenly moist except where otherwise noted; seasonally dormant plants <u>must</u> be kept dry
Soil: well drained organic compost
Fertilizer: balanced fertilizer twice monthly during active growth
Pests and diseases: Scale Insects, Mealy Bugs and Spider Mites can be a problem if plants are kept too dry; Soft Rots and Leaf Spots can occur if air movement inadequate
Propagation: division; seed; offsets

The Ginger family, Zingiberaceae, is large with about 40 genera. Most cultivated gingers are from the Old World Tropics. Among the many outstanding gingers for tropical gardens are Ginger Lilies, Torch Ginger, Pineapple Ginger, Spiral Flags, Garland Lilies, Hidden Lilies and culinary ginger. As well as having landscape potential, the Ginger family provides long lasting cut flowers and several species of culinary value.

True Root Ginger *Zingiber officinalis*, and Turmeric *Curcuma longa* are commonly cultivated in Caribbean gardens.

Gingers for your garden

CULINARY GINGER *Zingiber*

See Fruits, Vegetables, Herbs and Spices page 127.

GARLAND LILIES *Hedychium*

Seasonally dormant, tropical Asian herbs, Garland Lilies are showy specimens for any garden. Large, clump-forming plants, they bear terminal clusters of fragrant blooms that are traditionally used in garlands or (Hawaiian) leis. Propagate by division of the rhizome or from seeds using Method II.

BUTTERFLY OR WHITE GINGER *H. coronarium* is a spreading plant with large white fragrant blooms.

KAHILI GINGER *H. gardnerianum* has stiff stems bearing large leaves that are powdery beneath while young. The pale yellow, fragrant blooms are borne from a loose cluster of inflorescence bracts.

RED BUTTERFLY GINGER *H. greenii* has magnificent foliage and stout canes. Dark matt green above, coppery purple beneath, the leaves vie with the fiery orange flowers for your attention. This species would be a valuable addition to any garden.

SCARLET GINGER LILY *H. coccineum*, from Burma and Sri Lanka, is a large plant with stems over 2 m (6 ft) tall. The terminal inflorescence is crowded with red flowers.

YELLOW GINGER *H. flavum* is a bushy plant with long stately leaves. Valuable as a landscaping plant, Yellow Ginger bears showy, fragrant yellow flowers from the cone-shaped inflorescences.

GINGER LILIES *Alpinia*

RED GINGER *A. purpurata* is strictly a tropical plant, not tolerating temperatures below 10°C (50°F). Growing equally well in acidic or alkaline soil, Red Ginger flourishes where there is plenty of rain. It can grow to more than 2 m (6 ft). Heavy mulching will carry plants through periods of drought. Well-watered and fertilized plants will flower throughout the year. The dramatic vivid red inflorescence bracts are long-lasting. When cut, the inflorescence remains attractive for more than three weeks. The cultivar 'Tahitian Ginger' has massive inflorescences. Red Ginger was known in Barbados and the nearby islands before 1960. The pink varieties, introduced in the 1970s, have become increasingly popular. Pink cultivars include 'Eileen McDonald' and 'Pink Princess'.

Red and Pink Ginger Lilies are easily propagated vegetatively by division and also by bulbils that develop on old inflorescences. To divide a plant, lift the whole with a garden fork. Shake or wash off excess soil. Using a sharp, sturdy knife or cutlass, cut the branched rhizome, dividing the clump into two or more parts. Each part should have at least three shoots. Plant the divisions at their original depth in a prepared garden bed. To propagate Ginger Lilies from bulbils, resist the urge to cut off spent blooms. As the bracts lose their beauty and droop, small plantlets will arise in the axils. These bulbils grow rapidly while attached to the mother plant, developing two or three leaves and rudimentary roots. Remove matured plantlets using the fingers or if necessary, a sharp knife. Plant them in a shallow tray of damp sand. Do not plant them too deep! Place the tray in a location with filtered sunlight. Mist the plants daily until roots are well established. Rooted plants should be transferred to the garden nursery and grown to at least 50 cm (20 in) in height before planting them in their final location.

SHELL GINGER *A. zerumbet* is a handsome landscaping plant, growing to 1.5 m (5 ft). It can be cultivated in huge clumps for a bold effect or it can be used as a screening or hedging plant. The form *variegata* has outstanding striped foliage that will last over six weeks when cut and placed in water. The white, pink-tipped flowers of Shell Ginger are showy, resembling shells, hence the common name. The inflorescences are short-lived when cut.

VARIEGATED GINGER *A. sanderae* forms large clumps of handsome 45 cm (18 in) long green leaves, banded white. The leaves are useful in decorative arrangements.

GLOBBA *Globba*

Globbas are small, seasonally dormant plants. Charming as potted plants, they can also be grown in special beds where they should be left undisturbed during their period of dormancy. A rest is essential. Companion plants such as *Impatiens*, *Alternanthera*, Ground Orchids *Spathoglottis* and some Gesneriads can share the same well-drained and semi-shaded growing area. Propagation is by division while the plants are dormant, or from seed using Method II.

G. *agrosanguinea*: from Borneo; pendulous heads of purple red bracts; bright yellow flowers

G. *macrocarpa*: from Thailand; white bracts and flowers

G. *schomburgkii* (Yellow Dancing Lady): yellow bracts and flowers

G. *sessiliflora*: pale mauve bracts and flowers

G. *wintii*: pale purple bracts and yellow flowers

HIDDEN LILIES *Curcuma*

Rhizomatous herbs from tropical Asia, their common name signifies seasonal dormancy. Leafy shoots arise from the rhizome to 1.0–1.5 m (3–5 ft) in height. Some species have ornamental foliage, others are prized for their cone-like inflorescences, notable for their persistent coloured bracts. Propagation is primarily by division of the rhizome.

HIDDEN LILY *C. roscoeana*, from Burma and India, has showy ribbed, long-stalked leaves. Solitary erect inflorescences have purple bracts with orange-red flowers. The cultivar 'Jewel of Burma' has orange bracts and yellow flowers. Both make excellent cut flowers.

MINIATURE HIDDEN LILY *C. siamensis*, from Thailand, makes a very pretty pot plant. It is compact, the white inflorescence appearing in the centre of the plant.

QUEEN LILY *C. petiolata*, from Burma, has large grass-green leaves with 15 cm (6 in) long petioles. The terminal inflorescence has green bracts tinged with purple: the flowers are creamy yellow.

TURMERIC *C. longa*, from India, is widely cultivated throughout the tropics as a spice and as a dyestuff. The leaves are a dark, glossy green with a prominent midrib. The inflorescence bracts are an attractive pale green to white colour. The short, branched rhizomes are bright yellow and fragrant. Harvest Turmeric when the plants die down completely. Plant Turmeric in beds of rich loam, and mulch well. Provide adequate moisture and nutrients during the growing season.

RESURRECTION LILIES *Kaempferia*

Almost stemless perennial herbs, Resurrection

Lilies make good potted plants and ground covers. Seasonally dormant, the common name is associated with Easter, the season when the plants resume growth. Seasonally dormant plants have evolved in locations where such dormancy helps them survive drought or cold. To grow them well, we must respect their requirement for rest. The humid tropics have little or no definite dry season. Therefore we must go to the extreme of removing the dormant plant from the soil and storing it in a dry place until growth resumes. Following is a good example of how a Caribbean gardener can cope with seasonally dormant plants.

Kaempferia elegans, from Thailand, is a very rare plant. Small and exquisite, it has two beautifully feathered leaves. A daily succession of single, glistening white flowers begins as soon as the leaves are mature. Flowers are produced for about 25 days. The leaves continue to display their beauty for another four or five months: they then wither and fall off. Watering must cease at this time. The plant should be removed from the pot, cleaned of soil, and stored dry in a paper bag until June. In mid-June, a tiny green bud will appear, signalling time to pot it up and re-start the cycle.

PRETTY RESURRECTION LILY *K. pulchra* has very attractive broad, variegated ribbed leaves and mauve flowers. It is a good ground cover plant.

RESURRECTION LILY, TROPICAL CROCUS *K. rotunda*, from South East Asia, breaks its dormancy with a show of white and lilac fragrant blooms. The leaves develop afterwards. A feathered blend of greens on the upper surface, purple beneath, the striking foliage makes this species most desirable for edging narrow garden beds.

VARIEGATED GINGER LILY *K. gilbertii*, from southern Burma, is stemless and fleshy rooted. The green and white leaves grow in tufts. The flowers are white. This plant is a good ground cover for dry areas, and is useful as a pot plant.

SPIRAL FLAGS *Costus*

This genus has over 140 species from both the Old and New World tropics. Most attain 1–3 m (3–10 ft) in height unless otherwise noted. Propagation is by division of established plants or from seed using Method II (see page 38).

Costus productus has rich lime green foliage and bright red bracts and flowers. It is good as a ground cover in dappled sunlight.

Costus stenophyllus, from Costa Rica, is an unusual and interesting clustering plant with tall, green, cane-like stems banded brown near their base. The leaves are long and narrow. The yellow inflorescences arise from the base of the stems. This species has landscape potential.

FIERY COSTUS *C. igneus*, from Brazil, has stout maroon-coloured stems bearing spirally-arranged leaves which are green above and red beneath. Flowers are rich orange.

INDIAN HEAD GINGER *C. spicatus* originates in the West Indies. It is a good perennial landscape plant, tolerant of salt in the soil. The showy red bracts form a glossy cylindrical inflorescence from which arise yellow flowers.

SPIRAL GINGER, CANE REED *C. speciosus*, from India, is grown mainly as a landscape plant. The beauty of its variegated form, *C. speciosus variegatus*, should not be overlooked. The large, frilled white flowers common to both forms are borne from 7.5 cm long (3 in) red cones. In seasonally dry gardens, stems shed their leaves, at which time the plants should be cut back.

STEPLADDER PLANT *C. malortieanus*, from Costa Rica, bears yellow and red flowers on handsome plants. This species is very useful for landscaping.

VIOLET SPIRAL FLAG *C. sanguineus*, from Central America, is outstanding because of its foliage. Velvety bluish-green leaves, each with a silvery central vein and red lower surface, are carried by wine-red petioles. The flowers are red with a yellow lip.

TORCH AND PINEAPPLE GINGERS

Torch Ginger *Etlingera elatior* and Pineapple Ginger (Indonesian Ginger) *Tapeinochilos ananassae* are attractive members of the Ginger family. Their inflorescences do not appear at the end of the leafy stems as in *Alpinia*, but emerge as solitary erect stalks at the base of the parent plant. The very showy, long-lasting inflorescences of Torch Ginger range from blood red to the palest pink. Pineapple Ginger produces an inflorescence of recurved scarlet bracts, not unlike a pineapple. The foliage is a dark, glossy green.

These plants can grow to more than 3 m (10 ft). The inflorescence stalk is relatively short, 50–75 cm (20–30 in). Position the plants in beds along pathways, at the edges of the garden, or on a gentle upwards slope. Adequate sunlight, warmth, moisture and nutrients are required. Propagation is from seed using Method II, and by division.

GRASSES AND BAMBOOS

Ornamental Grasses and Sedges

The usefulness of ornamental grasses and sedges is limited only by our imagination and the availability of appropriate material. The varieties listed here are all recommended for their beauty. Plants with variegated foliage look particularly attractive as a contrast to dark green shrubbery, while those with grace-ful, arching feather-like plumes can be used as accent plants in a border or in island beds. Grasses that form clumps are easier to control than those that form runners. To control a potential invader, use a plastic or metal edging around the bed. The edging should be at least 30 cm (12 in) deep, the upper edge at the soil surface and disguised by mulch. Many ornamental grasses and sedges are perennial and can be propagated by division of clumps. Annual grasses must be propagated from seed.

AMERICAN PAMPAS GRASS
Cortaderia selloana 'Monstrosa'

The graceful white plumes of this South American perennial grass rise high above the narrow, dark green leaves. There are separate male and female plants: females produce the more attractive plumes. Propagate female plants by division; divide when new growth commences after the dry season or a drought. Grow in full sun; attains height of 2.5–6.5 m (8–20 ft).

CAREX 'Aureo-marginata' *Carex siderostricta aureo-marginata*

A handsome, moisture-loving sedge, it grows rapidly to form dense clumps of leaves broadly banded with yellow on green. Propagate by division; semi-shade; height is 25–30 cm (10–12 in).

FOUNTAIN GRASS *Pennisetum alopecuroides*

Related to Elephant Grass *P. purpureum*, this perennial shares many of the decorative characteristics but lacks the coarseness of its cousin. It is graceful, bearing silvery-rose spikes resembling bottle brushes at the tips. Plant divisions at least 1 m (3 ft) apart; grow in full sun; height is 1 m (3 ft).

NATAL RED TOP *Rhynchelytrum repens*

Feathery sprays of red bronze florets adorn this compact, drought-resistant grass. An annual easily propagated from seed. Particularly attractive when planted in drifts across gravel or stony land. Grow in full sun; attains height of 60 cm (2 ft).

RIBBON GRASS *Phalaris arundinacea*

The green and white striped leaves of this vigorous spreading grass make a beautiful ground cover. Propagate this perennial grass by removing rooted stolons from established patches. Excellent for erosion control. Grow in full sun to semi-shade; height is 60–120 cm (2–4 ft).

SAVANNAH GRASS *Axonopus compressus*

The variegated form of this creeping perennial grass can be an interesting addition to a garden. It must be kept mowed otherwise it tends to be overwhelmed by weeds. Grow in full sun; height is only about 5–15 cm (2–6 in).

SPANISH REED *Arundo donax*

A tall perennial grass with stout stems and 5 cm (2 in) wide green or striped foliage. The inflorescence is showy and golden brown. Propagate selected cultivars by division. Grow in full sun; very tall plant, attaining height of 3–6 m (10–20 ft).

Bamboos

Bamboos are woody tropical and sub-tropical grasses with jointed, often hollow stems. The stems, **culms**, arise from an underground rhizome. Bamboos are heavy feeders and use copious quantities of water when in active growth. Growth is rapid. They are propagated by division of a rhizome or a clump.

CHINESE GODDESS BAMBOO *Bambusa riviereorum*

An elegant clump-forming bamboo reaching only 3 m (10 ft) in height. It is adapted to moist soil and is suited to sunny gardens having a stream or pond overflow area.

COMMON BAMBOO *Bambusa vulgaris*

In height, this giant bamboo reaches 26 m (80 ft) or more in high rainfall areas or about 10 m (40 ft) in drier gardens. It can be used on large properties to establish a grove, create a boundary planting or to control erosion of river or streambanks. Yellow and striped culm cultivars exist. Culms are about 10 cm (4 in) in diameter. When propagating this species, first cut the mature culms to about 1 m (3 ft) – this makes it easier to divide the clumps.

HEDGE BAMBOO *Bambusa multiplex*

This bamboo forms compact graceful clumps, 3–10 m (10–40 ft) tall. The leaves are silvery beneath. Cultivars include 'Silverstripe Fernleaf' with white striped delicate leaves and 'Stripestem Fernleaf' with green stripes on reddish green culms. This species can be used as an informal hedge or as ornamental clumps.

LANCE BAMBOO *Dendrocalamus strictus*

A clump bamboo with nearly solid stems Lance Bamboo grows to 30 m (100 ft) in high rainfall regions, 20 m (80 ft) in drier locales. It forms a dense, impenetrable clump and is suitable for boundary planting or for groves. It grows well in semi-shaded, moist gardens.

Grasses recommended for lawns

CARPET GRASS *Axonopus furcatus*

This coarse grass is seldom planted except on difficult wet sites where growth of other species is limited. It adapts readily to boggy sites in sun or in partial shade.

CENTIPEDE GRASS *Eremchloa ophiuroides*

This drought-resistant, shade-tolerant grass reaches only 10–15 cm (4–6 in) in height. Recommended mowing height is 4 cm (1.5 in). It resents heavy fertilization and is well-suited to sandy coastal soils. Centipede Grass may be propagated vegetatively by sprigs or plugs or it may be seeded. Seed is in limited supply and is expensive. Sprigs or plugs may be planted in rows about 30 cm (12 in) apart. Sprigs should be planted 2–5 cm (1–2 in) deep with most green foliage left above ground.

DEVIL GRASS, BERMUDA GRASS
Cynodon dactylon

A very common, tough grass that is intolerant of shade. Devil Grass is used for cricket and football grounds, golf fairways and lawn tennis courts. It does best on near-neutral, fertile soils and must be fertilized, watered and mowed regularly to 'look good'. Recommended mowing height is 2.5–4 cm (1–1.5 in). While common Devil Grass can be propagated from seed, selected varieties must be propagated from living sprigs or stolons. These are scattered evenly on a prepared soil base at the rate of 40–200 litres (1–6 bushels) per 100 m^2 (approximately 1000 ft^2), topdressed with approximately 2.5 cm (1 in) topsoil and watered. Plugs may be planted from 15–30 cm (6–12 in) apart. The closer the plantings, the more rapid the lawn development. As the name Devil Grass implies, it can be 'a devil of a grass' to eradicate if it chooses your flower bed as its home!

FLAT GRASS, SAVANNAH GRASS
Axonopus compressus

Savannah Grass is perhaps the best choice for a small lawn. It needs less cutting, can tolerate some shade and is relatively easy to remove from flower beds. It stays green except during extended drought. Although more coarse and less attractive than finer-bladed species, Savannah Grass is tough and requires less maintenance.

JAVA GRASS *Polytrias amaura, P. praemorsa*

Java Grass has proved to be of considerable value for lawns but requires constant care. Although it is the best looking of all tropical grasses, it requires more cutting, more feeding, more weeding, more watering, and it goes brown more quickly during a drought. Recommended mowing height is 2.5 cm (1 in).

ST. AUGUSTINE GRASS
Stenotaphrum secundatum

A shade-tolerant coarse grass that keeps flat to the ground, St. Augustine Grass spreads by runners. It requires only moderate mowing. Recommended mowing height is 7.5 cm (3 in). St. Augustine Grass is valuable for covering steep slopes and rough land. It can be attacked by a variety of diseases and pests including Chinch Bug. Cultivar 'Floralawn' has greater Chinch Bug resistance. St. Augustine Grass is propagated vegetatively from sprigs or plugs planted in rows about 30 cm (12 in) apart. With fertilization and some weed control, a reasonable turf can be obtained in a few months of favourable growing weather.

SHADE GRASS *Paspalum breve*

Caribbean grass found in gullies and under trees. Shade-tolerant, it gives a very fine turf. Recommended mowing height is 7.5 cm (3 in). Propagate Shade Grass vegetatively from sprigs planted in rows about 30 cm (12 in) apart.

ZOYSIA GRASS *Zoysia tenuifolia*

Zoysia is an attractive salt-tolerant grass that makes a fine lawn. It is a slow-growing grass that spreads by runners making a tough, dense turf that requires careful regular mowing: otherwise it tends to produce a puffy growth liable to 'scalping' when mowed. A heavy-duty mower is recommended: mowing height is 2.5–4 cm (1–1.5 in). To establish a Zoysia lawn, plant sprigs or stems about three nodes in length at 15 cm (6 in) intervals. The pieces of grass should be almost completely buried in the prepared soil bed. The area should be watered and picked clean of weeds until the grass begins to sprout.

HELICONIAS

Heliconias are one of the most recently discovered of the horticulturally desirable tropical plants. Fifty years ago, fewer than 20 were described in the literature. Now more than 400 species are in cultivation. Exotic cousins of Bananas and Gingers, Heliconias are tall plants with clustered stems (pseudotrunks) and large paddle-shaped, waxy leaves. In their native habitat, Heliconias grow best in the light-gaps of warm, humid forests. They need adequate light and moisture to grow vigorously and to flower profusely. Where trees have fallen, where streams flow, or where paths have been established, more light is available and Heliconias thrive. In tropical latitudes, Heliconias are found growing at altitudes from 100–600 m (300–2000 ft) above sea level. Found both in the Old and New World tropics, the tropical American species are by far the most colourful having brightly coloured bracts in red, orange, yellow, cream, pink and green. Their flowers are hummingbird-pollinated: fruits are gentian blue. Those from Asia and South Pacific, such as *H. indica*, have less showy inflorescences, although some have very attractive foliage. They are pollinated by bats and have red fruits.

New World Heliconias are divided into groups based on shape and position of inflorescence and fruit structure.

1 Tortuosa group, for example *H. latispatha*, erect, spiral (rotate) inflorescence with red and yellow, red and gold, or orange bracts; fruits not exposed at maturity. Flower year-round with peak April to September.
2 Bihai group, for example *H. bihai* and *H. caribaea*, erect, distichous inflorescence with deep bracts of red, burgundy, chartreuse, cream or combinations thereof; long, curved flowers; fruits exposed at maturity; wavy leaf margins. Peak flowering April to November.
3 Pogonantha group, for example *H. mariae*, pendulous, distichous inflorescence; oblong fruits; massive shoots to 8 m (26 ft). Flowers year-round.

Most Heliconias are big plants and are best situated in larger gardens. A colourful alternative for the smaller garden is *H. psittacorum* which stands about 1 m (3 ft) tall. It is superb as a landscape specimen and as a source of cut flowers. Some Heliconias such as *H. chartacea* 'Sexy Pink' need acidic soils, however the majority of species will grow in almost any soil given plenty of organic mulch and high nitrogen fertilizer. They need sunshine and adequate moisture to grow and flower. Failure to flower is almost always due to lack of sunshine. Place Heliconias along broad walkways or on the edge of a clearing. Mulch them well leaving plenty of room for them to grow. Large suckers or divisions may be planted at any time; smaller suckers only at the beginning of the rainy season.

Heliconias have recently been transferred to their own floral family, Heliconiaceae. While this information is of no direct interest to gardeners, it can make a difference to those wishing to import plants. Members of the Banana family Musaceae are denied entry to certain countries in order to control Banana pests and diseases: Heliconias may only be subject to quarantine. Check with your local Agriculture Department for details.

HIBISCUS

Popular flowering shrubs throughout the tropics and sub-tropics, Hibiscus find a place in almost every sunny Caribbean garden. Hibiscus can grow to up to 4 m (13 ft) tall. The common red varieties of *H. rosa-sinensis* 'President', 'Psyche' and 'Bonaire Special' are especially vigorous. They can be pruned to a more manageable size for hedges and wind breaks. A sport of 'President', *H. rosa-sinensis cooperi* has attractive variegated foliage and red blooms. This variety can be also used for hedging or for specimen planting. Large-flowered hybrids are grown as specimen plants in pots or in beds. Hibiscus can be trained as a tree-like standard. Starting with a vigorous cultivar, remove any side branches that form while allowing the main stem to elongate. Once the stem reaches the required height, pinch out the terminal bud and allow it to branch. Pinch these branches to encourage even further branching. Once the form is established, allow the plant to bloom. You will be rewarded with an eye-catching display.

Whether you choose to grow Hibiscus as a hedge, specimen plant, standard or pot plant, one rule applies – Hibiscus flowers develop at the tips of new shoots. Regular pruning keeps the plant producing new growth and flowers. To prune Hibiscus, remove approximately one-third of each branch as well as any dead, diseased or damaged stems. Healthy cuttings can be used for propagation.

To propagate Hibiscus from semi-hardwood and hardwood cuttings, take 20–30 cm (8–12 in) sections of healthy stems. Dip the cut end in hormone rooting powder and plant in damp sand. Keep the cuttings shaded, misting frequently with water several times daily. Roots will form within four weeks. Transfer well-rooted cuttings to a nursery bed, to individual pots or plastic bags, or to a prepared hedge location. Feed weekly with a dilute liquid fertilizer (20–20–20). Encourage branching by pinching the growing point.

Friable, well-drained soil, moisture and sunlight are basic requirements of Hibiscus. Poor drainage, insufficient light and nutrient deficiencies can all contribute to poor growth and lack of bloom. Choose a sunny spot to grow Hibiscus. The soil should be a loam, neutral to slightly alkaline. Dig the bed well, incorporating some leaf mould or compost. Hibiscus need a vigorous root system to take up moisture and nutrients. Encourage deep rooting of newly planted stock by watering thoroughly rather than just lightly sprinkling the plants. Water the plants deeply during dry periods. Hibiscus are moderate feeders when in active growth and may require supplements of iron, manganese and zinc. Feed Hibiscus with a granular or liquid fertilizer according to manufacturer's instructions. If the foliage becomes chlorotic, apply chelated trace minerals. Such applications may be required especially after periods of heavy rain.

Root knot Nematodes are a major pest of Hibiscus. They attack feeder roots, rendering them incapable of nutrient absorption. Some Hibiscus cultivars are particularly susceptible to attack while others such as 'Sulphur Queen' are somewhat resistant. It is wise to pre-treat a new bed by planting Marigold several months prior to planting Hibiscus. Chemical nematicides can also be used although these very toxic substances should be applied only by trained professionals.

GARDEN HIBISCUS *Hibiscus rosa-sinensis*

Native to China, it is grown for its spectacular, although short-lived flowers. There are thousands of cultivars in a kaleidoscope of colours: vivid red, rich golden yellow, white with a red centre, pale pink, bluish mauve and tan, bicolours and picotees. The large 10–25 cm (4–10 in) flowers are single, semi-double or fully double. Some favourite cultivars are 'Harlequin' (cream flecked carmine and orange), 'Lavender Lady' and 'Black Beauty' (very dark red), 'Coeur de Creole' (crested), and 'Sulphur Queen'. There are many varietal names. It is probably best to choose the plants you like when they bloom. Hybrid Hibiscus are usually bud grafted onto a vigorous rootstock such as hedging variety 'President'. Look for well-branched plants with healthy foliage. Hibiscus varieties differ greatly in vigour. You should invest in a strong plant that will reward your care with abundant bloom.

New varieties arise as sports or from hybrid seed. Single Hibiscus flowers produce prominent anthers and a five-part stigma. To make your own hybrids transfer pollen from the anthers to the stigma using an artist's soft paint brush. Not all varieties will be fertile. Some semi-double and double flowers lack functional reproductive parts. With a good deal of patience and luck you may be fortunate to harvest viable seed. Germination takes approximately 15 days.

CORAL HIBISCUS *Hibiscus schizopetalus*

A tall shrub producing pendant rose-red flowers with deeply incised petals, this species can be grown as a hedge or as a specimen plant. Judicious pruning is needed to keep it shaped. Propagate by cuttings or by air layers.

SLEEPING OR TURK'S CAP HIBISCUS *Malvaviscus grandiflorus syn. M. arboreus*

An attractive, 3 m (10 ft) shrub, Sleeping Hibiscus bears an abundance of 6 cm (2.4 in) long bright red flowers that never open, hence the common name. The ten-part stigma and the stamens protrude from the unopened petals. These intriguing blooms are pollinated by hummingbirds with bills and tongues long enough to reach the flower nectaries. Bees cheat, making a hole at the base of the flower to rob it of its nectar! This species is readily propagated by cuttings.

IXORAS

Colourful, ever-blooming Ixoras are showy garden plants from the Asia-Pacific region. These sun-loving shrubs and small trees can be used as specimens or for hedging. *Ixora coccinea*, the most common variety used for hedging, bears large heads of long-lasting scarlet flowers atop glossy green foliage. Fragrant, white-flowered *I. finlaysoniana* grows into a small tree. Ixoras can be prone to chlorosis: applying chelated iron will correct the problem. Propagate by suckers, by cuttings, and by air layering.

ORCHIDS

Basic care
Light: shade, semi-shade or full sun
Water: Epiphytes – allow roots to dry out between waterings; use rainwater (in preference to domestic supplies with high dissolved mineral content); protect dormant orchids from rain
Terrestrials – keep compost moist when they are in active growth
Soil: Epiphytes – attach to trees, posts or grow in pots with pieces of charcoal, cork, tree fern, bark and other materials that do not retain water; do not grow in soil!
Terrestrials – compost, leaf mould, sand, grit

Fertilizer: weekly applications of dilute liquid fertilizer for actively growing plants; use fertilizers specifically recommended for orchids according to manufacturer's instructions

Pests: Blossom Thrips, Scale Insects, Spider Mites, Mealy Bugs, Bush Snails and Slugs; use solvent-based liquid pesticides with caution!

Bacterial and Fungal Diseases: Rots are spread by water; isolate affected plants and stop watering; excise affected parts plus a generous portion of healthy tissue with a sterile blade; if the causative fungus is known, treat plants with an appropriate fungicide

Virus Diseases: plants and flowers disfigured; there is no known cure!; destroy infected plants, their pots and potting materials by burning

Propagation: division; top-cuttings; offsets or keikis; seed (use method recommended for Orchids, Chapter 2 page 41)

The Caribbean is a paradise for growing most orchids. Orchids grow wild on nearly all of the islands and on the nearby mainland. In Trinidad, we find Cedros Bee *Oncidium lanceanum*, Virgin Orchid *Caularthron bicornutum* and Butterfly Orchid *Oncidium papilio*; in Barbados, Eyelash Orchid *Epidendrum ciliare*; in the Dominican Republic we might find the now endangered Bumblebee Orchid *Oncidium henekenii*; in Jamaica, the beautiful pink-flowered fan-leaved *Oncidium pulchellum*; and in the Bahamas, we see many *Encyclia* species.

There are more than 35,000 orchid species, many of these native to the tropical Americas. Horticultural selection and hybridization has given rise to many more thousands of colourful, showy plants that can be grown in a Caribbean garden. There are orchids for the amateur and for the specialist grower alike, many bearing flowers that last for weeks in perfect condition on the plant or that can be used as cut flowers. Fortunately for the gardener, many orchids can be naturalized on trees: they can also be grown in pots, in garden beds or in a shade house. Most are no more difficult to cultivate than Begonias, Ferns, Hibiscus or Palms.

Raising orchids in conditions similar to those of their native habitat encourages optimum growth and flowering. Like most other plants, orchids thrive within a certain range of temperature, humidity, air movement and light. Learning the particular requirements of each kind of orchid comes with experience, discussion with other orchid growers, experimentation and reading.

Culture

Most tropical orchids are **epiphytes** having adaptations which allow them to grow on other plants such as a tree trunk or a branch. The roots of epiphytic orchids are highly specialized, adapted to periodic dryness. Not only can they meander over the surface of the bark, holding the plant firmly in place, but they also can absorb moisture and nutrients. The roots, exposed as they are to the air, dry quickly after a rain. Orchids are not parasites, their roots extract nutrients from the compost of dead leaves, insect and bird droppings, caught in their tangled mass of roots. They simply use a tree branch as a means to hold them above the shaded forest floor. Here they have more light yet are still lightly shaded by the canopy of foliage above. To grow epiphytic orchids well, you must provide similar conditions to those to which they have become adapted. Such provisions include the use of a potting mix that drains quickly and dries out between waterings, frequent feedings of weak liquid fertilizer solution, shading appropriate to the plant type, some air movement, and high humidity.

Orchids that grow rooted in the soil, humus or leaf mould are referred to a being **terrestrial**. Ground Orchids *Spathoglottis* and *Bletia plicata*, Ladyslipper *Paphiopedilum* and Jewel Orchid *Haemeria* are terrestrials. Their roots are intolerant of dryness. While the Ground Orchids are popular choices as bedding plants, others are more suitable for pot culture. Terrestrial orchids can be rooted in humus, leaf mould, or sandy loam enriched with compost. The mix should be water-retentive but at the same time, porous and well-drained. Pieces of charcoal or chopped tree fern and coconut husk fibre can be added to the mix to improve its porosity.

LIGHT REQUIREMENTS

Orchids require sufficient light to grow and bloom well. *Vanda* and *Dendrobium* need almost full sunshine; *Cattleya* and *Oncidium*, moderate sunshine; while *Phalaenopsis* and *Paphiopedilum* need shade. As a general rule, those plants with tough, leathery foliage are the most sun-tolerant while those orchids with soft, pliable leaves are less so. If orchids are to be grown in the garden, site them where there is good air circulation. Orchid leaves adapt to available light, orienting to face towards the light. Be especially careful when moving orchids about in the garden, that the leaves remain similarly orientated. If plants such as *Vanda* or *Renanthera* grown in full sun are turned 90–180° from their original position, new leaves will become aligned differently from older leaves and to a similar degree. Not only will the symmetry of the plants be spoiled but also the foliage previously shaded by other leaves will now be exposed to full sun. Give newly acquired plants some shade until they become established. Failure to observe this simple factor can result in sunburned foliage.

SHADING

Shading can be provided by the branches and leaves of nearby trees, shade cloth or laths.

Shade cloth is a tough, woven polypropylene fabric that allows only a certain percentage of sunlight to pass through. The fabric comes in various grades that designate the per cent (%) shade. *Vanda* needs 25 per cent shade while 75 per cent shade is more suitable for *Phalaenopsis*. Shade cloth permits the uninterrupted passage of wind and rain. Additional protection is needed during the rainy season if watering is to be completely controlled.

WATER, HUMIDITY, AIR MOVEMENT

Orchids absorb moisture from the air and from the surfaces to which they are attached. Epiphytic orchids are dependent upon rainfall and humidity for water. A relative humidity of 60–70 per cent is considered good for orchid growing. Moisture evaporating from leaf surfaces results in substantial cooling, even more so when there is a light breeze to hasten evaporation. Various methods can be employed to maintain the moisture and high humidity required by orchids, even during dry weather. The simplest method to raise humidity is to spray the plants and their surroundings with water two or three times a day, once at approximately 8 a.m., then again at 11 a.m. and again at 2 p.m. if deemed necessary. Air movement about the plants will optimize the results and in fact is essential to avoid injurious bacterial or fungal rots. The last spraying should be timed so that the plants have a chance to dry off before dusk. For those unable to spray the orchids as required, an automated system may solve some of the problems. The most sophisticated systems employ a computerized timing mechanism, a light sensor and even a moisture sensor to detect a sudden afternoon shower.

The best water to use for spraying orchids is rainwater. Free of dissolved minerals, it leaves no unsightly salt deposits on foliage neither does it harm the plants. Epiphytic orchids are not particularly tolerant of water containing dissolved mineral salts. One way to solve the problem of supply is to collect rainwater over the rainy season, storing it in drums or in a reservoir. If you intend to store rainwater, be certain of the following:

1 the container should be large enough for your needs;
2 the container must be lined with polyethylene, butyl rubber or the equivalent to prevent leaching of minerals;
3 some mechanism, manual or automatic, should be in place to divert surplus rainwater once the container is full; and
4 the container should be screened to prevent mosquitoes from breeding.

TEMPERATURE REQUIREMENTS

Not all orchids will succeed or even survive in a Caribbean garden. Those deciduous species requiring a cold rest period, for example *Pleione* (4°C (39°F)) and *Dendrobium nobile* (10°C (50°F)) are impossible to grow well unless you wish to invest in refrigeration equipment. Others requiring a long dry rest period may succumb to rot. Night temperature, more specifically the difference between day and night temperature, can affect the health and flowering capability of some orchids. The few degrees between the minimum temperature at sea level and at an elevation of 200 m (600 ft) can make the difference between a magnificent show of the pink-flowered *Phalaenopsis schilleriana* and no show at all. This orchid requires cool nights, maximum 20°C (68°F) to flower.

FERTILIZERS

Orchids need a regular supply of mineral nutrients given in small doses and at regular intervals except when the plants are dormant. Fertilizers with formulations 18–18–18 and 20–20–20 have been designed for general purpose orchid feeding while blossom-booster formulations such as 10–30–20 are used on mature plants to promote flower production. If the product you intend to use has been especially designed for use on orchids, then follow the manufacturer's instructions. Apply other fertilizer products at one-quarter the recommended dilution. Ladyslipper orchids *Paphiopedilum* respond to occasional applications of Epsom Salts solution – 5 ml (1 tsp) Epsom Salts dissolved in 5 litres (1 gal) water. Epsom Salts (magnesium sulphate), available from the chemist, provides magnesium, an essential nutrient.

CONTAINERS

If orchids are to be grown in pots or baskets, choose clay pots over plastic, preferably those having holes or slits formed in the sides to permit efficient drainage and aeration. Baskets can be made of wire or wooden slats. Whatever the container, it should be large enough to permit two years growth before repotting is needed. Acceptable potting media include coarsely chopped tree fern, charcoal, broken terracotta tile (crock), pieces of Calabash *Crescentia* bark, or even chopped wine corks. *Cattleya*, *Dendrobium* and *Phalaenopsis* are more suited to pot culture. Often *Vanda* is placed simply in a wooden basket (raft) without any additional potting medium. As extreme as this may sound, it is a successful technique and one that ensures optimum root growth. Another potting technique that has been successfully employed with *Vanda* orchids is mounting them on vertical clay pipes (drainage tiles). The pipes are sealed at the bottom end and kept filled with water. The top can be fitted with a screen or lid to keep out mosquitoes. As the water diffuses through the porous clay it evaporates, creating both a cool and humid environment for the roots.

ESTABLISHING ON TREES

If orchid plants are to be established on trees then those trees should not only provide the necessary overhead shade but also their bark should promote root attachment. Suitable trees include Calabash *Crescentia cujete*, Flamboyant *Delonix regia*, Lignum Vitae *Guaiacum officinale*, Mango *Mangifera indica* and Frangipani *Plumeria*. Establishment of an orchid upon a tree is simply a matter of taking a healthy plant at the beginning of the growing season and fastening it in the desired location. The roots grow rapidly and attach the plant firmly to the surface. Orchids can also be established on non-living posts of Wallaba *Eperua falcata* or Tree Fern, or on slabs of wood and bark of the above mentioned trees.

Propagation

Orchids grow in two different ways. Those that have a single growing point grow continuously in one direction only, bearing leaves and roots along the length of the stem. Flowers or floral sprays arise from the leaf axils. Examples are Scorpion Orchid *Arachnis*, Moth Orchid *Phalaenopsis*, *Renanthera*, and *Vanda*. Such orchids can be propagated by top cuttings or from the side shoots produced at the base of an older plant especially if the growing point has been removed or has been damaged. **Side shoots can be removed once they have two or more roots, but it is preferable to leave them in place to grow into a beautiful specimen.**

Another group of orchids produce new shoots from a prostrate rhizome. These orchids including *Cattleya*, *Oncidium*, *Dendrobium* and *Paphiopedilum* can easily be propagated by division. When dividing the plant, ensure that the cutting tool is sterilized before use and that each planned division consists of at least three shoots. Smaller divisions may take a long time to re-establish.

Pests and diseases

Orchids can be subject to a variety of diseases including bacterial and fungal rots, a variety of leaf spots, leaf, stem and root decay. Some of these diseases can quickly kill a plant and spread to others nearby via water splashes. Special care must be taken during the rainy and hurricane seasons when the problem is more acute. Because the most dangerous causitive organisms move about in water, keeping the plants dry is the best way to control disease. As prevention is always easier than the cure, take care when watering your plants, especially when there is little breeze. Do not permit water to lie in the crown of leaves. If necessary, protect the plants from becoming wet by installing a translucent, overhead barrier or by moving the plants undercover for several days during storms. Fungicides can be used to control specific diseases.

One particularly troublesome disease of *Dendrobium* is Root Rot that eventually spreads upwards into the shoot. Often the first sign of a problem is the sudden collapse of a shoot. Fortunately Dendrobiums will often produce offsets from upper nodes before all is lost. These can be removed once they have developed a few roots. Water and fertilize *Dendrobium* only when in active growth.

While birds may pick at flowers and Slugs devour young shoots, the most troublesome pests are Spider Mites, Scale Insects and Thrips. One way to avoid the pest problem is to quarantine new plants; another way is to control infestations on nearby palms, *Citrus*, *Hibiscus* and *Ixora*. Careful examination of the orchids on a weekly basis will catch problems before they get out of hand. A good strategy is to have companion plants such as *Impatiens* growing with the orchids. As these particular plants generally become infested sooner than the orchids, periodic examination of them will provide an early warning system.

Thrips damage orchid flowers and foliage. Any insecticide that kills the pest will damage the flowers. Thrips can be effectively trapped by hanging sticky strips of bright yellow plastic (coated in vegetable oil) in amongst the plants. The bright yellow colour attracts quite a few flying insects: the oil holds them fast. Clean the traps daily and re-coat in oil (this is a more economical alternative to purchasing commercial Sticky Strips).

Slugs love the tasty, succulent orchid foliage and flowers. The best way to control them is to keep slug 'hiding places' to a minimum, and by treating your orchid growing area periodically with a metaldehyde bait or spray. Liquid preparations may damage thin-leaved Ground Orchids *Spathoglottis*. Be careful not to wet the foliage.

Favourite Orchids

BROUGHTONIA *Broughtonia*

B. sanguinea, a fine dwarf species, from Jamaica, is ideal for basket culture or for growing on plaques. Broughtonia can also be naturalized on trees. It produces long sprays of reddish purple flowers. White and yellow-flowered forms also exist. Broughtonias have been hybridized with Cattleyas *Cattleytonia* to produce larger flowers on miniature plants. Propagate by division of the rhizome.

CATTLEYA *Cattleya*

Some of the showiest orchids, Cattleyas are easy to grow in pots or naturalized in a tree crotch.

C. aurantiaca is a spring-blooming orchid from Central America. It is a drought and cold-tolerant species bearing clusters of clear orange, 2.5–3 cm (1.0–1.4 in) flowers from March to May. Selected plants have white, lemon yellow, apricot or cream-coloured flowers. The best varieties open their flowers fully. Popular hybrids include the glossy red Cattleya Chocolate Drop (*C. guttata* × *C. aurantiaca*), and the flame orange to burgundy purple *Sophrolaeliocattleya* (*Slc.*) Jewel Box (*C. aurantiaca* × *Slc.* Anzac). Propagate by division of the rhizome.

DENDROBIUM *Dendrobium*

D. phalaenopsis is native to northern Queensland, Australia where it is referred to as the 'Cookstown Orchid'. This species and its many hybrids are well suited to the Caribbean garden. Although most commonly grown in pots, they also may be naturalized on trees. Hybrids made in Australia, Thailand, and Hawaii have large, round blooms of dark purple (some almost black), white and mauve. They make wonderful cut flowers. Propagate by division of the rhizome and by keikis.

D. discolor syn. *undulatum* This large South Pacific species bears long sprays of golden blooms which last many months. It is virtually ever-blooming. The plants grow to 2 m (6 ft) and are admirably suited for a sunny cutting garden or display bed. The roots are intolerant of 'wet feet': potting should be done in heavy clay pots with pieces of broken tile or brick used to hold the plants in place. Coconut husks can be arranged around the pots to maintain humidity. Propagate by division of the rhizome and by keikis.

GROUND ORCHID *Spathoglottis*

Commonly referred to as the Ground Orchid, *Spathoglottis plicata* and its hybrids are a welcome addition to garden beds. Rose-pink *S. plicata* has lovely pleated leaves; the flowers of New Caledonia species *S. unguiculata* have a fragrance of grapes. Hybrid flowers may be pale pink to magenta, canary yellow or bicoloured. Ground orchids can be grown in beds or drums of compost and sand. They thrive on soils rich in lime derived from coral stone or limestone. Top dressing with well-rotted donkey or horse manure is beneficial. Although these orchids are evergreen and almost always in bloom, they show seasonal response to rain. The yellow-flowered forms are generally more delicate and best suited to pot culture. Propagation is by division of the onion-shaped pseudobulbs. Freshly harvested seed can be sown on moist, well-rotted compost. Seedlings will bloom within two years from sowing.

LADY-OF-THE-NIGHT *Brassavola*

Brassavola *nodosa*, a drought-tolerant Caribbean native, the white-flowered Lady-of-the-

Night produces a wonderful fragrance during the evening hours. It can be naturalized on suitable trees or grown in baskets. This orchid thrives in semi-shaded to dappled sunlight situations. Hybridization with Cattleyas has yielded some easy-to-grow, floriferous types including Brassocattleya (*Bc.*) Binosa (*Cattleya bicolor* × *B. nodosa*). Propagation is by division of the rhizome.

LADYSLIPPER ORCHID
Paphiopedilum

Tropical Slipper Orchids are showy terrestrials best grown in pots. They are so-named because of the slipper or boat-shaped petal (lip). The bright flowers last six to eight weeks. A few species and hybrids will grow in the warmer sea level localities: many more will thrive at higher altitudes where it is cooler. White-flowered *Paphiopedilum* F. C. Puddle is highly recommended for its vigour and heat-tolerance.

MOTH ORCHID *Phalaenopsis*

Moth Orchids are suitable for the novice grower. These relatively inexpensive, quick-blooming and floriferous orchids deserve a place in the garden. The most common colours are white, pink and yellow with some spotted and striped varieties as well. All are suited to pot culture in a shade house. Pink-flowered *P. schilleriana* may be naturalized in trees or along a shaded wall. Propagate by keikis formed on the inflorescence.

REED STEM EPIDENDRUM
Epidendrum

Easy-to-grow Reed Stem Epidendrums such as *E. ibaguense* make a wonderful display in a sunny location. The most common flower colour is orange but there are also many selected forms and hybrids available in shades of yellow, pink, mauve and white. This species will grow in a rich, fibrous compost or in blends of more coarse materials. The tall stems can reach 2 m (6 ft). The flowers are produced in clusters at the top of each stem. Often keikis are produced on the stems and in turn flower even while still attached to the parent plant. This orchid deserves more recognition for its potential as a landscape specimen. Propagate by division of the rhizome and by offsets. Seed may be sown on composted bagasse in the shade house to yield blooming-size plants in two years.

VANDA *Vanda*

Beautiful blue-flowered *V. coerulea* has been so admired and collected that it has become an endangered species in its native Himalayan habitat. White and pink-flowered forms also exist. This species has contributed many features to modern Vanda hybrids including floriferousness (blooming three to five times a year), colour pattern (tesselation) and bloom display. When crossed with *V. sanderiana*, the hybrid often carries the blue colour of one parent and the size and vigour of the other. Hybrids made in Florida, Hawaii, Thailand and Australia include the grape purple and raspberry-coloured Kasem's Delight, Fuchs Delight and Motes Indigo.

PALMS

Basic care
Light: semi-shade to full sun
Water: according to specific requirements; container-grown palms in sunny locations require most care in watering
Soil: garden loam with added humus
Fertilizer: container plants should be given a weak solution of 20–20–20 fertilizer at monthly intervals when the palm is actively growing; fast-growing garden palms should receive an application of granular fertilizer (7–7–7) containing trace elements, twice yearly, and at the beginning of the rainy season; fertilize slow-growing palms with care
Pests and diseases: Spider Mites and Scale

Growing Palms in the garden

Palms are one of the most useful plants for
Caribbean gardens. They can be divided into
two major groups based upon leaf shape: those
having feather-like (pinnate) leaves, for
example Coconut *Cocos nucifera*; and those
with fan-like (palmate) leaves, for example
Palmetto *Sabal palmetto*. The leaf form of
Fishtail Palm *Caryota mitis* is different in that
the leaves are bi-pinnate with leaflets being
further sub-divided into wedge-shaped
portions. The trunks of palms quite often
contribute to the overall beauty of the plant,
being sometimes smooth silvery grey as with
Roystonea spp., hairy fibrous as with Lady
Palm *Rhapis excelsa*, or very spiny as with
Macaw Palm *Aiphanes minima*. Remnant leaf
bases completely hide the trunks of Date Palm
Phoenix spp.

Some palms are slow-growing or compact,
making them appropriate for container culture. A good example is *Chamaedorea elegans*.
Other palms such as King Palm *Archonto-
phoenix cunninghamiana* grow quickly to form
handsome specimens. Most palms have a single trunk while others form suckers making a
clump of stems. Single-stemmed palms can be
planted in small groups of three to five specimens of one species such as MacArthur Palm
Ptychosperma macarthurii, or in rows along a
driveway as with Caribbean Royal Palm
Roystonea oleracea. Clustering palms such as

Golden Palm *Chrysalidocarpus lutescens* are
useful as an informal hedge. One of the most
wonderful palms for a garden focal point is
Sealing Wax Palm *Cyrtostachys renda* syn. *C.
lakka*. This colourful palm forms clusters of
shoots and is best suited to a semi-shaded,
moist, peaty soil.

Most palms can be raised from seed: the
clustering varieties may also be propagated
by division. You can grow your own plants
from seed or purchase seedlings. Do not
keep seedlings in an enclosed pot too long
or their growth may be curtailed. Except
where otherwise noted, palms grow best in a
well-drained loam well furnished with compost. It is important to place palms where
they can become established and grow without competition.

Palms for containers

These palms may also be grown in the garden.

BOTTLE PALM *Hyophorbe lagenicaulis*

A short 2–3 m (6–10 ft) palm with a flask-
shaped silvery trunk which narrows abruptly
near the top, this monoecious species has 2 m
(6 ft) long pinnate leaves with short petioles
twisted at base leading to a curious position-
ing of each leaf. Fresh seeds germinate easily.

CHAMAEDOREA syn. *Collinia*

These small, delicate, shade-loving palms, from
Mexico, are the ultimate container plants,
useful even indoors. Most of the cultivated
species have only a few pinnate leaves near
the crown. There are species such as C. *elegans*
and C. *erumpens* with clustered trunks, and
others with a single trunk. Fresh seeds germinate easily.

CHINESE FAN PALM *Livistona chinenis*

An attractive fan palm, the Chinese Fan Palm
is relatively slow-growing and suitable for
container culture. It has costapalmate,

roundish leaves with distinctive, long drooping tips. The dark green leaf surface contrasts with beautiful golden yellow veins. Adherent leaf bases form a characteristic spiral pattern on the trunk. Marble-sized fruits are jade green. This palm is best grown in semi-shade. Seeds germinate easily.

L. saribus is reputed to have the bluest fruits of all palms.

Drymophloeus beguinii

This short 3–5 m (10–16 ft), slender palm with unusual leaves comes from the Moluccas, Indonesia. It has pinnate leaves, the leaflets being wedge-shaped with the wider blunt end being notched and wavy. Flowers are produced below the crownshaft at an early age followed by red fruits. This lovely palm grows quickly from seed.

FIJI FAN PALM Pritchardia pacifica

Originating in the Fiji Islands, this small to medium-sized 9 m (30 ft) monoecious palm has large fan-shaped, palmate leaves that are divided along the edge and are deeply folded. They are covered in a white fluffy coating when young. The leaves are disproportionately large to the size of the entire plant. Dead leaves may accumulate on the trunk over time. This palm makes a suitable container plant for the patio where some wind protection will keep the leaves intact. These palms thrive in full sun. Seeds germinate readily.

LADY PALM Rhapis excelsa

The Lady Palm is a small, clustering palm from southern China. This dioecious palmate-leaved species has slender trunks covered in woven remnants of leaf bases giving a fibrous appearance. The leaves are formed of four to eight equal segments each being dark green, glossy and blunted at the tip. The arrangement is elegant. Flower stalks arise from the leaf mass and are branched. These palms prefer a moist, shady place: a sheltered patio is ideal. Lady Palm makes a wonderful container plant in the garden and in the home. Propagate by suckers or from seed.

LATANIA FAN PALM Latania loddigesii

Young specimens of this medium-sized, fast-growing dioecious palm from the Mascarene Islands of the Indian Ocean are especially attractive. The palm grows to 9 m (30 ft) with a slender 25 cm (10 in) thick trunk that can be slightly swollen at the base. The broad 1–2 m (3–6 ft) diameter costapalmate leaves are a dark grey green on top, lighter beneath. The 1–2 m (3–6 ft) long petiole is covered with a substantial quantity of white, woolly tomentum. Seeds germinate easily.

PRINCESS PALM, HURRICANE PALM Dictyosperma album

This medium-sized monoecious palm from the Mascarene Islands, has a dark grey trunk swollen at the base with many vertical grooves. The leaves are pinnate, 3–4 m (10–13 ft) long, with the new leaves bound together at their tips. This palm needs large quantities of water, especially during a dry period.

D. rubrum has dark red leaf veins and margins making it very attractive as a young pot plant.

ROUND LEAF PALM Licuala

These attractive fan palms have a variety of leaf forms according to the species. Their seeds germinate slowly – be patient!

L. grandis of Vanuatu, South Pacific, attains 2 m (6 ft) in height at maturity. The leaves are glossy green circular fans, notched along the edge. This palm is excellent for pot culture in a shade house or on a sheltered patio. The foliage arches from the trunk making a splendid specimen even with a young plant. The flower stalk bears pea-sized red fruits.

L. spinosa of Malaya, is a clustering palm growing to a maximum of 3 m (10 ft). Its leaves are palmate, circular with square-ended leaflets that are joined near the point of petiole attachment. The spiny petiole is almost 2 m (6 ft) long. Grow this palm in semi-shade.

SENTRY PALM *Howea forsteriana*

Originating in the South Pacific, namely Lord Howe Island, located between Australia and New Zealand, this medium-tall 12–15 m (40–50 ft) palm is monoecious, has 3 m (10 ft) pinnate leaves on 2 m (6 ft) long arching petioles. The leaflets emerge in such a way as to give the leaf a flat appearance. Leaflets are naturally spotted beneath. Seeds germinate freely.

Palms for shady gardens

FISHTAIL PALM *Caryota mitis*

This medium-sized palm, from India is widely grown and easily recognized. It is the only palm with bipinnate foliage, the leaf edges folding upwards to give a ruffled appearance. The palm clusters freely. Flower stalks, which should be removed after blooming, are produced from the upper leaf axils downwards over a 5–10 year period. Only the flowering trunk dies, other trunks of the same cluster are unaffected. Take care when handling the red fruits. They have STINGING, needle-like crystals in their covering that cause severe irritation. Germination of fresh seeds can take 3 months or longer. Grow this palm in full sun to semi-shade. Propagate from seed or from suckers.

KING PALM, MAJESTIC PALM *Archontophoenix*

This fast-growing, tropical Australian palm is distinguished by having deep rings of leaf scars on the trunk. Flower spikes arise around the junction of the crownshaft and trunk. Leaves are pinnate, about 1 m (3 ft) long. This is a very handsome palm for the semi-shaded garden. The seeds germinate with ease.

MACAW PALM *Aiphanes*

These medium-sized palms, native to the West Indies and South America, have rings of sharp, black spines on the trunk, leaf stalks, and pinnate leaves. Fruits are bright red. As the **palms mature, the leaves develop a graceful, ruffled appearance.** In the Lesser Antilles *A. minima* begins its life as a seedling in gullies **and** similar damp, shady locations. Mature plants may develop prop roots. If this palm is being raised from seed, shade must be provided for the first few years before planting the seedling into the final semi-shaded location. The seeds germinate in less than 60 days.

Pinanga kuhlii

This small, pinnate-leaved palm comes from Sumatra and Java. The slender trunks cluster; the leaves seem disproportionately large to the trunk. The crownshaft is obvious and larger in diameter than the trunk. A bright red flower stalk arises amongst the leaves of mature specimens. Grow this species in the shade beneath other tall palms. The seeds germinate with relative ease.

Syagrus schizophylla syn. *Arikuryroba schizophylla*

This distinctive Brazilian palm, short and graceful, 1–3 m (3–10 ft) tall, has a trunk covered with erect, purplish-black remnants of leaf bases. The pinnate leaves are gracefully arched, the long leaflets being notched at their apex. Young leaves have large terminal lobes. Flower stalks arise from the lower leaf axils and later produce golden clusters of fruits. The seeds germinate in one month. This palm is best grown in semi-shade.

WINDOWED PALM *Reinhardtia elegans* syn. *R. latisecta*

This small, shade-loving palm from Central America is an interesting subject for the collector with a sheltered patio. The 'windows' appear near the base of the leaflets. The leaves are pinnate, almost 1 m (3 ft) long and are composed of on average four leaflets, the two terminal ones being joined at the base only. Petioles are clothed in reddish-brown scales. Windowed Palm forms clusters of shoots and can attain 7 m (23 ft) in height if grown with a free root run. Propagate from suckers and from seed.

Palms for sunny spots

ARECA NUT, BETEL NUT PALM
Areca catechu

From Malaya, a medium-sized palm Areca Nut has soft pinnate leaves which are sometimes fastened near the tip. Flower stalks arise from the lowest leaf base, hanging down below the crownshaft. The fruits are an attractive orange. For propagation purposes, use only very fresh seed.

Note The name Areca Palm is often wrongly attributed to *Chrysalidocarpus lutescens*.

Arenga

Distinctive, fast-growing, medium-sized, monoecious palms from South East Asia, *A. engleri*, *A. microcarpa* and *A. mindorensis* have trunks clothed in the brown-black fibrous remnants of leaf bases. These palms are curious in that they flower, starting at maturity (10+ years from seed), from the uppermost leaf axils, descending axil by axil until after the last and lowermost flowering, then the palm dies (monocarpic). Seeds are easy to germinate.

COCONUT PALM *Cocos nucifera*

A palm of economic importance, Coconut is an interesting and useful tree for the sunny garden and seaside locations. This pinnate-leaved palm begins flowering at a young age and will bear fruits within 10 years of planting. The cultivar 'Malayan Dwarf' is resistant to Lethal Yellowing, a disease caused by mycoplasma organisms. Propagate by seed.

Coccothrinax dussiana syn. *C. barbadensis*

The trunk of this medium-sized West Indian palm is enveloped with a mass of persistent leaf bases. The palmate leaves have a distinctive silver backing. Seed germinates readily enough but the plants grow slowly.

DATE PALM *Phoenix* spp.

Distinguished by the fact that spines replace the lower leaflets and that the leaflets are folded upwards, the Date Palms make interesting garden subjects. All of the species are drought-tolerant and should be grown in full sun. The seed germinates readily.

CANARY DATE PALM *P. canariensis* is a tall dioecious palm that can attain 20 m (66 ft). The thick trunk has a shingled appearance because of the adherent leaf bases. The pinnate leaves measure up to 7 m (23 ft) long.

EDIBLE DATE PALM *P. dactylifera* from North Africa, is very tall, 30 m (100 ft), suckering at the base. Suckers can be removed to be planted elsewhere or left to grow as a group. This palm grows best in neutral to slightly acidic soil. Because this species is dioecious, separate male and female plants are required for fruit production. The dark orange fruit will decay prematurely in the humid tropics.

DWARF DATE PALM *P. roebelinii*, from southern Asia, grows just 2 m (6 ft) tall at maturity. The pinnate leaves are about 50 cm (20 in) long. This species is easy to raise from seed.

SENEGAL DATE PALM *P. reclinata* is an attractive, medium-sized cluster palm from West Africa. It has a slender trunk and can grow to 8 m (26 ft) in height.

PALMETTO *Sabal*

Many species of Palmetto are found in Caribbean gardens. Their costapalmate leaves are arched and twisted downwards because of a curved midrib. These palms are medium-sized with massive trunks. Popular species include: Palmetto *S. palmetto*, native to Florida; Puerto Rico Hat Palm *S. causiarum*, very stout 1 m (3 ft) diameter ringed trunk; *S. mauritiiformis*, from Columbia.

Seeds of all of these species germinate readily.

PETTICOAT PALM *Washingtonia filifera*

This drought-tolerant palm from California is not suited to high rainfall areas but will thrive in some of the drier locations of the Caribbean. Flowers are hermaphrodite. A medium-sized palm, it attains 20 m (66 ft) with age. The dead leaves are adherent, giving the trunk a skirted appearance. Dead leaves can be removed without injury to the plant. The palmate leaves are large and are draped with long thread-like strands when young. Grow this palm only in drier localities, where there is full sun and excellent drainage. Seeds germinate easily.

Ptychosperma

SOLITAIRE PALM *P. elegans*, from tropical Australia, is a medium-sized tree, 7 m (23 ft) tall with a prominently ringed trunk. The pinnate leaves are 2 m (6 ft) long having leaflets with blunt, jagged ends. Fruits are bright red.

MACARTHUR PALM *P. macarthurii*, from New Guinea, is a short, clustering palm having a prominently ringed trunk and pinnate leaves with soft, square-ended leaflets. The flower stalk is branched, bearing oblong yellow fruits that become bright red. This species is very popular for landscaping in sunny locations. The seeds of both species germinate readily.

ROYAL PALM *Roystonea* spp.

Palms of the New World tropics, these stately monoecious palms have long pinnate leaves often reaching 4 m (12 ft) in length. The trunks are an attractive whitish grey. These palms can be grown in full sun wherever water is available year-round. Their seeds germinate easily.

CARIBBEAN ROYAL PALM *R. oleracea*, from South America, is by far the largest of the Royal Palms. This species attains 36 m (118 ft) in height.

CUBAN ROYAL PALM *R. regia* has a curious irregular bulging of the silvery grey trunk. Under favourable conditions they may reach 20 m (66 ft) in height.

FLORIDA ROYAL PALM *R. elata* prefers wet ground. With adequate water it grows quickly to 30 m (100 ft) or more in height. The trunk does not bulge.

PUERTO RICAN ROYAL PALM *R. borinquena* is medium tall, reaching 20 m (66 ft). The trunk bulges noticeably towards the top.

SAW PALMETTO *Serenoa repens*

This palm, short and clustering, from South Florida, is prized for its exquisite foliage. Selected clones having the most attractive glaucous blue green palmate leaves can be reproduced from suckers. The oval fruits are bluish black. Easy to grow from seeds and suckers.

Syagrus coronata

This attractive Brazilian species has adherent leaf bases that form an interesting spiral pattern on the trunk. The long pinnate leaves arch only at their tips, the leaflets emerging at many different angles to give a bushy appearance. The orange fruits are edible. Fresh seeds germinate within three months.

TALIPOT PALM *Corypha umbraculifera*

This tall 10–25 m (33–82 ft) hermaphrodite

palm from Sri Lanka exhibits an extraordinary lifestyle. It grows slowly at first and then faster, achieving maturity in 25–75 years. The leaves are palmate, measuring 3 m (10 ft) long by 5 m (16 ft) wide. The mature plant blooms only once then it dies (monocarpic), but first you are rewarded with a magnificent 7 m (23 ft) long flower stalk that grows vertically from the top of the palm. The fruits take up to one year to develop atop the dying parent. To propagate this species, you must have fresh seed.

THREE-SIDED PALM *Neodypsis decaryi*

Originating in Madagascar, this beautiful sun-loving palm has a distinctive three-sided appearance to the trunk because of the protruding petiole bases arranged as they are in three rows. It is reasonably drought-tolerant. The 3 m (10 ft) long grey-green pinnate leaves arch upwards gracefully. Propagate from fresh seed.

Veitchia merrillii

From the South Pacific, this medium-sized palm is a popular garden plant, attaining 15–20 m (50–66 ft) at maturity. It flowers while still young, bearing bright red, 3 cm (1.2 in) long, egg-shaped fruits. All *Veitchia* species are easily raised from seed.

Verschaffeltia splendida

An unusual palm, it stands on stilt roots. Attractive if somewhat awkward looking even when young, this palm eventually attains 20 m (66 ft). The pinnate leaves when first formed are almost entire although deeply incised at the tip: a truly splendid sight. They measure 3 m (10 ft) long by 2 m (6 ft) wide. Plant this exquisite palm in a well-drained, sheltered location as it is intolerant of 'wet feet' and also because the magnificent foliage becomes easily torn in the wind. Seeds germinate only with difficulty.

Palms needing a moist environment

Prestoea pubigera

This pinnate, monoecious, slender-trunked, rainforest tree comes from Trinidad. It is a palm with no crownshaft. It can reach 4 m (13 ft) in height. The leaves, resembling a fish tail, are most interesting and variable, being over 1 m (3 ft) long with terminal leaflets joined and deeply indented at the tip. Grow this palm in upland gardens of Caribbean islands such as Trinidad, Grenada, Martinique and St. Lucia.

QUEEN PALM *Syagrus romanzoffianum* syn. *Arecastrum*

The smooth and attractively ringed trunk of this Brazilian palm makes it especially attractive. It is occasionally used for street planting. The flower stalk of this monoecious palm emerges from axils of the lower leaves followed by conspicuous bundles of red fruits. Long, soft and graceful pinnate foliage is borne from petioles set in a mass of fibres. A fast grower in wet soil. Seeds of this species germinate readily.

RAFFIA PALM *Raphia farinifera* syn. *R. ruffia*

Originating in Madagascar, this interesting monocarpic palm is noted for the fibre produced from the leaf bases, its long spiny pinnate leaves, and large, scaly fruits resembling cones. The attractive fruiting inflorescence is pendulous with sessile fruits and branchlets of male flowers. One plant produces many suckers. Plant this palm in wet areas or provide water whenever rain is lacking. Seeds germinate poorly.

SEALING WAX PALM *Cyrtostachys renda* syn. *C. lakka*

A small-growing cluster palm from the coastal region of west Malaysia, this species is grown primarily for its bright red leaf bases and petioles. The trunks become very attractive with alternating red and green portions. It normally inhabits wet areas near rivers and streams and must have rich moist acidic soil to succeed. The red flower stalks of this monoecious palm develop below the leaves. Fresh seed germinates quickly. This species resents being moved or divided once established.

Palms for boundaries and hedges

GOLDEN PALM, BAMBOO PALM
Chrysalidocarpus lutescens
This species grows in clumps, the arched pinnate foliage hiding the trunks. The palm is dioecious, medium-sized and originates from Madagascar. It is often used where hedging or a boundary planting is required. It also makes an excellent specimen plant. The petioles are a lovely golden yellow. Seeds germinate within two months.

SHRUBS

Basic care
Light: semi-shade to full sun; variegated foliage plants generally need more light to enhance their colour
Water: water weekly during the dry season except where otherwise noted
Soil: well-drained loam with added compost
Fertilizer: fertilize after pruning to promote new growth
Pests and diseases: Aphids, Spider Mites, Scale Insects, Slugs, Nematodes; fungi, bacteria or virus diseases may attack particular species
Propagation: cuttings; layering; seed
See also Shrubs page 58.

Shrubs with decorative foliage

ARALIA *Polyscias*
Commonly called Angelica, Aralias such as *P. balfouriana* and *P. filicifolia* have a wide variety of leaf shapes and patterns including variegated white and green, golden yellow and heavily ruffled. Aralias may be used for hedging, as specimen shrubs or as pot plants. Careful attention should be paid to pruning as the more vigorous kinds can quickly become unsightly. Propagate from semi-hardwood or hardwood cuttings.

CROTON
See Crotons, page 86.

ERANTHEMUM *Eranthemum*
Small shrub with ornamental foliage, *E. atropurpureum* has dark purplish foliage attractively marked and blotched with cream and pink. Flowers are magenta red. Foliage colour is more pronounced on new growth and on plants grown in full sun. Suitable for informal hedging. Prune regularly to encourage bushiness and flushes of colorful new growth. Fertilize after pruning. Water during dry periods. Propagate from hardwood cuttings.

MATCH-ME-NOT *Acalypha*
Acalyphas are shrubs or small trees that can be grown either as specimen plants or as colourful hedges. The common name Match-me-not refers to their mottled leaves: no two look alike. A red-splashed leaf form is the most commonly seen although there are many more varieties with differing leaf shapes, sizes, edges and colour patterns.

Especially during the rainy season, Acalyphas usually grow quickly and luxuriantly. They can survive neglect, but for best results, be certain that they have a sunny location, moisture, fertilizer and protection from too much wind. They will reward you with a year-round splash of colour. Prune Acalyphas heavily at the end of the dry season. Once new growth is underway, regular trimming will keep them tidy. The young growth produced as result of the pruning is even more vividly coloured. Feed with a general purpose fertilizer once growth commences. Propagate by 25 cm (10 in) hardwood cuttings.

A. hispida is sometimes referred to as the Chenile Plant because it is graced with long-lasting, pendulous (25 cm (10 in)) red inflorescences that resemble lengths of scarlet rope. The foliage is an undistinguished green colour.

A. marginata has many attractive cultivars including two forms of 'Ceylon'. Both have a creamy white leaf margin that resembles picotee edging to the curved and twisted leaves: 'Fire Dragon' has bronze-red foliage; and 'Hoffmanii' has grass-green leaves.

'Java White' is used as a street hedge in Singapore. Its leaf colours are yellow, cream and pale green with never a trace of red or bronze. Yellow tones predominate when this form is grown in full sun. 'Torta', similar to cultivar 'Ceylon' only smaller-leaved and more twisted, the purple-brown foliage is admired by florists to highlight brightly coloured flowers such as Anthuriums.

A. wilkesiana RED MATCH-ME-NOT (COPPER LEAF) has large flat leaves coloured crimson and russet-brown. The young leaves are more red, the older more brown. The variety 'Heart Copperleaf' is similar with crinkled heart-shaped leaves.

PLEOMELE *Pleomele*

The clustering stems of slow-growing *P. reflexa variegata* make it a welcome addition to a small garden. The tough cream and green striped foliage grows in whorls about the stem much like *Dracaena*. Removal of the growing point will encourage branching. Pleomele will do best when located in a semi-shaded position although they tolerate more direct sun. Propagate from cuttings or air layers (see pages 35–36).

PONY TAIL PLANT *Beaucarnea recurvata* syn. *Nolina*

Sometimes referred to as the Bottle Palm, although not a true palm, Pony Tail Plant is a true succulent. Long, slender foliage grows in a tuft from the top of a swollen stem. It is commonly used as a specimen 'shrub' in gardens or as a pot plant specimen. This drought-tolerant plant is a welcome addition to the dry garden. It grows slowly to 3 m (10 ft) and will sometimes branch with age. Propagate from seed using Method II.

PSEUDERANTHEMUM *Pseuderanthemum*

Small shrubs with colourful foliage, Pseuderanthemum make useful hedging plants or individual specimens in mixed borders. *P. reticulatum* has yellow-veined leaves, the youngest leaves being entirely bright golden yellow. Pruning encourages new growth and hence added colour. The shrub bears small, upright spikes of white flowers attractively marked with magenta purple. These shrubs grow best in full sun. Water during dry periods. Fertilize after pruning and at the beginning of the rainy season. Propagate by hardwood cuttings.

Shrubs with attractive fruits

ANNATTO *Bixa orellana*
Annatto is a plant of the American tropics that has considerable value when grown as a boundary planting, where the ground is continually moist. It can also be grown as a specimen, attaining 5 m (16 ft) in height. This shrub is more suitable for planting on larger properties because of its size. One of its most striking features are the bright red, bristly fruits. Propagate from seed using Method II. Transplant seedlings when they are 15 cm (6 in) high.

GOLDEN DEWDROP *Duranta repens*

Golden Dewdrop is a tall, 5 m (16 ft) Caribbean shrub with semi-drooping stems tipped first with attractive lilac flowers followed by golden bead-like fruits that give the plant its name. It can be grown as an informal background hedge or as a specimen bush. Propagate from hardwood cuttings or from seed using Method II.

Shrubs with attractive flowers

BAUHINIA *Bauhinia* spp.

Bauhinias are small leguminous trees and shrubs with beautiful white, purple or red flowers. Each leaf is a pair of leaflets joined for nearly their whole length. Situate Bauhinias in full sun. Propagate from seed using Method III.

B. acuminata has white flowers and grows to 3 m (10 ft) high. Gather seedlings under this shrub for planting elsewhere.

B. galpinii syn. *punctata* is a sprawling shrub with nasturtium-red blooms. Use judicious pruning to keep it in shape. This species rarely produces seeds so must be propagated by air layers.

B. purpurea is a fast growing tree that can be pruned to make an attractive flowering specimen. The showy flowers are purple and fragrant. Propagate from seed.

BOUGAINVILLEA

See Bougainvilleas, page 79.

CASSIA *Cassia*

CHRISTMAS CANDLES *C. alata* is easy to raise from seed. This handsome shrub has pea-green, pinnately compound foliage and upright spikes of bright yellow flowers followed by brown winged pods. Flowering begins in November. Plant this shrub in full sun.

It is naturally bushy and will adequately screen a wire fence or other unsightly areas. Propagate from seed using Method II.

CHINESE HAT *Holmskioldia sanguinea*

This small shrub, just 1.5 m (5 ft) tall, is often covered with flowers, each with hat-like, papery orange calyx and curved red blooms. Flowering is seasonal after the dry season. The blooms will fade but each papery calyx remains for months. There are two colour forms, the common orange red and a lime green-yellow. The 'paper hats' can be used for miniature floral arrangements. Plant this shrub standing alone in a sunny spot. Prune hard every year after flowering. Propagate from hardwood cuttings.

CLERODENDRON *Clerodendron* spp.

Small to medium-sized shrubs and scramblers with tubular flowers, sometimes a conspicuous, persistent calyx, cultivated Clerodendrons are vigorous plants well suited for use in decorative flower beds and borders.

PAGODA FLOWER *C. paniculatum* is a small shrub to 2 m (6 ft) in height producing a huge terminal inflorescence 50 cm (20 in) or more in length. Cut this shrub back after blooming to control its growth and to encourage branching. Plant in a sunny spot with space for an all-round view or massed in a sunny border.

C. speciosissimum is a shrub with heart-shaped, velvety foliage and a terminal inflorescence bearing long-lasting scarlet flowers. Propagate both these species from cuttings.

HIBISCUS
See Hibiscus, page 99.

IXORA
See Ixoras, page 100.

JATROPHA
See Euphorbias, page 87.

MUSSAENDA *Mussaenda*

Mussaendas are attractive 2 m (6 ft) shrubs featuring flower clusters typified in that one sepal of each bloom is larger, forming a leaf-like lobe (bract) coloured white, yellow, pink or scarlet. *M. erythrophylla* with scarlet blooms has tolerance for wet swampy land. Other Mussaendas thrive in a sunny but sheltered garden, especially when planted in a rich loam with plenty of water during times of drought. Prune after flowering is finished. Propagate from hardwood cuttings.

OLEANDER *Nerium oleander*

Tall shrub that can reach 5 m (16 ft) but it is best cut back every 18 months or so to keep it bushy and floriferous. Plant Oleanders in full sun. They are drought-tolerant and require no special soil mix but do respond to fertilizer application especially after pruning when new growth commences. They make a very effective hedge or screen. As well as the common single pink, there are many varieties with red, white, yellow and double pink flowers. All parts of Oleander are POISONOUS. Propagate from semi-hardwood cuttings which are easily rooted in wet sand or from air layers.

PLUMBAGO *Plumbago auriculata (capensis)*

This is a sprawling 2 m (6 ft) shrub that is best kept clipped to 1 m (3 ft) as a driveway edging or as a low border to taller plants. It has pale blue or white flowers, blooming more profusely during the dry season. Grow Plumbago in full sun or in semi-shade. Keep it trimmed and fertilize after each hard pruning for optimum blooms. Propagate by softwood cuttings or by division of pruned older plants.

POINSETTIA

See Euphorbias, page 87.

POMEGRANATE *Punica granatum*

The very pretty scarlet blooms are followed by globe-shaped fruits with many seeds each surrounded with a juicy red pulp. The foliage is glossy green. Dwarf forms of the drought-tolerant Pomegranate are suitable for pot culture. They can also be used to make a Bonsai. Propagate from hardwood cuttings or softwood cuttings taken during periods of active growth.

PRIDE OF BARBADOS, FLOWER FENCE *Caesalpinia pulcherrima*

An attractive informal hedging plant, Pride of Barbados has lacey compound foliage and brightly-coloured flowers with long drooping stamens. Flowers are borne year-round on upright spikes and vary from red, yellow, into bicolours. Prune regularly to keep the shrubs tidy. Plant Pride of Barbados seedlings in a sunny location. They thrive even in poor soil. Grow them in rows or groups for effect. Propagation is from seed using Method III.

QUEEN OF FLOWERS *Lagerstroemia indica*

This plant often grows to 6 m (20 ft) but may be cut back annually and contained to 3 m (10 ft) when it will bloom. Clusters of ruffled flowers are mauve, white or various shades of pink, borne at the tips of branches. Prune heavily after flowering is finished. This shrub makes a nice informal hedge to screen the garden from the roadway. It is especially recommended for high rainfall regions. Propagate from hardwood cuttings and air layers.

ROSE Rosa spp.

Mildew-resistant, fragrant roses are sometimes found in Caribbean gardens. Roses are a temperate rather than a tropical plant: only certain varieties will succeed. The right varieties must be chosen and planted in a sunny location. Equally important are a day and night temperature differential of 3–6°C (5–11°F), good air circulation and light to moderate rainfall. Some old-time varieties that have succeeded include 'Etoile de France', 'Paul Neyron', 'Etoile de Lyon', 'La Tosca', and hybrid polyanthas such as 'Else Poulsen'. Finding suitable named varieties may be difficult. Instead, try to obtain rooted cuttings of roses known to be successful in your locality. Grafted Hybrid Tea roses are sometimes imported. These may grow and bloom but rarely reach their full potential. Try bud grafting a vigorous, mildew-resistant tea rose onto a local rose. Propagate successful varieties by semi-hardwood cuttings, heel cuttings or air layers.

THUNBERGIA *Thunbergia erecta*

A flowering shrub to 2 m (6 ft) tall, having dark blue flowers with a contrasting throat. It flowers best when left to grow naturally and will tolerate semi-shade. This shrub may be used as a hedge or with superior results as a specimen flowering plant. Propagate from hardwood cuttings.

WILD SAGE *Lantana*

Native to the West Indies, Central and South America, Wild Sages, such as the Rock or White Sage *Lantana involucrata* prefer dry gardens or seashore locations. They thrive here with little special attention yet are controlled. When grown in a moist garden, *Lantana* becomes an invasive weed. Keep these sprawling shrubs clipped for maximum bloom. Lantanas produce flat clusters of flowers in shades of yellow through orange and red to mauve. Propagate from softwood cuttings and from seeds using Method III. Soak seeds one day before planting.

SUCCULENTS

Basic care
Light: light shade to full sun
Water: when plants are actively growing; shelter potted plants from rain
Soil: well-drained sandy loam
Fertilizer: incorporate slow-release fertilizer in soil mix
Pests and diseases: root Mealy Bugs, Scale Insects, Spider Mites; Rots
Propagation: cuttings; offsets; seed

True succulents are plants which have evolved with a physiological mechanism to tolerate drought. They are able to survive long periods without water and are ideal subjects for the dry garden. Succulents will also grow in humid sites, but they do not enjoy having 'wet feet'. Good drainage is important whether the plants are grown in the garden or in pots. Soils should be based on coral rubble or lava rock, coarse sand or gravel, with additional loam and leaf mould. Some succulent plants such as *Sansevieria*, thrive in filtered sunlight: plant these kind close to shrubs or large boulders so that they may have some protection. Many succulents grow best in full sun where their foliage will attain its full colour and condition. Plant succulents in groups or as individual specimens. Watering the plants should not be a concern except for those specimens grown in pots. Water potted plants whenever the soil is dry: fertilize them monthly with a very dilute solution of 20–20–20. Garden specimens seem to do better without additional fertilizer. Most succulents are easy to propagate by cuttings, division or removal of offsets; less common ones can be grown from seed using Methods I or II.

ALOE *Aloe* spp.

The wonderful Aloes produce attractive rosettes of succulent leaves. Pendant, bell-like flowers are borne on tall upright spikes. Garden plants should be grown in full sun; pot specimens may require very light shading. Some of the lovely large species, 1–3 m (3–10 ft) tall, are suitable for landscaping. These include *A. arborescens* with dark green foliage and scarlet flowers, and Barbados Aloe *A. vera*, whose thick grey-green leaves exude a sap reputed to have a myriad of medicinal properties. Miniature Aloes can be grown either as pot plants or in a rockery. One favourite is the red-flowered *A. variegata*, also known as the Partridge-breasted Aloe because its markings resemble those on a bird's breast. Offsets quickly form a colony of plants.

Aloes can be propagated by division into individual rosettes or from seed.

CENTURY PLANT *Agave* spp.

Reputed to bloom only after one hundred years, Century Plants are long-lived, magnificent specimens for a dry garden. Most mature plants are monocarpic: they die after flowering but only after producing seed and numerous offsets both on the flower stalk as well as around the base of the parent plant. Many of the smaller species make interesting pot plants. Propagation is by division, offsets and from seeds.

A. americana is impressive with its glaucous blue-grey foliage. The leaf tips and edges are armed with brown thorns. This Agave forms a rosette more than 2 m (6 ft) in diameter. Underground branches form numerous plantlets which can be removed for propagation. The variety *mediopicta* has dark blue-green leaves with a white mid-stripe.

A. attenuata has soft, pale green, succulent leaves. It could be easily mistaken for an Aloe. The 2 m (6 ft) long brush-like inflorescence will be produced by mature plants. This species appreciates an especially rich soil.

A. filifera is a solitary, slow-growing species having dark green foliage with white markings and marginal white hairs that make the leaf margins appear shredded. With a free root run in well-drained fertile soil it can produce some offsets. This species is also suitable for pot culture.

A. victoriae-reginae, ornamental and slow-growing, this small Agave, 50 cm (20 in) diameter, has dark green leaves with white edges and attractive markings. It is prized as a pot plant. Propagation is from seed.

DESERT ROSE *Adenium obesum*

An East African relative of Frangipani *Plume-ria*, Desert Rose is a stem succulent. It forms a thick succulent basal stem, half of which is below ground, with thinner branches in the crown. Plants bear lovely clear pink flowers and attractive glossy green leaves. During unfavourable periods, the plants become dormant and leafless. Propagation can be difficult: seeds are seldom produced. Cuttings treated with hormone rooting powder form roots very slowly. Propagation is much more successful if *Adenium* is grafted onto Oleander *Nerium* but the swollen stem does not form.

KALANCHOE *Kalanchoe* spp.

The Kalanchoes are succulent plants with opposite leaves and a propensity to produce plantlets from mature leaves, either as a matter of course or if the leaf is severed from the plant and placed on damp sand. Mexican Hat Plant *K. daigremontianum* bears a row of plantlets along the edge of mature leaves. The leaves are dark reddish green, the flowers a dusky pink. *K. marmorata* has attractively mottled rounded waxy leaves. It can be readily propagated by rooting a leaf. These and the many other species can be naturalised in the dry garden. All Kalanchoes are very easy to propagate either by leaf offsets, or by leaf and stem cuttings.

SNAKE PLANT *Sansevieria* spp.

Closely related to the Agaves, *Sansevieria* species are tolerant of a wide range of garden conditions. True succulents, they can survive for months without water. Of the wide variety of species in cultivation, there are forms with long sword-like leaves, with cylindrical leaves, and those that form miniature rosettes. The foliage may be solid green, mottled, striped or silver. Yellow or silver-leaved forms need a little more sunlight than other forms which do best in semi-shade. Species to grow in the garden include:
S. cylindrica: cylindric dark green leaves; tall; pink flowers

S. stuckyi: small, marbled foliage; many off-sets

S. trifasciata 'Hahnii': rosettes with golden yellow variegated foliage; 20 cm (8 in) tall; abundant offsets; lends itself to mass planting;

S. kirkii: undulating leaves sporting a rich blend of grey, green and brown blotches

S. parva: miniature species for pots.

Growing and spreading from thick, prostrate rhizomes, these plants are easily propagated from offsets. They can also be propagated by leaf cuttings in damp sand although this process is much slower.

STAPELIADS *Edithcolea, Huernia* and *Stapelia*

The Stapeliads are a group of African succulent plants allied to the Milkweed family (Asclepiadaceae). Many of the species bear flowers smelling of carrion: blow flies are attracted by the smell and thus pollinate the flowers. Stapeliads are generally found growing in the shade of a shrub or amongst rocks. Similar to cactus, this group has succulent leafless stems. With the exception of *Frerea indica* which has deciduous functional leaves, Stapeliads have only minute deciduous leaves and in their place remains a 'tooth' of variable length. All are readily propagated from cuttings and seeds.

Edithcolea grandis originates from Somalia. This beautiful tropical succulent is best grown in a basket. The branched stems are difficult to handle with bare hands covered as they are with many sharp teeth. The 8 cm (3.2 in) diameter flat beige flowers are attractively marked and edged in dark brown. As with all Stapeliads grown in the humid tropics, this species must be grown under cover so that the gardener controls the frequency of watering and avoids destructive rots.

Huernia is a large group of African succulents prized by collectors not only for their plant form but also for their interesting flowers. Variable in colour, the flowers can be open, bell-shaped, or may have a brilliantly coloured raised ring or annulus. Those species with an annulus, for example *H. confusa*, are referred to as the 'lifebuoy' types. While most Huernias are suited to culture in shallow pots, some of the more vigorous species, such as *H. schneideriana* and *H. kirkii*, can be planted in a semi-shaded location of a dry garden.

Stapelia gigantea forms immense mats in its native habitat (Natal, Transvaal, South Africa). This species has softly pubescent, square stems up to 20 cm (8 in) tall. The flowers are beige, lined reddish-brown and very hairy. The large 45 cm (18 in) diameter flowers are some of the largest produced by green plants. The flowers smell of carrion and attract flies. This vigorous species can be grown in a tall clay pot or it can be planted in a well-drained garden location. Some shade should be provided. Because of the size of the blooms and the semi-pendant nature of the stems, the pot must be tall enough to carry the bloom over its side. Place some rocks in the bottom of the pot (for stability) and fill with gritty humus.

TREES

Basic care

Light: full sun except where otherwise noted

Water: especially freshly planted trees during dry periods

Soil: well-drained loam

Fertilizer: apply balanced fertilizer around drip line either at beginning of rainy season or as specifically noted

Pests and diseases: sucking insects, such as Leaf Hoppers and Scale Insects may occasionally cause problems including the spread of disease

Propagation: cuttings; grafts; seed

See also Trees and Palms page 54.

Trees grown for their flowers

AFRICAN TULIP TREE, FLAME OF THE FOREST *Spathodea campanulata*

Growing to 20 m (66 ft) high African Tulip Tree forms an upright trunk with a flaring crown topped with orange scarlet blooms. It is almost always in bloom with a flowering peak from September through to May. This splendid fast-growing West African tree suckers freely although it may not set seed. Propagate from root suckers, or from seed using Method III.

CANNONBALL TREE *Couroupita guianensis*

Examples of this curious tree can be found growing in Trafalgar Square, Bridgetown, Barbados, or opposite Queen's Royal College in Port of Spain, Trinidad. South American in origin, it forms a large upright trunk to 20 m (66 ft) with massive pendant inflorescences. The large salmon-red flowers 10 cm (4 in) in diameter are followed by large fruits resembling cannonballs. This tree makes a very attractive specimen for a large garden. Propagate from seed using Method III.

CASSIA *Cassia* spp.

APPLEBLOSSOM, PINK CASSIA C. *javanica* grows to 10 m (40 ft), having a spreading and arched canopy and bearing clusters of lovely pink flowers in April, May and June. Keep this tree trimmed of dead branches. Propagate from seeds using Method III.

GOLDEN SHOWER, PUDDING PIPE CASSIA C. *fistula* is a fine upright tree with a spreading crown. This seasonally deciduous tree bears long drooping racemes of bright yellow flowers together with a flush of new leaves from April to June. The flowers are followed by long dark brown cylindrical pods. Propagate by air layers of large branches, or from seed using Method III.

CHACONIA *Warszewiczia coccinia*

The national flower of Trinidad, Chaconia is a small tree that bears clusters of flowers each with an enlarged red sepal. Flowers are brilliant and long-lasting. A very desirable double form was discovered in Trinidad in 1957 by David Auyong. Grow in full sun. Propagate by hardwood cuttings, or from seed using Method III.

CORAL TREE, BOIS IMMORTELLE *Erythrina* spp.

Coral Trees can often be seen blooming on the hillsides of drier regions in the Caribbean. A variegated leaf form offers an interesting contrast to the flame-coloured flowers. Propagate from large semi-hardwood cuttings, and from seed using Method III.

CORDIA *Cordia sebestena*

Cordia is a drought- and salt-tolerant Caribbean tree that brightens each day with a colourful display of fresh orange-red flowers. The leaves are large, oval, rough, with a texture like sandpaper. The bark is thick, corrugated and ideal for naturalizing orchids. This handsome tree grows to 7 m (23 ft). Propagate by seeds using Method II.

FLAMBOYANT *Delonix regia*

This leguminous tree, seasonally deciduous, has a lovely spreading crown of lacy foliage and bears large red flowers during the period April to September. Yellow and salmon-coloured varieties are also cultivated. The large, flat dark brown pods are distinctive. Allow 36 m² (400 ft²) or more for this spreading tree to grow as a specimen. The tree will provide excellent shady place for pot plants beneath its boughs, and its trunk is suitable for naturalizing orchids. Propagate easily by seed using Method III.

FRANGIPANI *Plumeria rubra, P. alba*

Small trees native to the Caribbean and Central America, Frangipanis grow to 5 m (16 ft). They have large, leathery leaves and terminal clusters of sweetly fragrant white, cream, yellow, pink or red flowers. Although seasonally deciduous, these multi-branched trees are admirable for a small garden. Branches, leaves and flower stalks produce a POISONOUS milk white latex (avoid contact with eyes). Propagate from large cuttings planted in barely moist sand, air layers, and seed using Method II.

LIGNUM VITAE *Guaiacum officinale*

Native to South America, Lignum Vitae is the national flower of Jamaica and the Bahamas. This heavily branched, slow-growing, shapely tree makes a pleasing specimen for small or large gardens. The compound leaves are a dark glossy green, the flowers, medium blue, followed by bright orange fruits. Propagate from seed using Method II.

MAHOE *Thespesia populnea*

Drought- and salt-tolerant tree reaching 10 m (33 ft), the handsome Mahoe is also known as Tulip Tree Mahoe, Seaside Mahoe, or Mahault de Londres. Its bright yellow flowers turn purplish late in the day. Seeds are produced in flattened capsules. Propagate from seed using Method II.

ORCHID TREE *Bauhinia purpurea*

This small tree from South East Asia has distinctive bilobed leaves and large rose-violet flowers. Propagate from air layers, softwood or semi-hardwood cuttings, or from seed using Method III.

POUI *Tabebuia* spp.

YELLOW POUI *T. rufescens* is known as the Apamata in Trinidad. This tree presents a brief but glorious display of yellow flowers at the end of the dry season in April–May. There are no leaves on the tree at the time of flowering.

PINK POUI *T. pentaphylla* bears clear dark pink blooms. Both trees grow to 20 m (66 ft) in height. As they are normally deciduous, withhold water until after blooming is finished. Propagate from seed using Method II.

PRIDE OF INDIA *Peltophorum ferrugineum*

Up to 20 m (66 ft) tall with a large, spreading crown, Pride of India bears masses of golden yellow flowers followed by small reddish brown pods which are distinctive even at a distance. Propagate this tree from seed using Method III.

Trees grown for their foliage

BEARDED FIG TREE *Ficus citrifolia*

This Barbados native is reputed to be origin of the island's name. Massive aerial (adventitious) roots cascade from over-hanging branches. This huge spreading tree should only be planted in a large garden. Propagate from hardwood cuttings, air layers, or from seed using Method II.

CALABASH *Cresentia cujete*

Drought-tolerant, native of the Caribbean, Calabash has spreading branches clothed in attractive mid-green foliage. The large oval fruits measure 25 cm (10 in) in diameter and when ripe have a hard, dry shell. The mature fruits can be hollowed and used as bowls. The rough, corrugated bark of this tree is a suitable substrate for orchid naturalization. Propagate from seeds using Method III.

MILE TREE *Casuarina equisetifolia*

Also known as Whistling Pine, Ironwood or Pine, Mile Trees are flowering plants and should not be confused with conifers. They are tall trees, over 20 m (66 ft) in height, and native to Australia. The 'foliage' consists of green scaly branches, the tiny red flowers are inconspicuous and the fruits resemble cones.

These trees are salt- and drought-tolerant, often being used for wind breaks, plantings along inner dunes or in other coastal locations. They can be used for hedging but require early and frequent pruning to achieve the required effect. Propagate from seed using Method II, or *C. cunninghamiana* from air layers.

PALMS

See Palms page 106, see also Trees and Palms page 54.

SEA GRAPE *Coccoloba uvifera*

Most common along shorelines where it forms large mounds of tangled branches, Sea Grape can also become a handsome tree 15 m (50 ft) when grown away from continuous wind. The leaves are thick, leathery rounds that can be dried for interesting floral arrangements. The flowers are borne on long racemes followed by conspicuous, grape-like, green to purple fruits. This tree is 'a must' in coastal gardens making a very effective windbreak. Propagate from seed using Method III.

SEASIDE ALMOND *Terminalia catappa*

An interesting drought- and salt-tolerant tree from the Asia-Pacific region, which can reach 18 m (60 ft). Seaside Almond has horizontal whorls of branches and large glossy leaves. The flowers are inconspicuous. The fruits resemble almonds. Propagate by seed using Method II.

TAMARIND *Tamarindus indica*

Prized as a shade tree and for its edible fruit, the Tamarind is a large leguminous tree that can reach 20 m (66 ft). Swollen brown pods follow inconspicuous flowers. The pods contain large brown seeds surrounded by flavourful but astringent pulp. The pulp can be mixed with sugar to form tamarind balls or diluted with sweetened water to make a refreshing drink. Tamarind fruit is also a useful additive to chutneys and condiments. Collect the fruits as soon as they are ripe as the seeds are a favourite food for weevils! Propagate from seed using Method III.

TRAVELLER'S TREE *Ravenala madagascariensis*

The Traveller's Tree is a large tree-like plant native to Madagascar. Related to the Bird of Paradise plant *Strelitzia*, and to Banana *Musa*, it is sometimes erroneously referred to as a palm. Ravenalas reproduce mainly by suckers, although they also flower and produce viable seeds. The plants illustrated in Plate 17 were grown from seed brought from Martinique and planted at Andromeda Gardens, Barbados, in about 1970. After 20 years they had not flowered although more than 9 m (30 ft) tall. Much younger plants flower and set seed in Martinique. Grow these plants in full sun, in a well-drained organic compost and provide plenty of water during dry periods. This tree grows best in high rainfall regions. Propagate by suckers, or from freshly harvested seeds using Method II.

VINES AND SCRAMBLERS

Basic care
Light: semi-shade to full sun
Water: as necessary during dry periods
Soil: garden loam except where noted
   otherwise
Fertilizer: apply twice yearly
Pests and diseases: Slugs
Propagation: cuttings; seed

ALLAMANDA *Allamanda cathartica*

Yellow-flowered Allamanda, a straggler rather than a climber, must be supported on a trellis, fence or wall. The lower parts can be unsightly. Plant small shrubs at the base to hide this. Encourage new growth by pruning the vine immediately upon planting to a new location. Propagate from woody cuttings.

BLUE AND WHITE PEA *Clitoria ternatea*

The Blue and White Pea is a slender perennial vine that will bloom in four months from seed. Brilliant dark blue, white, single or double 5 cm (2 in) flowered forms are available commercially. Grow this colourful delicate vine in full sun to semi-shade. It climbs easily and will quickly cover a light support with dark green foliage and blooms. Pinch to keep it bushy and productive. *Clitoria* will thrive in a protected garden near the sea. Grow seedlings in individual pots and plant them where they are to grow without disturbing the roots. Fertilize at planting time and when flowering commences. Propagate from seed using Method II.

BOUGAINVILLEA

See Bougainvilleas, page 79.

CHALICE VINE *Solandra guttata*

The Chalice Vine is a very showy perennial climber. The large creamy yellow, cup-shaped blooms are about 25 cm (10 in) long. The vine is heavy requiring sturdy support. This vine can be trained into an umbrella shape with the flowers hanging all around or grown against a wall. Plant it in full sun. Fertilize at the beginning of the rainy season and directly after pruning. Water during dry periods. Propagate by hardwood cuttings.

CLERODENDRON *Clerodendron*

One of the most handsome Clerodendrons is Bleeding Heart *C. thomsonae*. This perennial scrambler grows to 4 m (13 ft) in semi-shade and needs a well-drained soil. Support the weak stems by tying them to a fence or tree limbs. Propagate from hardwood cuttings.

CORALLITA *Antigonon leptopus*

Flourishing in full sun, Corallita, a vigorous perennial vine, climbs by means of flower stem tendrils. Flowers may be pink, white or two-toned. Consider where you want this vine to grow and take care to train it accordingly. It can easily take over a garden but responds well to judicious pruning. Propagate Corallita from the nut-like seeds using Method II or from semi-hardwood cuttings. White-flowered types do not come true from seed.

GLORIOSA LILY *Gloriosa superba*

This perennial vine climbs by means of leaf tendrils to over 4 m (13 ft). It has a tuber-like root and thrives in rich, well-drained soil. The root should be shaded by a supporting shrub or planting of annuals. As the vine grows, it will use the branches or trellis for support. Flowering will begin after 12 or 15 weeks. After blooming is finished, the leaves will yellow signalling the onset of dormancy. Watering should be restricted or the tubers lifted to avoid rotting. The red and gold flowers last well for cutting. Propagate Gloriosa Lily by division of the tuber.

HOYA *Hoya*

Hoyas are climbing plants native to Asia and the South Pacific. Many of the species are true succulents. *H. carnosa* and *H. pallida* prefer a cool dry rest period whereas most of the other species thrive in a warm humid climate. Hoyas produce clusters of fragrant, waxy flowers, blooming from the same inflorescence stalk (peduncle) annually. They are weak climbers and should be supported on a trellis or arch or grown in hanging baskets. Propagate by cuttings.

IPOMOEA *Ipomoea*

Many popular garden plants belong to the genus *Ipomoea*. A favourite is *I. horsfalliae* var. *briggsii*. This attractive perennial vine has glossy dark green foliage and wonderful wine-red blooms borne in clusters. Grow this vine on a wall or strong trellis. Propagate from cuttings and suckers.

JADE VINE *Strongylodon macrobotrys*

Known as the Jade Vine because of its magnificent long blue-green pendant inflorescences, *S. macrobotrys* can be trained onto a sturdy trellis so that its inflorescences will be attractively displayed. Some plants bloom year-round whereas others are seasonal bloomers. Plant this leguminous vine in well-drained loam enriched with compost. The roots should be shaded or well mulched; the upper portions of the vine should receive at least four hours of direct sunshine a day. Fertilize monthly during the rainy season. Propagate by seeds and by cuttings.

JASMINE *Jasminum*

If fragrance is required in the garden plant a Jasmine Vine. Most Jasmine are twiners or sprawling shrubs. They need support and careful pruning so as not to interfere with the flowering cycle. Prune the vines after flowering is finished. Flowers are produced on new growth.

SPANISH or POET'S JASMINE *J. officinale* is one of the most fragrant, producing masses of 3 cm (1.2 in) white flowers; this species propagates readily from softwood cuttings.

ROYAL JASMINE *J. rex* has magnificent white blooms measuring 5 cm (2 in). It is not scented but makes up for this short-coming with showy flowers. Plant the vine in a sheltered sunny location against a tall 2 m (6 ft) support. This species can be difficult to propagate; try hardwood and heel cuttings.

MOON VINE *Calonyction aculeatum*

Moon Vine is a perennial twiner with large white saucer-shaped blooms that open 'before your very eyes' at dusk. The flowers are very fragrant. Plant this vine on a trellis near your hospitality area or patio. Propagate from seed using Method III.

PETREA, QUEEN'S WREATH *Petrea volubilis*

Growing up to 8 m (26 ft), *Petrea*, a woody perennial twiner presents a cascade of foliage and blue or white blooms on a bank or wall. Prune it seasonally to maintain a neat appearance. Repeat blooming can be encouraged by heavy watering after periods of dry weather. Propagate with difficulty from softwood cuttings and air layers.

PHILODENDRON *Philodendron*

See also Aroids, page 69. There are many climbing varieties of *Philodendron*, some large enough to be planted at the foot of a tree and allowed to climb. Smaller types make excellent specimens for hanging baskets. Plant Philodendrons in a rich loam with a high humus or leaf mould content. Propagate from cuttings.

RANGOON CREEPER, LAD'S LOVE *Quisqualis indica*

Rangoon Creeper is a perennial woody vine that requires a sturdy support. The flowers are fragrant at night, opening white then changing to a rich pink and later to red. Long-tongued moths visit the clusters of blooms for nectar and thus enact pollination. This vine can be established on a wall either in semi-shade or in full sun. It will bloom periodically, year-round in either location. Propagate from root suckers.

RED HOT POKER, BEACON *Norantea guianensis*

Native to the Caribbean, *Norantea*, a vigorous woody perennial climber is sometimes known as the Beacon plant. The attractive flower spikes are orange red. This vine can become massive: judicious pruning will be required to keep it in check. Plant it close to a rocky cliff where it can cascade or grow it as a large shrubby specimen. Propagate by hardwood cuttings and by air layers.

THUNBERGIA, *Thunbergia*

T. alata BLACK EYED SUSAN is a quick-growing delicate annual vine. The flowers are orange or white, sometimes with a dark contrasting blotch in the throat. It can be grown in a hanging basket, balcony planter or as a quick cover plant. Propagate from commercially available seed using Method II.

T. grandiflora is a vigorous perennial woody climber that bears a daily supply of large blue flowers on pendant racemes. It will grow anywhere from sea level to 1000 m (3000 ft) altitude. Train the vine on a trellis, arch or pergola so that the flowers hang from above. It responds well to pruning. Propagate from hardwood cuttings or suckers.

URECHITES *Urechites lutea*

This slender woody vine bears 5 cm (2 in) bright yellow flowers resembling those of *Allamanda*. The floral displays are equally impressive: the vine is much more attractive and less heavy than *Allamanda*. The oval leaves and green stems are softly pubescent. This vine is attractive on a garden path archway or trellis. Propagate from hardwood cuttings.

WATER PLANTS

Basic care
Light: semi-shade to full sun depending upon the plant
Water: fresh water; depth can be critical for some species; Water-lilies dislike splashing water
Soil: garden loam with well-rotted cow manure or compost
Fertilizer: granular slow-release product; bone meal
Pests and diseases: Snails and some Fish may cause noticeable damage to Water Plants when a pool population is ecologically unbalanced; diseases are not common
Propagation: division; removal of offsets produced by viviparous species; seed.

LOTUS *Nelumbo lutea*

Stately leaves, yellow flowers and seed heads carried high above the water mark this plant as a speciality for your garden. If not kept in check it can easily become the dominant plant in a larger pool. Lotus should be planted as the sole occupant of a small or larger shallow pool where it can grow and bloom unchecked. Small pools of Lotus can be placed at strategic intervals along or at the end of a garden path or within a border. The seed heads are prized for decorative arrangements. Propagate by division or from very fresh seed planted as for Water-lilies (see page 41).

PAPYRUS *Cyperus*

C. papyrus is an imposing aquatic African sedge that can reach 2–3 m (6–10 ft). Each stem is topped with a decorative plume of green flowers and thread-like bracts. Umbrella Sedge *C. alternifolius* is a smaller-growing, more leafy relative reaching up to 1 m (3 ft) in height. It is more suited to smaller pools. Both species thrive in wet soil, mud or in shallow water situations. Propagation is by division of the clumps.

SNOWFLAKE WATER-LILY
Nymphoides indica

This dainty water plant is suitable for a small, shallow pool. It has small, round, floating leaves and 2 cm (0.8 in) wide fringed white flowers. Propagate by division.

WATER HYACINTH *Eichhornea*

Inflated leaf petioles keep this plant afloat. Water Hyacinth has attractive upright spikes of rose-purple blooms. It often escapes from cultivation and can become a menace in freshwater canals, rivers and lakes. Keep this vigorous plant under control. Propagation is by division.

WATER LETTUCE *Pistia*

This attractive floating plant resembles a head

of lettuce. The pleated leaves are lime green with a velvety surface. It spreads quickly by runners and can easily become invasive: keep it under control. It is best grown as the sole occupant of a small pool. Propagation is by division.

WATER-LILY *Nymphaea*

There is something undeniably exotic about a fragrant Water-lily blooming in a tropical pool. Whether they are night-blooming varieties capturing and reflecting moonlight, or day-bloomers in any one of a rainbow of colours, tropical Water-lilies deserve a place in your water garden. Ranging in colour from the purest white through yellow, peach, pink, blue, and purple, Water-lilies also have interesting foliage which can be green, bronze or maroon, and even speckled.

Water-lily varieties differ in the size, number and colour of flowers, in leaf spread, and their preferred depth of water. Some varieties, such as 'Panama Pacific' (purple) and 'Mrs Martin E. Randig' (deep blue) are compact 0.1–0.6 m² (1–6 ft²) and can easily adapt to a small pool or sunken tub. Other varieties such as 'General Pershing' can attain a leaf spread of 1.2 m² (12 ft²).

The following varieties (see top of next column) are the recommendations of Charles B. Thomas, President, Lilypons Water Gardens, Maryland, U.S.A., and one of the foremost breeders of Water-lilies.

Tropical Water-lilies require 15–50 cm (6–20 in) of still water over the rootstock and at least six hours of sunshine daily. All Water-lilies should be planted in a container, the whole being placed where appropriate in the pond. The extra effort will be rewarded when it comes time to divide the plants or clean the pond.

Some Water-lilies provide fertile seed for propagation; others are viviparous, producing plantlets in the centre of the leaf. These plantlets eventually develop adventitious roots. Propagate by seed (see page 41) or by plantlets.

Day-blooming	Night-blooming
'Albert Greenberg' (rosy yellow)	'Emily Grant Hutchings' (rose)
'Blue Beauty' (blue)	'Red Flare' (Red)
'Blue Capensis' (blue)	'Texas Shell Pink' (pink)
'Charles Thomas' (blue)	'Wood's White Knight' (white)
'Dauben' (blue)	
'General Pershing' (pink)	
'Madame Ganna Walska' (pink)	
'Panama Pacific' (purple)	
'White Delight' (cream)	
'Yellow Dazzler' (yellow)	

WATER PLATTER, AMAZON WATER LILY *Victoria amazonica*

This immense-leaved water plant is native to the mineral-rich lakes associated with the Amazon River floodplain of South America. The 2 m (80 in) wide leaves have upturned margins. The strongly-scented flowers are each open for two successive nights. They open as white flowers at sunset the first day, gradually changing colour to deep pink and closing the following morning; the now dark pink flowers open the evening of the second day and close for the last time before the next morning. To hand pollinate, take pollen from second night flowers and using an artist's brush, transfer this to the stigmas found in the base of first night blooms. To prevent further pollination, remove the anthers and bag the flowers. Grow this magnificent plant in a large pool, providing 50–150 cm (20–60 in) water over the growing points. These plants are heavy feeders. Fertilize individual plants using small cloth bags of fertilizer (20–20–20) pressed into the soil around the plants. Feed every three months. Propagate by division and by seed (see page 41).

FRUITS, VEGETABLES, HERBS AND SPICES

Trees grown for fruit

AVOCADO PEAR *Persea americana*

The Avocado bears large edible fruits rich in fat. Ripe fruit can be spread on bread as a tasty butter substitute. Within the pear-shaped fruit is one large seed. The tree can reach 15 m (50 ft) in height and be equally wide. Provide enough space for this tree to grow. Grafted trees will begin to bear after five years whereas seedlings require at least seven years to come into production. Pick full size fruit about nine to 10 months after flowering. Allow the fruit to stand several days to fully ripen before eating.

Avocados are susceptible to *Phytophthora* Root Rot. They must be grown in well-drained locations otherwise they will succumb to disease. Disease-tolerant rootstock may be available in your region. A balanced fertilizer should be applied twice yearly. Occasionally, if chlorosis develops, apply iron chelate according to manufacturer's instructions. Propagate by wedge grafting selected varieties on to resistant rootstock (see page 35).

BANANA *Musa* spp.

Tree-like in size but not at all woody, Bananas produce short-lived pseudostems that grow quickly to flower and fruit once before dying in approximately 18 months. New suckers emerge from the large corm at the base of the plant. Bananas can be grown for their attractive foliage as well as for their delicious fruit. Most Bananas and their relatives, Plantains, Figs, and Bufas form fruits without pollination and are thus seedless. All have a common need for rich, well-drained compost that has been heavily mulched to encourage rooting and nutrient absorption. Bananas are heavy feeders requiring once or twice yearly applications of potassium chloride and super phosphate. A balanced 7–7–7 granular fertilizer should be applied monthly according to manufacturer's instructions. Bananas can become deficient in trace minerals such as manganese or boron. To avoid these problems, ensure that the fertilizer you use is formulated with additional trace elements.

Bananas can be subject to a variety of diseases and are also prone to damage by high winds. The 'Dwarf Cavendish' cultivar is not only resistant to Panama Disease but also is short enough to avoid wind problems. The fruit is excellent for home use but does not ship well. Once a banana flowers, fruits will develop gradually over the next six to nine months. Some varieties take longer to mature. Bananas should be picked at the 'full green' stage. There is a distinct colour change from dark to lighter green when the time is right. Cut the fruiting stalk and suspend the stalk in a covered place protected from rodents. Green bananas can be boiled as a vegetable or **allowed to ripen and eaten as dessert.**

After the fruit has been harvested, the fruiting pseudostem should be removed and suckers allowed to develop. Remove surplus suckers leaving no more than three to a clump at any one time. Prepare a new bed and plant with disease-free stock every five years. This rotation helps interrupt the development of populations of harmful Root Knot Nematodes in the soil. Bananas are propagated by suckers.

BREADFRUIT *Artocarpus communis*

The Breadfruit is a large tree 20 m (66 ft) tall, with magnificent, glossy leaves. The limbs can break easily in storms. The large fruits each weigh up to 4 kg (9 lb) and are produced year-round. Fruit can be harvested about three months after flowering. Propagation of the seedless Breadfruit is by root suckers removed from the parent plant or by root cuttings or stem cuttings. Breadnut produces edible seeds which can be boiled or roasted. Reproduce this cultivar from seed using Method II.

Grow Breadfruit in well-drained locations where the soil is of sufficient depth to allow the trees to become deeply rooted. Allow enough space for this tree to grow. Be certain that limbs do not overhang buildings.

LIME *Citrus aurantifolia*

Many kinds of citrus fruit are grown in the Caribbean including West Indian Lime, Lemon, various Oranges, Grapefruits, Tangerines, Tangelos and Shaddocks. Although the trees vary in size and fruiting period, their culture is otherwise very similar. The advent of grafted stock has made the productive garden orchard possible. Lime trees can be started from seeds using Method II. Most other *Citrus* are propagated by bud-grafting (see page 33) selected varieties onto disease-free and disease-resistant rootstock.

Citrus trees should be planted about 6 m (20 ft) apart in well-drained locations and kept growing vigorously. Preferably the soil should be a fertile sandy loam with neutral to slightly acid pH. *Citrus* trees are heavy feeders. Provide a balanced fertilizer recommended for citrus, three times a year. Apply the fertilizer along the canopy line of the tree and

water in thoroughly. Occasionally the leaves will become chlorotic in which case iron chelate should be applied according to manufacturer's instructions. Water should be provided during dry periods to prevent fruit drop.

MANGO *Mangifera indica*

Mangoes are medium-sized trees with attractive foliage, the new leaves being reddish orange and drooping. They bear clusters of flowers followed by pendant stems of fruit. It is an ornamental landscape specimen; the fruits are an added bonus. Beware of monkeys that will pay a visit to this tree: they bite almost every fruit to test for ripeness before discarding it. Fruits develop two to three months after flowering. Selected varieties may be available as grafted stock. These will begin to bear about four years after planting in your garden.

This tree is tolerant of drought and needs relatively little care to survive, however some care is advantageous. Fertilize the trees four times a year using a balanced commercial product according to manufacturer's instructions. Propagate by budding selected cultivars using the inverted-T technique (see page 34).

PAPAW, PAPAYA *Carica papaya*

This species is native to the Caribbean. Mostly separate male and female trees (dioecious), but hermaphrodites are becoming more common. Flowers and fruits are borne close to the green trunk. Selected varieties have large flavoursome fruits with orange or salmon-coloured flesh. Papayas are subject to a variety of diseases, the most serious is Bunchy Top. Remove the affected top of a diseased plant using a sterile knife. Enclose valuable stock in a cage to exclude flying insects which transmit the disease agent. Fertilize Papaya trees three times each year using 10–15–10 (or equivalent) according to manufacturer's instructions. Propagate by seed harvested from self-pollinated hermaphroditic plants: this gives the greatest yield of fruit-bearing stock.

Germinate seed using Method II. Selected varieties may be available locally.

Other fruit

PINEAPPLE *Ananas comosus*

The pineapple is the delicious fruit of a drought-tolerant bromeliad native to tropical America. Pineapples are propagated by suckers that form at the plant base, from suckers (slips) found beneath a fruit, or from leafy top cuttings (crowns). Planting stock should be healthy and from better quality, vigorous cultivars. The preferred soil is slightly acid (pH 5.0–6.5), sandy and well drained. Plant Pineapple suckers or crowns in a sunny location, about 60 cm (2 ft) apart. Potassium, nitrogen and trace elements, especially iron and zinc, are needed to produce good fruits. Fertilizer rich in potassium should be applied before planting by mixing it into the soil. Muriate of potash (potassium chloride, KCl) is applied at the rate of approximately 600 g/m^2 (about 1 lb/yd^2): the exact amount needed will vary according to local soil conditions. A commercial fertilizer such as 21–3–9 is applied according to manufacturer's instructions starting four weeks after planting and every three months thereafter. Frequency of application will depend upon rainfall, with smaller, more frequent applications needed in high rainfall gardens. Foliar sprays containing the elements iron and zinc can be applied if leaf chlorosis develops. Keep the garden free of weeds that may harbour pests and diseases. Pineapples take about 12 months to produce fruit.

Vegetables

EGGPLANT *Solanum melongena*

SWEET AND HOT PEPPERS
Capsicum annuum and C. frutescens

TOMATO *Lycopersicon* spp.

Eggplant, Sweet and Hot Peppers and Tomato are all closely related members of the same family of tropical American plants. Eggplant is an excellent lowland tropics crop, tolerating a high night temperature and not requiring much temperature variation from day to night to produce fruit. Peppers are similar, but Tomato does require a variation between night and day temperature to grow well and to set fruit. All the above vegetables are subject to the same pests and diseases. Disease and nematode-resistant varieties are available. Method of propagation – all of the above are best started from seed using Method II.

PIGEON PEA *Cajanus cajan*

A short-lived, drought-tolerant perennial shrub growing to 3 m (10 ft). It has dull green hairy leaves, yellowish red flowers and forms a utilitarian hedge alongside the vegetable plot. Pigeon Pea tends to bloom year-round but more so when day length is less than 12 hours. Longer days inhibit flowering. The pods contain 2–8 seeds and can be harvested when green ripe or when dried. It will take approximately nine months from seed to harvest. Pigeon peas prefer a neutral to slightly acid soil. If the soil is especially poor, fertilizer (10–15–10) or compost can be dug into the soil before planting. Plant seeds 2–3 cm deep (about 1 in) in hills or in rows. Thin seedlings, allowing about 1 m (3 ft) between plants. Keep the seedlings free of weeds.

SPINACH (MALABAR, INDIAN OR CEYLON SPINACH) *Basella alba*

A vigorous, heat-tolerant vine producing thick, juicy, dark green leaves that may be eaten raw in salads and sandwiches or steamed. Spinach is propagated from seeds (or whole fruits) started in a nursery bed or with 25 cm (10 in) stem cuttings. Seeds or fruits should be sown using Method II. Plant cuttings or 10 cm (4 in) seedlings in rich loam containing added organic matter. The vines require full sun and warmth: they can be trained to climb a fence or trellis. Shade newly planted stock with branches or cloth for several days. Keep the soil evenly moist throughout the growing period. Young shoots with leaves can be harvested two to three months after planting. Mature leaves can be harvested during a period of six months or more.

Seed of the less commonly grown red-stemmed *Basella rubra* is now commercially available. Established on a pillar support at the entrance to the vegetable garden, red-stemmed spinach is both decorative and productive. Spinach is rarely affected by pests and diseases.

SWEET POTATO *Ipomoea batatas*

This Central American vegetable has been cultivated for more than 3000 years. Some selected cultivars, for example 'Nemagold' and 'Carolina Lee' have firm, dry flesh, and others, for example 'Centennial', have soft moist flesh. Varieties differ in skin colour, colour of tuber flesh, time to maturity and disease resistance.

Sweet potatoes need full sun, growing best in sandy loam with pH 6.0 and excellent drainage. Where soils are heavy, the plants should be grown on hills or ridges. Propagation is by stem cuttings of selected healthy stock. Take cuttings, length 25–50 cm (10–20 in), and plant two or three cuttings to a mound – early in the rainy season for best results. Control weeds until the vines become established. Fertilize at planting time and one month later with 10–15–10, applying more potassium on volcanic or non-calcareous soils and less on coral or limestone-based soils. Manures and compost can also be worked into the mounds. Sweet Potatoes take from three to eight months to produce a crop depending on variety. Avoid wounding or bruising tubers when digging to harvest them as they are very prone to decay. Air cure the tubers in a sheltered location for about one week before using.

Black Rot appears as dark circular depressions developing in stored tubers and renders them potentially toxic. If this problem arises, contact your local Agriculture Department for a source of resistant varieties. Do not grow Sweet Potatoes in the same place for several years. Sweet Potato Weevil larvae can also attack the tubers, tunnelling and also spreading rot organisms. Do not allow the tubers to lie close to the soil surface where they can be reached by egg-laying female weevils.

Herbs and Spices

BLACK PEPPER *Piper nigrum*

Grow the Black Pepper vine on a small trellis in a semi-shaded location. The soil should be a rich, well-drained compost. Keep the soil evenly moist at all times. Fertilize four times a year with 7–7–7 applied according to the manufacturer's instructions. The racemes of inconspicuous flowers are borne year-round and are followed by green fruits changing to red when ripe. Dry the fruits in the sun to make black pepper; scrape off the pulp and dry the hard inner seed to obtain white pepper. Propagate by seed using Method II, and by 15–25 cm (6–10 in) cuttings.

CULINARY GINGER *Zingiber*

Z. officinalis is a low growing herbaceous perennial native to Asia, grown on a small scale throughout the West Indies. Propagation is by division of rhizomes of the choicest clones. As 'a rule of thumb', the best quality rhizomes are a dull yellow within; poorer quality rhizomes have a bluish tint. Ginger plants take about ten months to produce a crop of rhizomes. Plant Ginger rhizomes about 60 cm (2 ft) apart in a well-prepared bed enriched with compost and leaf mould. Grow the plants in full sun to dappled shade, keeping the bed evenly moist throughout the productive season. Harvested rhizomes should be washed carefully and dried in the sun before use.

SHALLOTS, ESCHALOTE, CHIVES
Allium ascalonicum

Shallots are widely grown throughout the Caribbean and are used in place of their close European relative, Chives *Allium schoenoprasum*. Both the leaves and the small bulbs are used as 'seasoning' in the preparation of fish and pork. A single parent bulb produces a cluster of secondary bulbs which mature as the leaves yellow. Propagate shallots by dividing clumps of mature bulbs. The bulbs are air-dried and stored in a sheltered area for at least six weeks before planting. Plant single bulbs 20 cm (8 in) apart in well-drained sandy loam with added organic matter. Press the bulbs into the soil, covering the bed with netting to stop birds from uprooting what has just been planted. Remove the netting once leaves appear. Fertilizer (7–7–7) should be applied at the time of planting and every three weeks thereafter. Bulbs will take two or three months to mature. Shallot plants may be trimmed or dug as needed beginning about one month after planting. Allow some to mature for propagation purposes.

THYME *Thymus vulgaris*

Leaves of this Mediterranean shrub are used in many Caribbean dishes. Fortunately it grows well in most gardens. The dark green plants make an attractive border to vegetable plots and even to flower beds. If using this plant as an ornamental, keep it clipped like a miniature hedge. Propagate by seed using Method II, and by cuttings. Plant the seeds directly in a prepared bed or start seedlings in pots to later transplant to the garden. Thyme prefers a well-drained sandy soil. Fertilize twice a year with 7–7–7 or similar all-purpose fertilizer. Clip plants for new growth of foliage and to provide you with fresh herb. Excess herb can be sun-dried and stored in a sealed container or in the freezer.

CHAPTER 5

Plant Competitors

'You can put things on paper, lay out a beautiful garden, you may even pay a consultant to tell you what to do. You may acquire the most desirable and expensive plants, use pricey soil mixes and fertilizers, but if you do not care for those plants, weed and keep your newly planted plot in order, very little will result from your efforts and expense.'

I.B.

When you plant a garden, you want your chosen plants to flourish. Uninvited plants (**weeds**) invading flower beds become competitors with the cultivated ones for water, nutrients and light. Specimens planted too close together can likewise become competitors with each other. Weakened plants are often more susceptible to attack by **pests** and **diseases**.

The two initial steps you can take are

1 choose plants suited to your garden environment and give them space to flourish – such plants are more likely to be pest-tolerant;

2 know your enemy; learn how to recognize weeds, pests and diseases that can afflict your plants – prevention through observation is the best method for control.

Regular inspection will reveal problems before they become serious. Some of the most destructive pests and the most persistent weeds have been introduced quite innocently with imported plant material. Plant Quarantine Rules and Regulations exist for the protection of indigenous flora and cultivated crops. Your Agriculture Department can provide you with more detailed information and advice especially concerning new or uncommon pests, diseases or weeds.

Knowing the cause of a garden problem is essential to your developing strategies to deal with it. Integrated management is the most successful way to deal with plant competitors.

WEEDS

Weeds are plants growing where they are not wanted. Thus when Devil Grass (Bermuda Grass) *Cynodon dactylon* invades your flower bed it is considered a weed. Likewise, when Shrimp Plant *Beloperone guttata* flourishes in a damp, shady spot where you would rather grow grass, it might be considered a weed. Weeds are successful plants which have evolved with various strategies to survive and thrive where less adaptable cultivated plants might have difficulty. Production of vast quantities of seed, extended seed longevity, and physiological mechanisms to survive drought are some of the means by which weeds succeed. Certain weeds can reproduce vegetatively; every chopped-up piece of stem is capable of forming a new plant. Lawn and garden weeds may be introduced to your garden through either planting grass seed contaminated with weed seeds, or adding soil, manure or compost from a weedy place.

Weeds are competitors for moisture, nutrients and sunlight. They may be host to insect pests and plant diseases that can also affect garden plants. Controlling weeds can be as simple as pulling them by hand, cutting, mowing, hoeing or otherwise physically disrupting the plants. Mulch may sometimes be appropriate to cover annual weeds. The use of weed-killers (herbicides) should be considered only with full knowledge of the weed species to be eliminated, its particular life cycle and most vulnerable stage. Integration of all the possible weed control practices is probably the most successful approach.

Some common Weeds

ANNUAL WEEDS

Hand-pulling, mowing or otherwise destroying annual weeds before they set seed will prevent an increase in the weed seed population in the soil. Careful, regular cultivation can all but eliminate them. The use of a mulch of straw, cacao bean or rice hulls, chipped tree bark, burlap, or landscape fabric may be effective in controlling annual and biennial weeds. Mulching is often appropriate between rows of vegetables or between plants in an established flower bed.

MILKWEED *Euphorbia prostrata* and related species

Vigorous, low, matted annuals, Milkweeds often appear in yards, driveways and between paving stones. They exude an IRRITANT milky sap when broken. Wear protective gloves and eye covering to avoid exposure to the sap. Hand-pull before they set seed. Milkweeds are resistant to most selective herbicides.

PIGWEED *Amaranthus* spp.

Pigweeds produce 100 000 or more seeds per plant if allowed to mature. Hand-pull or hoe before seed forms.

PURSLANE, PURSLEY, PUSSLEY *Portulaca oleracea*

Prostrate and drought-tolerant with tiny yellow flowers, this succulent annual is sometimes fed to hens. Hand-pull and remove the plants before they set seed. Be aware that broken pieces of stem can root to form a new plant.

SANDBUR *Cenchrus* spp.

Annual grass with sharp-spined fruits, Sandbur is common in sandy, loose soils. Hand-pull young plants before they set seed.

SHEPHERD'S PURSE AND OTHER MUSTARDS *Capsella, Lepidium* and other genera

These annuals and biennials form rosettes of leaves and then upright flowering stems. Hand-pull or hoe these weeds.

PERENNIAL WEEDS

Perennial weeds are those plants that grow for a number of years, either as woody plants or as recurrent herbs from an underground tuber, rhizome or other perennating organ. Even the most persistent perennial weeds such as Bindweed *Convolvulus*, can be eliminated if you are diligent in hoeing the new shoots as they appear. Eventually all the food reserves in the underground storage organs will be used up and the plants will die. It should be noted roots may remain dormant for two or more years during unfavourable conditions. Mulches are generally ineffective against vigorous perennial weeds.

BINDWEEDS, MORNING GLORY *Convolvulus*

Perennial vines spread both by seed and by production of shoots from an extensive underground root system. Flowers are white, pink or yellow. Regular digging to remove all roots and hoeing to remove the parts above ground will eventually eliminate this persistent weed.

BROOM WEED *Sida, Malvastrum*

Tough and shrubby, these perennials have small, 2 cm (0.8 in) yellow flowers (like a miniature Hibiscus); they are rarely a major problem. Digging or hoeing is required to remove established plants.

DEVIL GRASS, BERMUDA GRASS
Cynodon dactylon
Sometimes used as a lawn grass, Devil Grass tolerates flooding and grazing. It may be used to stabilize ditch banks. Hand-pull plants in flower beds before they become established. Every tiny portion of stem can set root. To be sure that no stolons are left, remove an extra 10 cm (4 in) band of soil around each plant.

LOVE VINE, DODDER *Cuscuta americana* and *C. indecora*

Tiny flowers are produced on the slender, orange-stemmed parasitic vines. Hand-pull and destroy all vines and parasitized plant material.

NUT GRASS *Cyperus rotundus*

Numerous small, hard, brown, underground tubers are formed. Complete plants including all tubers must be dug out. Generally Nut Grass is resistant to herbicides.

WILD CUCUMBER *Coccinia grandis*

A perennial vine that produces white flowers on separate male and female plants. Green fruits turn scarlet at maturity. Dig and destroy the tuberous stem to control this weed.

STRATEGIES FOR WEED MANAGEMENT

Choice of the most appropriate weed control method will depend upon:
1 the weed species, its life cycle and stage of growth;
2 how abundant it is;
3 where the weed is growing;
4 with what it is growing; and
5 what the future plans are for the affected garden area.

Herbicides

Chemicals used to control weeds are called herbicides or weedkillers. The use of herbicides should be considered as a supplement to good cultural practices and cannot be expected to correct the results of poor soil preparation, lack of fertility, drainage problems, inappropriate plantings or neglect. When appropriately and correctly used, chemical weed control can reduce competition so that garden plants will grow better and produce more. In parks, large gardens and fruit plantations the effective use of herbicides can reduce labour requirements. The same saving of time and effort can be realised by the home gardener through the judicious use of herbicides.

Weeds are often persistent problems in driveways, thriving between cracks in the cement. These weeds require repeated removal by hand, a never-ending task. In the past, motor oil, creosote, and soil-sterilant herbicides were used. Today there is a greater concern for the environment, realizing that these materials wash off the driveway or patio to the lawn, flower beds or vegetable garden, and ultimately into fresh water supplies.

The most effective and least intrusive method to kill a few weeds growing between cracks is to pour boiling water on them. Preparations of glyphosate kill all plants they touch within 14 days. It is not possible to give specific recommendations for gardens as often the desired flowering plants are as equally susceptible as the weeds to herbicides. Before purchasing a specific product, read the manufacturer's recommendations and the limitations. All herbicides are poisonous – see Appendix 5 Pesticide Precautions.

Herbicide alternatives

MECHANICAL DISRUPTION
Nothing is better than the old-fashioned hoe to disrupt weeds at their vulnerable early stage

of growth. Hand-pulling likewise can destroy weeds before they begin to reproduce. Although labour-intensive, mechanical disruption is still the safest and most dependable means of weed control.

ORGANIC MULCHES

Well-rotted bagasse, sawdust, chipped wood, bark, straw, cacao or rice hulls are among the most commonly used materials as mulches. Organic mulches decompose to become part of the soil substance. At the same time, a thick layer will smother all but the most aggressive perennial weeds. Organic mulches may need to be replenished frequently.

BLACK POLYETHYLENE (PLASTIC) SHEET

Light, water and fertilizers can only penetrate the plastic where you have made openings. Plastic mulches are an inexpensive way to kill patches of weeds. Polyethylene degrades on exposure to sunlight and will have to be replaced annually.

LANDSCAPE FABRIC

Porous landscape fabric blocks all but the most aggressive weeds while letting water, air, fertilizers and systemic pesticides pass freely. Landscape fabric must be covered with about 10 cm (4 in) of organic mulch, decorative bark chips, gravel or soil to protect it from the destructive effects of sunlight. Aesthetically pleasing and long-lasting when properly installed, landscape fabric may be your solution to weed control in flower beds and vegetable gardens.

PLANT DISEASES

BACTERIAL INFECTIONS

Wilts, foul-smelling stem and root rots, and leaf spots are characteristic symptoms of bacterial infections. Wet and warm conditions associated with the lowland tropics are favourable to the development of disease caused by bacteria. Good cultural practice and careful attention, especially during the rainy season, will reduce the chance of infection. Bacteria causing plant diseases produce enzymes that destroy the physical barriers to their passage within plant tissues. Infections can quickly overwhelm a susceptible host.

Controlling Bacterial Infections of potted plants

The general procedures are given below.
1 Isolate infected pot plants; withhold water; keep them dry and under cover.
2 Remove all infected tissue plus a generous portion of healthy plant using a sterile knife.
3 Destroy infected tissue by burning.
4 Treat the cut edges of the plant with a bactericidal powder such as Flowers of Sulphur.
5 Drench or spray the whole plant including the roots and soil with a bactericidal product, such as Natriphene (sodium phenyl phenate) according to manufacturer's instructions.

Bordeaux Mixture is another product that can be used to control bacterial and fungal diseases. Plant damage may occur when the mixture is applied at temperatures above 25°C (80°F).

FUNGAL DISEASES

Fungi are a group of living organisms without chlorophyll. They are generally filamentous, reproducing both by sexual and asexual means with spores. While certain fungi are parasites, infecting living organisms to obtain their food, the majority are capable of surviving on dead organic material. Mushrooms (Duppy Parasols) are the reproductive structures of certain species of fungi.

Diseases, caused by fungi, spread in water

Contributing factors:
    rainy season; stagnant air (foliage remains wet);
    crowded, unthrifty plants (low disease-resistance).

Look for these signs:
    moist rots, rapid withering of plant tops, shoots, and stems;
    fruit decay.

Control methods:
    destroy diseased material by burning;
    isolate infected pot plants and withhold water;
    improve air movement amongst plants by altering garden design;
    remove unthrifty, susceptible plants from the garden;
    keep susceptible pot plants (cactus, succulents, certain orchids) under cover during the rainy season;
    use a fungicide when appropriate.

White Rusts and Downy Mildews are destructive plant parasites with motile spores that move from infected to uninfected plants through water splashes or by swimming in thin water films on the plant surface.

Damping-off disease of seedlings, caused by *Pythium debaryanum*, is encouraged by wet soil, poor sanitation, inadequate air circulation, high humidity and thick mats of competing seedlings. Seedlings may even be killed before they emerge from the soil, leading one to believe that they have planted poor seed.

Pythium palmivorum may attack Coconut Palm *Cocos*. The earliest sign of disease is one of the recently expanded leaves turning white. Withering follows. As other leaves are attacked in turn, the whole top withers and falls off.

Careful removal and burning of infected plant material at an early stage in the infestation is an effective means of controlling the spread of this destructive disease.

Downy Mildews may cause damage to susceptible Cucumbers, Melons *Cucumis* and Squash *Cucurbita* although disease-tolerant Cucumber and Melon cultivars are now commercially available. Eddoes and other edible forms of *Colocasia esculenta* may be injured by Downy Mildew *Peronospora trichotoma*. The disease attacks the tubers after they are lifted. Tubers should be thoroughly dried before storage. Only sound tubers should be used for propagation. Land that has produced a diseased crop should not be planted with *Colocasia* again for two or three years.

Black Rot of *Cattleya* orchids and their relatives is caused by *Phytophthora cattleyae*. Other *Phytophthora* species produce smelly Black Rot of Palms, Root Rot of Avocado *Persea* and of Stapeliads. When weather or cultural conditions are favourable and spores are present, these fungi can destroy a prized collection of Orchids, Cactus or Succulents in a matter of hours. Special care must be taken during the rainy season to shelter the plants from rain. After a hurricane, examine plants for damage and infection, immediately isolating and treating those infected.

Diseases, caused by fungi, spread by air-borne spores

The spores of some fungi are released into the air spreading disease from the original infected plants.

Contributing factors:
    diseased host plants in or near garden;
    foliage remaining wet for more than several hours;
    susceptible plant varieties.

Look for these signs:
  fungal tissue and spores evident on foliage and stems;
  spots, blotches or streaks of yellowed tissue;
  spore-bearing structures;
  defoliation.

Control methods:
  remove and burn all infected material;
  control weeds that could serve as alternate hosts;
  avoid susceptible cultivars;
  use a fungicide when appropriate.

Powdery Mildews may be recognized by white powdery fungal growth on leaves, stems and floral parts. Spores spread by air currents require high humidity for germination and infection.

Sooty Mold found on the surface of leaves and fruit, lives on the honeydew secretions of insects and is not at all parasitic. Controlling the insects producing the sugary secretion controls the fungus.

Rose Mildew *Sphaerotheca pannosa* develops on roses *Rosa* – the Multifloras are particularly susceptible. Leaves, young shoots and even flower buds may be covered with a fine white fungal net. Severely infected rose bushes will die. The best control measure is to plant only mildew-resistant varieties.

Rusts are parasitic fungi, often having two unrelated hosts for different stages of their life cycle. They can attack Rose *Rosa*, Snapdragon *Antirrhinum*, Canna Lily *Canna*, Orchids, and a wide variety of Grasses including Bamboo, for example *Dendrocalamus*. Rusts may be easily diagnosed by the numerous orange spots and streaks they produce on leaves of the host. These orange spots soon split releasing many tiny, dust-like, yellow or orange spores. Severe rust attacks are difficult to control.

MYCOPLASMA DISEASES

Mycoplasma organisms are microbes without cell walls. Over 100 plant diseases, including yellows and witches' broom, once believed to be caused by viruses, have been attributed to mycoplasmas. Sucking insects such as Leaf Hoppers and Aphids transmit these diseases. Bud or scion-grafting onto infected rootstock will also result in disease.

Coconut Lethal Yellowing disease is one example of the destructive nature of mycoplasmas. It has destroyed Coconut Palm *Cocos* in Cuba, some of the Cayman Islands, Jamaica, Florida and in West Africa. Over 20 other Palm species are susceptible. The symptoms and effects can be significantly suppressed by treatment with the tetracycline group of antibiotics followed by a systemic fungicide such as benomyl. Treatment results in a remission of symptoms, not in a cure. Coconut cultivar 'Malayan Dwarf' is highly resistant to Lethal Yellowing.

Bunchy Top of Papaya *Carica papaya* is a rare instance of mycoplasma successfully eliminated by surgery from the host plant. Removal of the bunchy top and a portion of the stem with a sterile knife leaves the plant free of disease. Disease-carrying Leaf Hoppers *Empoasca papayae* must be prevented access if the plant is to remain disease-free. Home gardeners can use cheesecloth or similar screens to save superior fruiting plants.

VIRUS DISEASES

Viruses are major plant parasites, producing symptoms such as flecking and streaking of foliage and flowers and failure to thrive. Viruses can be transmitted by insects, mites, fungi, nematodes, and even by the gardener working amongst the plants. Some viruses, such as Tobacco Mosaic Virus, are carried on the surface of seeds whilst others are transmitted within the seed embryo. Cymbidium Mosaic Virus is spread by the orchid grower on tools, pots and potting materials contaminated with infected plant juices.

Tests have been developed for the detection and identification of plant viruses. Heat therapy and/or meristem tip culture are methods used to obtain virus-free stock. Virus-free plantlets grown in test tubes of sterile culture media present a safe and convenient means for the importation of planting material, and at the same time complying with stringent quarantine measures. The procedure for removing such virus-free orchids from sterile culture flasks is described on page 42.

Strategies to Control Viral Infections in Your Garden

1 Plant only virus-free seeds and plants.
2 Eliminate weed plants that might be reservoirs of virus infection.
3 Control pests, see later, (for example Leaf Hoppers and Aphids) that could transmit viruses.
4 Sterilize secateurs, knives, cutlasses and other tools before working with another plant. Immerse tools in a 10% solution of chlorine bleach or trisodium phosphate for 10 minutes before cutting another plant. Prepare fresh solution daily or whenever the original becomes discoloured.
5 Disinfect seeds before sowing in a solution of 10% liquid bleach for 10 minutes. Rinse the seeds with fresh water and sow in sterilized soil or soilless mix.
6 Remove and burn any plants showing symptoms suspicious of virus infection.

PESTS

INSECTS

Many insects feed on plants although there is a great variation in the extent to which different plants are attacked by insects. Certain cultivated plants such as ferns are affected by only a few pests whereas other plants such as Cacao *Theobroma cacao* can be host to numerous different insects feeding on the leaves, stems and fruits. Some insects may feed on only one plant species whereas others such as locusts feed on many different unrelated plants. Scouting the garden for insect damage gives advance warning but you have to know what to look for and what are the most appropriate control measures. An integrated approach to pest management, by using more than one method, is the most successful.

Leaf eaters

Damage done by leaf-eating insects is largely proportional to their size and numbers. Leaf eaters have biting and chewing mouthparts and are found mainly among the Grasshoppers and Locusts, adult Beetles and their larvae, as well as the caterpillar larvae of Moths and Butterflies. The types of damage done to a leaf often gives a clue as to the perpetrator. Chewing insects can be controlled by hand-picking and stomach poisons.

Bachac or Parasol Ants *Acromyrmex octospinosus* and *Atta cephalotes* of Trinidad, can devastate a *Hibiscus* bush or chop a wide path through garden beds in a few hours. The pieces of leaves and flowers gathered so industriously and destructively are not intended as parasols but are gathered solely for the purpose of making a compost heap on which is grown a fungus used by the ants as food. You must follow the ants, find and destroy the nest.

Gardening in the Caribbean

Flea Beetles *Epitrix* can produce very small, scattered, round holes feeding on the leaves of Eggplant *Solanum melogena*, Cabbage *Brassica* and Tomato *Lycopersicon*; shredded leaf margins may result from Grasshopper and Locust attack. Examine damaged leaves, looking carefully at their undersurface as well as along the petiole and stem. Some insects mimic plant parts. Hold a sheet of paper beneath the leaves as you examine them in which to catch any insects that may drop.

Leaf rollers

Certain caterpillars construct for themselves a retreat of a rolled leaf edge. The Arrowroot Leaf Roller *Calpodes*, which also attacks the Canna Lily *Canna*, is one such pest. The very first work done by the tiny leaf-rolling caterpillar after hatching from the egg is to eat two parallel cuts at right angles to the edge of the leaf. The resulting flap is pulled over its body and attached to the leaf surface. As the caterpillar grows, a larger flap is cut and rolled. Canna Lily leaves suffer considerable damage, particularly if many caterpillars are present.

Leaf-miners

Leaf-mining insects feed on leaf tissue between the upper and lower epidermis. Holding a suspicious leaf up to the sun will reveal the insects feeding within. The majority of leaf miners are the larvae of Moths and Flies: mines can be serpentine or restricted to a single blotch. Beet, chard and spinach *Beta* spp. leaves are often subject to severe miner attacks rendering the leaves inedible. Leaf miners are difficult to control, protected as they are within a leaf. Systemic insecticides may be used on certain ornamentals.

Sucking insects

The (true) Bugs (Hemiptera) and their allies, the Leafhoppers, Aphids, Mealy Bugs and Scale Insects are all sucking insects. Many produce toxic saliva, resulting in serious leaf damage, defoliation and even loss of flower buds. Sucking insects have been implicated in the transmission of virus and mycoplasma diseases such as Aster Yellows and Papaya Bunchy Top. Aphids, Mealy Bugs, Scale Insects and White Fly excrete a sugary solution (honeydew), an attractive food for ants. Infested *Citrus*, *Hibiscus*, and *Ixora* become unsightly because black Sooty Mold fungi flourish on the honeydew-drenched leaves. Sucking insects can be controlled by natural predators or systemic insecticides that poison the plant juices.

Leaf and Flower Raspers (Thrips)

Gladiolus and orchid flowers are a favourite food of Thrips. The epidermis is scraped from the petal or leaf surface, resulting in a mottled silvery appearance. Severe attack by Thrips often indicates that the infested plant is otherwise stressed, by drought, too much water at the roots, or inadequate shade for a shade-loving species. Thrips can be controlled with contact poisons.

Seed damage

Insects can damage seeds both during their formation as well as afterwards during storage. Many leguminous crops such as Pigeon Pea *Cajanus cajan* and beans, for example *Phaseolus*, are subject to attack by the weevil-like Bruchid larvae. Harvested seeds may not show outward signs of infestation. Gardeners should keep seeds cool, dry, and stored separately in sealed containers, examining them at intervals for signs of infestation.

Stem borers

Found in the stems of herbaceous and woody plants, stem borers are mostly larvae of Beetles and Moths. Various Weevils, for example *Stethobaris* attack orchids such as *Dendrobium* and *Schomburgkia*. Larvae of Goat Moth *Cossus cossus* can attack *Cassia*, causing such damage as the tree will die from their extensive borings. Wood-boring beetle larvae attack trees. Often the only sign of attack will be the presence of the insect faeces (frass) at the bore hole. Digging the larvae from the trunk using a penknife is one way of controlling a few borers.

Lawn damage

Lawns are subject to damage by insects which include Chinch Bugs *Blissus* that suck juices from succulent stems and roots, and White Grubs, larvae of various beetles, that chew the roots. In both instances, unsightly bare or brown patches appear in lawns. The dead and dying grass can be easily pulled up.

MITES

Tiny, eight-legged cousins of Spiders, Mites can cause severe leaf damage when their population suddenly expands. Mites damage *Citrus*, *Hibiscus*, Croton *Codiaeum*, Orchids, Palms and a variety of other ornamental and crop plants. Look for Mites on the undersurface of leaves. Use a magnifying glass! Finely speckled foliage may be your first clue that an infestation is underway. Mite infestations are most frequent during hot, dry weather when plants are stressed. More than four Mites per leaf indicates the need for spraying with an acaricide. Dicofol provides rapid control of the most common mite species. Mite predators such as *Phytoseiulus persimilis*, are also used with success.

SLUGS AND SNAILS

Slugs are basically snails without shells. Beige, grey, black or brown, they range in size from babies of a few millimeters (0.5 in) to giants of 10 cm (4 in) or more in length. They reproduce by eggs. While juveniles will feed mostly on decaying vegetation, the adults rasp leaves, stems and flowers, leaving a tell-tale slime trail from their hideout to the plant then back again. The more moist and humid the garden, the more active the slugs. One giant slug can devour all the orchid buds in one night; several giant slugs can defoliate a Bougainvillea plant overnight. The key word is 'night'. Slugs hide during the day, when they are at greater risk of dessication. Slugs breathe through their moist skin: if the skin dries they suffocate.

In a small garden, patio or lath house, the slug population can be kept in check by keeping hiding places to minimum, removing rotting vegetation, fallen leaves and organic debris, and by hand-picking and killing any slugs found in the area. You can even provide place for them to hide then raid them during the day, killing any slugs found there. Slug-killing pesticides such as metaldehyde can be used as pellet baits, impregnated tapes or as sprays to control large infestations, however, there is no substitute for good garden hygiene.

Snails range in size from tiny brown Bush Snails to larger, striped individuals. Snails feed on a variety of plant material and are controlled like slugs.

NEMATODES

Plant-parasitic nematodes are tiny, thread-like worms that feed mostly on roots. Plants attacked by root nematodes become stunted, produce fewer flowers, and may be more prone to wilting; damaged roots lose function and die. Nematodes inhabiting the soil surrounding roots have been implicated in virus transmission.

Nematodes can be controlled by the use of chemical nematicides applied to the soil in either liquid or fumigant formulations. A novel and less ecologically disruptive method uses solar radiation to raise soil temperature to partially sterilizing levels. Developed in Israel, the technique called soil solarization, is based on covering very moist soil with clear poly-ethylene (plastic) sheeting for one month or more. The soil must be thoroughly wetted, the plastic must be transparent, without holes and firmly held in place around the edges with soil or sod. The garden bed also must be exposed to full sunlight. Sunlight will heat the soil to approximately 40°C (104°F), effectively suppressing nematode infestation. This technique is to be recommended for pre-treatment of flower and vegetable beds where nematode infestation has been a problem. Inter-planting with Marigold *Tagetes* may also prove useful.

Root knot and cyst nematodes live within roots. Nematode-tolerant cultivars of Tomato *Lycopersicon*, Sweet Potato *Ipomoea batatas* and other garden plants can be selectively planted to improve productivity. The Sweet Potato cultivar 'Nemagold' produces repellant root exudates that reduce contact with nematode larvae. The hybrid Tomato cultivars, 'Ultra Girl', 'Ultra Boy', and 'Red Star' are known to be nematode-tolerant.

Leaf-burrowing nematodes can occasionally be a problem with *Begonia* and other ornamental plants. The small brown water-soaked spots and discoloured veins resulting from infestation can easily be confused with symptom caused by bacterial or fungal infection. Nematodes swim in water films on the plant surface and enter leaves via leaf pores. Diagnostic assistance should be available from your local Department of Agriculture.

LARGE ANIMALS

Crabs

Various species of Land Crab can be destructive in a garden. They may chop down plants, damage foliage and fruits, as well as being a general nuisance with their burrows. They will generally be more active during the rainy sea-son and will be more of a problem if the garden is located near a wet forested area. It is important to know that crabs are important scavengers and decomposers. Their droppings and their burrowing improves the soil. In spite of the fact that crabs are beneficial, large populations have no place in a cultivated garden. They can be trapped at night when they leave their burrows to feed. Alternatively, a poison bait can be put in the burrows and the hole covered with earth. Baiting may have to be repeated several times to achieve control.

Birds

During the dry season when food is scarce, birds may become pests, feeding on flowers, fruit and vegetables. Some species will gather the 'hair' from certain cactus such as *Cephalocereus* to line their nests. Screening affected plants, enclosing a lath house with netting, or moving the plants to a more protected location are appropriate strategies for what is basically a seasonal problem.

Monkeys

Monkeys can be very destructive of fruit and vegetables. Not content with eating one mango or tangerine, they will pick, bite and throw away many fruits, ruining the crop. There may be a Control Program in force in your region.

PESTICIDES AND ALTERNATIVES

Chemicals used to control pests and diseases (also known as insecticides, acaricides, fungicides etc.) have two different modes of action.

See also Appendix 4 Some pesticides and their use, and Appendix 5 Garden Safety.

Contact pesticides kill when they come in contact with pests. Their protective effect may be either short-lived or up to several weeks dependent upon the particular chemical and the weather. Contact pesticides can be applied as a fine spray or dust in order to achieve total plant coverage.

Systemic pesticides are toxic to pests on contact but are also absorbed by the plant and give protection for several weeks after treatment. Once absorbed they cannot be washed off. Systemic pesticides are applied as a coarse spray or as a dip. Runoff will enter the soil surrounding the plants and be absorbed by plant roots.

PESTICIDE RESISTANCE

Occasionally you will experience poor control of an insect or disease-causing organism. Of course, the pesticide could have become inactive due to improper storage, or you may have made the solution too dilute, or applied it incorrectly. Before you leap to rectify the situation with another application (stronger this time!) be aware that pesticide resistance can occur after continuous use of the same chemical, especially if that chemical has a very specific mechanism of action. Pesticides should not be used repeatedly without assessing the effects of their application. Development of pesticide-resistant populations can be delayed or even prevented by alternating pesticides of different chemical groups (Appendix 4).

Chemical pesticide alternatives

All of the following products or substances are insecticides: they kill insects.

BACILLUS THURINGIENSIS – THURICIDE

A preparation of spores of the insect disease-causing *Bacillus*, this bacterial product is toxic to leaf-chewing caterpillars of Butterflies and Moths. Research workers aim to produce genetically engineered pest-resistant cultivars before the end of the twentieth century.

DIATOMACEOUS EARTH

The sharp-edged, silicaceous diatom skeletons contained in this material are able to pass between folds on the insect body, rupturing the body wall, causing dehydration and death. As it kills all insects, it should be used only directly on infestations and not scattered about randomly.

SOAP, INSECTICIDAL SOAP AND DETERGENT

Various formulations have been recommended for natural control of plant pests. A dish-washing liquid detergent (1.0–1.5 per cent solution in tepid water) can be sprayed or used as a dip to kill soft-bodied Aphids, Spider Mites, and Mealy Bugs. Do not apply if natural predators are present otherwise these may be killed also. Some ornamental plants are particularly sensitive to the soapy spray. Rinse plants several minutes after treatment with plain water.

ROTENONE DUST AND SPRAY

A botanical insecticide, rotenone is derived from the South American *Derris* plant. It can be used safely on leafy vegetables to control chewing insects such as caterpillars and beetles. Roots of the *Derris* plant are used by indigenous peoples to kill fish. This insecticide is lethal to fish! Do not use it near pools containing fish!

STICKY PREPARATIONS, STRIPS AND TRAPS

Entomologists have discovered that flying insects, including winged Aphids, Leaf Hoppers, Whiteflies and Leaf Miners, are attracted to the colour yellow. Yellow strips covered with a sticky substance (for example the commercial product Sticky Strips) trap insects that alight on them. Sticky Strips are recommended as an highly effective way to trap insects, indoors and out. Other traps include those baited with insect-attractant hormones. Traps are used mostly for agricultural purposes or on large estates.

BENEFICIAL INSECTS

Learn to recognize the beneficial insects in your garden that are predators, parasites and natural enemies of insect pests. These are your friends.

LADYBIRD BEETLES

The bright orange or scarlet beetles are often found amongst groups of Aphids, Mealy Bugs or Scale Insects. Adults can consume 50 to 100 pests a day.

BRACHONID AND CHALCID WASPS

These tiny parasitic wasps, for example *Trichogramma minutum*, lay their eggs in their host caterpillar, cutworm or insect egg. They do not sting people! The wasps can be attracted to a 'predator patch' of suitable nectar-producing flowers including small daisies, Dillweed *Anethum*, Coriander *Coriandrum* and Anise *Pimpinella*.

SYRPHID (HOVER) FLIES

Hoverflies are strongly attracted to groups of Aphids. Their predatory slug-like larvae feed voraciously on the aphid pests. Hoverflies can also be attracted to your garden if you provide 'predator patches'.

LACEWING FLIES AND THEIR LARVAE

Lacewing larvae are excellent predators feeding on a variety of pests including Aphids, Red Spider Mites, Mealy Bugs, Thrips and insect eggs.

PRAYING MANTIS

Praying mantids are named from their 'praying' attitude while waiting to catch and feed on Grasshoppers, Leaf Hoppers, Crickets and various beetles. Egg cases can be placed in gardens to increase the predator population.

RESPONSIBLE MANAGEMENT OF PLANT COMPETITORS

STRATEGIES FOR PEST AND DISEASE MANAGEMENT

The sequence of steps for effective control is:
1 identify the pest or disease;
2 identify any factor(s) that contributed to the outbreak;
3 determine the most effective immediate solution to the problem; and
4 develop a strategy to avoid similar problems in the future.

COMPANION PLANTING

Companion plants can affect microclimate; vary air movement and humidity about their neighbours; warn, by being attacked first, that there are plant enemies about; and they may even control plant pests.

Common Garden Marigold *Tagetes* produces a root secretion that suppresses egg-laying by plant parasitic nematodes. As the effective range is about 90 cm (35 in) about each marigold, they should be planted throughout the garden for optimal effect. Marigold foliage has also been shown to be deterrent to Mexican Bean Beetles.

Annual Nasturtium *Tropaeolum* plants are companion to Radish *Raphanus*, Cabbage *Brassica*, Cucumber and Melon *Cucumis*. Nasturtiums are reputed to deter Wooly Aphids and Squash Beetles.

Careful observation of companionships that work has led to significant discoveries. Pests feeding on a companion plant may be deterred from feeding further. Any discoveries that you make concerning effective companionships should be shared with your gardening community.

THE INTEGRATED APPROACH

Attitudes toward pest management have changed markedly since the 1960s. Now there is a greater awareness of the delicate ecological balance that exists in a garden, and the ability of natural predators and parasites to regulate populations of pests.

Many insects feed on dead, decaying or damaged plant material. From minute Springtails to the gigantic larvae of the Rhinoceros Beetle, scavengers play a very important role in an healthy garden, a role that cannot be ignored. Adult Ladybird Beetles and their larvae voraciously consume numerous harmful insect pests. Unfortunately all these beneficial insects can fall victim to pesticides as easily as the target organism.

Free-living fungi and bacteria are important components of the composting process. Both disease-causing fungi and beneficial micro-organisms can be destroyed with fungicidal and bactericidal sprays. Mycorrhizal fungi, necessary to their host plants for optimum absorption of mineral nutrients, have been shown to affected by systemic fungicides.

Some controversy may exist as to when a natural control measure is most appropriate. If any population of plant competitors becomes overwhelming, an integrated approach combining both natural and chemical means of control may be more successful.

Appendices 1–6

APPENDIX 1   pH of soils found in some Caribbean Islands

Island or group	pH range
Antigua	alkaline
Aruba	alkaline
Bahamas	alkaline
Barbados	alkaline
Bermuda	alkaline
British Virgin Islands	alkaline/mixed
Carriacou	mixed
Cayman Islands	alkaline
Cuba	mixed
Curacao	alkaline
Dominica	acidic
Dominican Republic	mixed
Grenada	acidic
Guadeloupe, Basse Terre	acidic
Guadeloupe, Grande Terre	alkaline
Haiti	mixed
Jamaica	mixed
Martinique	acidic
Montserrat	acidic
Puerto Rico	mixed
Saba	alkaline
St. Lucia	acidic
St. Vincent	acidic
Tobago	mixed
Trinidad	mixed
U.S. Virgin Islands	mixed

APPENDIX 2   Availability of plant nutrients according to soil pH

Plant nutrient	Availability with soil pH
Nitrogen	Available over normal range. Decreased availability below pH 6.0 and above pH 8.0
Phosphorus	Optimum availability between pH 6.5 and 7.5. Sharply diminished availability below pH 6.3 and above pH 7.5
Potassium, Sulphur	Available
Calcium, Magnesium	Decreased availability below pH 6.5
Iron	Decreased availability above pH 6.0
Manganese	Decreased availability above pH 6.5
Boron, Copper, Zinc	Decreasing availability below pH 7.0

APPENDIX 3 Germination guide for ornamental foliage and flowering plants

Name	Method[a]	Time	Light or dark conditions[b]
Achimenes	I	14 days	
African Violet *Saintpaulia*	I	21 days	light
Aloe	II	28 days	
Alyssum *Lobularia*	I	3 days	light
Amaranthus	II	10 days	
Asparagus	III	30 days	
Bachelor's Buttons *Gomphrena*	II	15 days	dark
Balsam *Impatiens balsamifera*	II	8 days	
Barbados Pride *Caesalpinia*	III	30–60 days	
Bauhinia	III	30 days	
Begonia	I	15–30 days	light
Bromeliads	II	28 days	
Cactus	Cactus	14 days	
Canna	III	variable	
Celosia	II	5 days	
Cleome[c]	II	10 days	
Clitoria	III	21 days	
Coleus	I	7 days	light
Cosmos	II	14 days	
Crossandra	I	30 days	light
Croton *Codiaeum*	Croton	14–21 days	
Cuphea	I	7 days	light
Dahlia	II	7 days	
Datura	II	14 days	
Desert Rose *Adenium*	I	14 days	light
Dracaena	I	50 days	light
Eucalyptus	II	21 days	
Euphorbia	II	21 days	
Ferns (spores)	Ferns	3–6 months	
Ficus	I	1–3 months	light
Flamboyant *Delonix*	III	1–3 months	
Forget-me-not *Myosotis*[d]	II	10 days	dark
Four O'Clock *Mirabilis*	II	5 days	
Gerbera	I	28 days	light
Gingers (e.g. *Hedychium*)	II	28 days	
Helichrysum	I	14 days	light
Heliconia	Heliconia	6 months	
Hibiscus[e]	III	15–30 days	dark
Ipomoea see Morning Glory			
Kalanchoe	I	10 days	light
Lotus *Nelumbo*	Water Plants	25 days	
Marigold *Tagetes*	II	5 days	
Moon Vine *Calonyction*[f]	III	7 days	
Morning Glory *Convolvulus*[f]	III	5 days	

Gardening in the Caribbean

Name	Method[a]	Time	Light or dark conditions[b]
Orchids	Orchids	21 days	
Ornamental Banana *Musa*[g]	III	21 days	
Palms	Palms	1–6 months	
Papaw *Carica*	III	1–2 months	
Passion Flower *Passiflora*	II	28 days	
Patience Plant *Impatiens wallerana*	I	14 days	light
Pentas	I	21 days	light
Periwinkle *Catharanthus*	II	14 days	dark
Petunia	I	10 days	light
Philodendron	II	28 days	
Plumbago	II	21 days	
Portulaca	I	10 days	light
Queen of Flowers *Lagerstroemia*	II	14 days	
Snapdragon *Antirrhinum*	I	10 days	light
Stephanotis	II	1–2 months	
Thunbergia	II	21 days	
Tithonia	II	10 days	dark
Torenia	II	14 days	
Water-lily *Nymphaea*	Water Plants	7–21 days	
Water Platter *Victoria*	Water Plants	7–21 days	
Wild Sage *Lantana*	III	30–90 days	
Zinnia	II	5 days	

[a] Methods I, II, III and those specified for Cactus, Croton, Ferns, Heliconia, Orchids, Palms and Water Plants are described in Chapter 2.

[b] Some plants require either the presence of light or darkness to germinate.

[c] Pre-chill seed 4°C for 5 days before sowing.

[d] Germinates best between 15°C and 20°C.

[e] Germinate in complete darkness with soil temperature varying between 12°C and 25°C.

[f] Nick seed coat with file and soak for 3 or 4 days before sowing. Change water daily. Sow seeds as soon as they swell.

[g] Clean seed and soak 48 hours before sowing.

APPENDIX 4   Some pesticides and their use

Pesticide group	Common name	Use
Acaricide/Miticide		
Organochlorine	dicofol	Effective against Spider Mites. Apply as spray or dip.
Fungicides		
Aromatic hydrocarbon	quintozene	Effective against *Rhizoctonia* and certain soil-borne diseases especially of *Gerbera* and *Chrysanthemum*. Apply to soil or as a dip.
Benzimidazole	benomyl	Systemic. Effective against a wide range of fungal diseases. Resistance may occur. Apply as spray or dip.
Dinitrophenol	dinocap	Effective against Powdery Mildews and also against some Spider Mites. Usually only available in a multi-purpose mixture. Apply as a spray or dust at 5 to 10 day intervals or as directed by manufacturer.
Phthalamide	captan, folpet	Effective against many Leaf Spot fungi. Apply as dust or spray at 7 to 10 day intervals.
Thiadiazole	etridiazole	Used to control soil-borne diseases especially Damping-off. Apply to or incorporate into soil.
Insecticides		
Carbamate	carbaryl	Effective against chewing insects. Toxic to honey-bees. Apply spray or dust when pests are noticed.
Organochlorine	gamma-HCH, lindane	Effective against insects on contact. Resistant pests exist. Persists in soil. Apply as spray.
Organophosphorus	diazinon	Effective against a wide range of insects including Aphids, Scale, Cutworms and root maggots. Apply as spray or granules.
	dichlorvos	Fumigant. Toxic. Resistance known. Use as pesticide-impregnated strip or as a smoke.
	malathion	Effective against a wide variety of pests including Mites. Some resistance. Some plant damage may occur. Apply as spray at 7 to 14 days intervals.
Synthetic pyrethroid	permethrin	Effective against a wide number of pests. Acts on contact and following ingestion. Apply as a spray.

APPENDIX 5   Garden safety

Gardening is a pleasant endeavour provided that common sense prevails and attention is paid to the potential hazards that exist. A little planning and forethought can save a gardener much grief.

Power tools

1 Read the operator's manual before starting work.
2 Cool petrol-powered engines before refuelling.
3 Turn off engines before adjusting blades or removing jammed objects.
4 Ground protect electric-powered tools; clip flex out of way of moving parts.
5 Never operate any mower barefoot.

POISONOUS popular garden plants

1 Poinsettia *Euphorbia pulcherimma*, *Euphorbia* spp., Frangipani *Plumeria* spp. and Manchineel *Hippomane mancinella* (irritating sap)
Wear protective eyewear when pruning: latex can spurt or drip from cut surfaces.

2 Fishtail Palm *Caryota mitis* (stinging crystals on fruits)
Wear protective gloves for working with any plant material and wash the hands afterwards. Warn children not to touch these plants.

3 Datura *Datura*, Dumb Cane *Dieffenbachia* and Oleander *Nerium* (toxic substances)
Do not eat or even put to the mouth.

Absence of a particular plant from this list does not imply that it is non-toxic.

Biting and stinging creatures

1 Venomous snakes: infrequent visitors in tropical gardens
2 Large centipedes: common, frequently encountered in fernery; painful bite
3 Wasps (Jack Spaniards): launch vicious attack when disturbed; be alert for nests before starting to trim or prune shrubs
4 Stinging Ants: common in lawns, especially while mowing

Wear shoes and gloves. Pay attention to where the hands and feet are to be placed while clearing bush and plant debris, working in the shrubbery, hedges and tall grass, and moving potted plants. Apply insect repellant to socks and ankles.

Pesticide precautions

Consider all pesticides as POISONOUS chemicals able to harm people, pets, fish and other friendly plants and animals.

1 Read the label before opening a pesticide container. Follow all the instructions and precautions. If uncertain, ask for assistance.
2 Avoid applying sprays or dusts on windy days.
3 Never smoke, eat or drink while handling or applying pesticides.
4 Always wear waterproof rubber gloves to handle liquid or granular pesticides, spray equipment and when preparing sprays.
5 Avoid inhaling pesticide dusts and sprays. Wear a mask when applying dusts.
6 Avoid spilling pesticides on the skin or clothing. Remove contaminated clothing and immediately wash affected skin with soap and plenty of clean water.
7 Avoid contamination of wells, ponds, pools, streams and rivers with pesticides.
8 Know the symptoms of pesticide poisoning. These include weakness, salivation, incoordination, tremors, and blurred vision. If you experience any of these symptoms using pesticides, find medical help immediately. The Medical Unit will want to know the name of the pesticide recently used.
9 Always store pesticides tightly closed in their original containers and in a secure building. In flood-prone areas, store pesticides above the likely highwater mark. Do not dispose of leftover spray in streams, ponds or in the sea.
10 Keep pesticides out of reach of children.

APPENDIX 6 Useful addresses

American Hibiscus Society
1615–24th Ave N
St. Petersburg, Florida 33713–4455
U.S.A.

American Orchid Society, Inc.
6000 South Olive Avenue
West Palm Beach, Florida 33405–4159
U.S.A.

Bromeliad Society, Inc.
P. O. Box 3279
Santa Monica, California 90049
U.S.A.

Heliconia Society International
c/o Flamingo Gardens
3750 Flamingo Road
Fort Lauderdale, Florida 33330
U.S.A.

International Aroid Society, Inc.
P.O. Box 43–1853
Miami, Florida 33143
U.S.A.

Lilypons Water Gardens
P.O. Box 10
Lilypons, Maryland 21717–0010
U.S.A.

Palm & Cycad Societies of Australia
P.O. Box 1134, Milton
Qld. 4064
Australia

The Cryptanthus Society
3629 Bordeaux Court
Arlington, Texas 76016–2809
U.S.A.

The International Palm Society, Inc.
P.O. Box 368
Laurence, Kansas 66044
U.S.A.

The Royal Horticultural Society
80 Vincent Square
London SW1P 2PE
England

Glossary

Adventitious Roots arising from places other than the base of the plant, as in *Philodendron*.

Areole Referring to the specialized nodes of cactus stems that can give rise to spines, glochids, hairs, branches and flowers.

Air layering (marcotting) Method of plant propagation: a wounded stem is induced to produce roots by wrapping it with damp moss and a plastic sheet cover.

Alkaline Soil or another substance with a pH greater than 7.0.

Annual Plant that grows from a seed to maturity, flowers, produces seeds, then dies, all in one growing season.

Anther Pollen-producing male structure of a flower.

Aphids Sucking insect pests; also called greenfly, black fly or plant lice.

Apical The uppermost and principal bud or shoot. This bud or shoot is said to have apical dominance.

Axil The space found between the main stem and a leaf or branch. Buds that arise in the axil are called axillary buds.

Bagasse The remnant fibre produced after crushing and grinding cut sugar cane stems. Bagasse must be composted for several months before use as a mulch.

Balanced fertilizer A fertilizer that contains all the major plant nutrients (nitrogen, phosphorus and potassium) and all of the minor nutrients.

Botanical name A plant has two names by International Convention, the genus and the species. Both names are italicized. Occasionally, a plant has a third italicized varietal name, indicating a distinct form which occurs naturally in the wild.

Bract Leaf-like structure associated with the protection of a shoot or a flower bud. Occasionally the bract becomes enlarged and brightly coloured as in Poinsettia *Euphorbia pulcherrima* or *Bougainvillea*.

Budding (bud grafting) Process of grafting the bud of a desirable plant onto the rootstock of another compatible plant.

Bud wood Propagation material with a single bud.

Bulbil Swollen offset produced in an inflorescence, as in Red Ginger *Alpinia purpurata*.

Calyx Whorl of separate or fused leaf-like structures found outermost in a flower. The calyx is sometimes colourful and persistent, as in *Petrea*.

Cambium Generative layer of tissue found within the stem and root that gives rise to conductive tissue (xylem and phloem) and growth in girth.

Capsule Seed container of certain plants including orchids.

Cephalium Specialized flower-bearing structure of certain cactus such as *Melocactus*.

Chelated iron and trace elements (sequestered iron) Product where iron and other reactive minerals are chemically bound remaining soluble and available to plants.

Chlorosis Development of pale yellow-green foliage, often caused by mineral deficiency or unavailability. The most common cause is alkaline soil.

Clone Individual plant that can be reproduced only by vegetative means.

Coconut cloth The fibrous remnant of Coconut Palm leaf bases resembling jute or hemp canvas (burlap cloth).

Compost To recycle and decompose organic matter. Material prepared by composting is referred to as compost.

Conifer Cone-producing plant.

Costapalmate Refers to palm leaves in which the petiole extends across the leaf as a major rib.

Crotch Juncture between a main stem or trunk and a branch.

Crownstalk Top of a palm trunk, often glossy green, formed by the clustered leaf bases wherein lies the growing point.

Crozier Coiled immature fern leaf resembling the staff of a Christian bishop.

Cultivar Cultivated plant variety selected for superior foliage, flowers or fruit. Cultivars are reproduced by cuttings, grafts, marcots or by tissue culture.

Damping-off Seedlings may be damaged or killed by various fungi that attack the stems at soil level.

Deciduous Plant that drops its leaves in response to changing seasons, drought or stress.

Deficiency Mineral nutrient deficiency caused by absence or unavailability of one or more substances.

Dehiscence The opening or splitting of a mature fruit to release seeds.

Dessicant Substance such as silica gel that absorbs atmospheric moisture. Silica gel can be dried in a warm oven or solar sterilizer for reuse.

Dioecious Having the male (pollen-producing) flowers and female (seed-producing) flowers on separate plants.

Distichous Characteristic arrangement of tightly overlapping leaves or floral bracts.

Division Propagation method whereby a plant is divided into two or more rooted parts.

Dormancy Certain trees, shrubs and herbs periodically cease active growth and sometimes also drop their leaves. The dormant period often coincides with a dry season.

Drip line (canopy line) Outside edge of a tree where rain drips from the canopy.

Endemic Plants unique to a particular region or island, not exotic or introduced.

Epiphyte Plant that lives rooted on the bark of trees and not rooted in soil.

Equitant Fan-shaped leaf arrangement of certain orchids, as in *Oncidium pulchellum*.

Fernery Shade or lath house where ferns are cultivated.

Fertilizer Source of plant mineral nutrients that may be added to soil to correct possible deficiencies.

Foliar feeding The application of dilute fertilizer solutions to leaf surfaces for absorption into the plant.

Fungicide Product used to control plant disease caused by fungi (sing. fungus).

Genus Group of closely related species. The generic name is the first of the two botanical names; always it is given a capital initial letter.

Germination Process by which a seed becomes a plantlet.

Glaucous Granular wax reflective covering of leaves causing them to appear whitish or bluish.

Glochid Barbed spine of *Opuntia* cactus.

Grafting Method of propagation: a piece of the desirable plant (scion) is united with a more vigorous rootstock.

Hardwood cutting Piece of stem with developed bark.

Herbicide Product used to kill weeds.

Hermaphrodite Flower having both male (pollen-producing) and female (seed-producing) structures.

Hormone rooting powder (*see* rooting hormone)

Host plant Plant that is attacked and weakened by fungi, bacteria or viruses.

Hybrid Cross between two species in an attempt to obtain an improved plant.

Infestation Condition when attacked by numerous pests.

Inflorescence Stem of flowers.

Juvenile state Immature plant not yet capable of reproduction.

Keiki Offsets produced by orchids; Hawaiian word for 'baby'.

Latex Milky white or coloured liquid product of certain plants such as *Euphorbia* and rubber *Hevea*.

Leaching   Action of water or rain to dissolve soil minerals and carry them away.

Loam   Soil consisting of sand, clay and organic matter in ideal proportions.

Marcot (air layer)   Procedure by which roots are induced to form along a stem without removing it from the parent plant.

Micronutrient   Plant nutrients such as magnesium, manganese and zinc that are required in small quantities for plant growth and development.

Mites (Spider Mites)   Tiny plant pests, related to Spiders, that attack leaves and suck plant juices.

Monocarpic   Refers to plants that live for many years to reach sexual maturity, then flower only once and die, as in Talipot Palm *Corypha umbraculifera*.

Monoecious   Having separate male (pollen-producing) flowers and female (seed-producing) flowers on the same plant.

Monopodial   Orchid plants having one perennial growing point, as in *Vanda*.

Mulch   Layer of organic matter, partially or fully composted, that is applied to soil to protect the surface from erosion, to conserve moisture and to reduce weed infestation.

Nectary   Nectar-producing area of a flower.

Nematicide   Product used to kill nematodes.

Nematode (eelworm)   Microscopic worm that attacks plant roots.

Node   Point along a stem where buds, shoots and flowers originate.

Nutrient   Substance used by a plant to grow.

Offset (offshoot)   Shoot arising from the base of a plant or occasionally from a stem (as in orchids), or from an inflorescence (*Alpinia purpurata*). *See also* keiki.

Palmate   Leaf that has several veins arising from a central point, resembling the human palm.

Parasite   Plant or animal that is dependent upon another living organism for nourishment, such as Dodder *Cuscuta*.

Pathogen   Organism that causes disease, for example bacteria and virus.

Perennial   Plant that once mature, maintains a yearly reproductive cycle.

Perlite   White, porous pumice that can be used as a soil substitute or in combination with other materials to make a rooting medium.

Pesticide   Product used to kill insects. The term may also be used for products used to kill slugs, other non-insect pests, weeds and organisms causing plant diseases.

Petiole   Part of a leaf that extends from the flattened blade to the stem.

pH   Symbol used to describe the relative acidity or alkalinity of a substance.

Pinch   (pinch back) Removal of growing points to induce bushy growth.

Pinnate   Leaf that has one central vein from which lesser veins arise, resembling a feather.

Pistillate   Female (seed-producing) flowers. *See also* monoecious and dioecious.

Pollination   Process by which the pollen of one flower is transferred to the stigma of the same or another flower.

Porosity   Refers to spaces between soil particles which allow passage of water and air.

Propagation   Method by which a plant is multiplied. This may be by seed, cuttings, grafting or division.

Pruning   Process by which a tree or shrub is trained by the removal of excess branches or of excessive growth.

Pseudobulb   Annual swollen shoots of certain orchids, as in *Cattleya*.

Pseudostem (pseudotrunk)   Furled leaves and their bases by upright growth form the 'stem' of plants such as Banana *Musa*: the true stem is found at the base of the plant.

Pup   (*see* Offset)

Relative humidity   Percentage saturation of the air at a particular temperature.

Resistance   Natural means by which a plant wards off pests and diseases.

Rhizome   Prostrate underground stem.

Rooting hormone   Preparation of one or more auxins in a powder, liquid or paste form: when applied, to an appropriate plant part, will accelerate the formation of roots.

Rosette   Whorl of leaves clustered about a shortened stem, as in *Gerbera*.

Scale insects   Sucking insect pests covered by a protective shell or scale.

Scion   Desirable plant that may be propagated by grafting onto a rootstock.

Seasonal dormancy   (*see* dormancy)

Self-heading   Refers to Philodendrons that form clumps and do not climb.

Semi-hardwood cutting   Piece of stem that has just begun to form woody tissue and bark.

Shadehouse Building or shelter that provides shade.

Slow-release fertilizer Product formulated to release mineral nutrients slowly over several months.

Softwood cutting Piece of stem yet to form woody tissue and bark.

Spadix Specialized cylindrical reproductive structure of aroid plants having separate staminate and pistillate flowers.

Spathe Protective and sometimes colourful bract associated with the spadix of aroid plants, as in *Anthurium*.

Species Group of closely related plants. Species are subdivisions of a genus. Each species will breed true from seed. The species name is the second of two botanical names; it is always written in lower case letters and *italicized*.

Spore Tiny reproductive body produced by ferns, mosses and their relatives. Fern spores are produced in a special structure (sorus) usually found on the underside of the leaves. Fungi and certain bacteria also produce spores.

Sport Spontaneous mutation in a plant bud leading to the production of leaves and/or flowers that are markedly different to those produced on other parts of the same plant.

Staminate Male (pollen-producing) flowers.

Standard Shrub or small tree trained, by pruning or created by grafting, to have all the branches clustered at the top of a single stem.

Stigma Female portion of a flower that receives pollen.

Stock (rootstock) Plant chosen to receive grafting material (scion or bud).

Subtropical Climatic zone next to the tropics: plants growing in this zone experience seasonal temperatures below 10°C (50°F), but rarely below freezing.

Sucker Shoot or offset produced by a plant from the base of a stem or from the roots.

Succulents Group of plants having special adaptations to reduce water loss during drought including closure of leaf pores during the day and storage of water.

Sympodial Orchid plants having annual shoots from a perennial rhizome, as in *Cattleya*.

Temperate A climatic zone: plants growing in this zone experience seasonal temperatures at or below 0°C (32°F).

Terete Reduced leaf surface area of certain plants such as *Vanda teres* with cylindrical leaves.

Terrestrial Plants such as certain orchids and bromeliads that grow rooted in the soil and not attached to trees as epiphytes (which see).

Tomentum Woolly covering of leaves and stems of certain plants.

Top cutting Cutting taken from the uppermost part of an orchid plant such as *Vanda*. A top cutting should have one or more adventitious roots.

Tuber Subterranean stem bearing nodes and buds, and acting as a food storage organ during dormancy.

Variegation Variable striped or blotched colouration of leaves most frequently seen as white on green.

Variety Horticulturally desirable plant often bearing a varietal name.

Vermiculite Expanded mica particles sometimes used as a soil substitute or in a soilless rooting medium.

Viviparous Plants giving rise to plantlets on their leaves as in certain tropical water-lilies and ferns.

Xerophyte Plant having adaptations allowing it to survive in dry environments.

Bibliography

Adams, C. Dennis, *Caribbean Flora*, Thomas Nelson and Sons Ltd., Sunbury-on-Thames, England (1976)

Agusiobo, O. N., *Vegetable Gardening*, Macmillan Publishers Ltd., London and Basingstoke, England (1984)

Berry, F. and Kress, W. J., *Heliconia: an identification guide*, Smithsonian Institution Press, Washington and London (1991)

Brown, B. F., *Florida's Beautiful Crotons*, Undersea Press, Eau Gallie, Florida, U.S.A. (1960)

Collett, J., *Bermuda: her plants and gardens 1609–1850*, Macmillan Publishers Ltd. and Bermuda National Trust, London and Basingstoke, England (1987)

Gooding, E. G. B., *The Plant Communities of Barbados*, Government Printing Office, Barbados (1974)

Handbook on Orchid Pests and Diseases, 1st revised edn, American Orchid Society, West Palm Beach, Florida, U.S.A. (1990)

Kenny, J., *Native Orchids of the Eastern Caribbean*, Macmillan Publishers Ltd., London and Basingstoke, England (1988)

Kochhar, S. L., *Tropical Crops*, Macmillan Publishers Ltd., London and Basingstoke, England (1981)

Light, M. H. S., Doing your part for Conservation – 3: Doing it! Sterile Technique, Flasking, The Works, *American Orchid Society Bulletin* vol. 59, no. 10, (1990) pp. 1014–22, American Orchid Society, West Palm Beach, Florida, U.S.A.

Macmillan Caribbean Certificate Atlas, revised edn, Macmillan Publishers Ltd., London and Basingstoke, England (1986)

Matthew, I. P., and Karikari, S. K., *Horticulture: principles and practices*, Macmillan Publishers Ltd., London and Basingstoke, England (1990)

Onwueme, I. C., *The Tropical Tuber Crops*, John Wiley & Sons, Chichester, England (1978)

Pal B. P. and Swarup, V., *Bougainvilleas*, Indian Council of Agricultural Research, New Delhi, India (1974)

Rowley, G., *The Illustrated Encyclopedia of Succulents*, Salamander Books Ltd., London, England (1978)

Rice, R. P., Rice, L. W., and Tindall, H. D., *Fruit and Vegetable Production in Warm Climates*, Macmillan Publishers Ltd., London and Basingstoke, England (1990)

Seaborn, B., *Bromeliads: tropical air plants*, Gick Publishing Inc., Laguna Hills, California, U.S.A. (1976)

Seddon, S. A. and Lennox, G. W., *Trees of the Caribbean*, Macmillan Publishers Ltd., London and Basingstoke, England (1980)

Uhl, N. W. and Dransfield, J., *Genera Palmarum*, The L. H. Bailey Hortum and The International Palm Society, Lawrence, Kansas, U.S.A. (1987)

Williams, R. O., *The Useful and Ornamental Plants of Trinidad and Tobago*, 4th edn, Government Printery, Trinidad and Tobago (1969)

Index of Common Names

B. coccinea, B. nitida,
B. ulmifolia 75
Bermuda Grass *Cynodon dactylon*
97, 132, 134
Betel Nut Palm *Areca catechu* 110
Bignonia *Bignonia* spp. 32
Macfadyena corymbosa 26, 60
Bindweed *Convolvulus* spp. 133
Bird of Paradise *Strelitzia* spp.
122
Bird Pepper *Capsicum frutescens*
38, 129
Bird's Nest Fern *Asplenium nidus,*
A. nidus crispafolium 89
Bishop's Cap Cactus *Astrophytum*
capricone, A. myriostigma,
A. ornatum 83
Black Pepper *Piper nigrum* 130,
Plate 19
Black Eyed Susan *Thunbergia*
alata 60, 124
Blechnum Fern *Blechnum*
occidentale 90
Bleeding Heart Vine *Clerodendron*
thompsonae 60, 123
Blue African Lily *Agapanthus*
africanus 24
Blue and White Pea *Clitoria*
ternatea 60, 60, 123
Bois Immortelle *Erythrina* spp.
56, 120, Plate 27
Boston Fern *Nephrolepis* spp.
89, 90
N. biserrata, N. biserrata var.
turcata, N. cordifolia,
N. cordifolia var. *duffii* 178
Bottle Palm *Hyophorbe*
lagenicaulis 107
Bottlebrush *Callistemon*
lanceolatus 56, 57
Bougainvillea *Bougainvillea* spp.
16, 17, 22, 26–29, 32, 47,
52, 53, 60, 77, 79–80, 140,
Plates 2, 27
B. glabra 53, 59, 79–80, Plate
2
B. peruviana 79–80, Plate 2
B. spectabilis 79–80
B. × *buttiana* 80
Bowstring Hemp *Sansevieria* spp.
16, 32, 117, 118, Plate 15
Bread and Cheese *Pithecellobium*
unguis-cati 52
Breadfruit *Artocarpus*
communis 17, 28, 30, 128
Breadfruit Fern *Polypodium*
aureum 90
Breadnut *Artocarpus*
communis 17, 28, 30, 128

Bridal Wreath *Spiraea cantoniensis*
25, 26
Bromeliad *Aechmea* spp. 157
Cryptanthus spp. 51, 82
Guzmania lingulata 82, Plate
3
Neoreglia carolinae 81, 82
Nidularium innocentii 82,
Plate 3
Tillandsia spp. 80, 81
T. baileyi, T. ionantha,
T. seleriana 81
Vriesia spp. 81
Broom Weed *Malvastrum*
spp. 133
Broom Weed *Sida* spp. 133
Broughtonia *Broughtonia*
sanguinea 66, 105
B. negrilensis 66
Bumblebee Orchid *Oncidium*
henekenii 101
Butter Bean *Phaseolus vulgaris*
139
Buttercup Tree *Cochlospermum*
vitifolium 26
Butterfly Ginger *Hedychium*
coronarium 92
Red *Hedychium greenii* 92
Butterfly Orchid *Oncidium*
papilio 101
Button Mangrove *Conocarpus*
spp. 12, Plate 21

C. erectus 65
Cabbage *Brassica oleracea*
143
Cacao *Theobroma cacao* 138
Cactus *Astrophytum capricorne*
83
A. ornatum 83
Cephalocereus spp. 41
Cereus spp. 52, 84, Plate 4
C. peruvianus 52
C. variabilis 84
Hylocereus spp. 23, 33, 84
H. cubensis 84
Myrtillocactus geometrizans
84
Opuntia argentina 84
O. dillenii 12, 39, 52, 84
O. microdasys, O. vestita,
O. rubescens, O. santa-rita
84
Parodia spp. 85
Pereskia aculeata 23, 82,
Plate 4
Pilocereus barbadensis 84
Pilosocereus nobilis 52
Rhipsalis spp. 84

Selenicereus spp. 84
Trichocereus macrogonus 84
Cactus Hedge *Euphorbia lactea*
52
Calabash *Cresentia cujete* 56,
84, 103, 121, Plate 24
Caladium *Caladium* spp. 30, 61,
70
Callathea *Calathea* spp. 29, 51
Calceolaria Cassia *Cassia*
spectabilis 26
Canary Bush *Galphimia glauca*
26
Canary Date Palm *Phoenix*
canariensis 110
Canna Lily *Canna* spp. 38, 75,
137, 139, Plate 6
C. indica 75
Cannonball Tree *Couroupita*
guianensis 56, 57, 120
Carex 'Aureo-marginate' *Carex*
siderostricta aureo-
marginata 190
Caribbean Royal Palm *Roystonea*
oleracea 16, 56, 107, 111
Caricature Plant *Graptophyllum*
pictum 58
Carnation *Dianthus* spp. 38, 67
Carpet Grass *Axonopus furcatus*
96
Cassia *Cassia* spp. 16, 26, 38,
68, 77, 120, 139
C. biflora, C. multijuga,
C. polyphylla 26
Appleblossom *C. javanica* 56,
120
Calceolaria *C. spectabilis* 26
Golden Shower *C. fistula* 57,
120
Horse *C. grandis* 57
Casuarina *Casuarina equisetifolia*
12, 36, 46, 56, 65, 77, 121
Cat's Claw Creeper *Macfadyena*
unguis-cati 23, 26, 60
Cattleya *Cattleya* spp. 102, 103,
104, 136, Plate 12
C. aurantiaca 23, 105
Cattleytonia *Cattleytonia* 105
Cauliflower *Brassica oleracea*
143
Cedros Bee Orchid *Oncidium*
lanceanum 101
Celosia *Celosia* spp. 38, 72
Centipede Grass *Eremochloa*
ophiuroides 66, 96
Chaconia *Warszewiczia coccinia*
56, 57, 120
Chalice Vine *Solandra guttata*
60, 123

Index of Common Names

Index of Botanical Names

General Index

air layering   35–36
altitude   3
annuals   22, 71–73
arch   59
Aroid   36, 69–71
auxin   21

Bamboo   16, 95–97
Banana   16, 28
bark   16, 25, 30
Bedding plants   20, 61, 71–76, 102
Begonia   74–75
Bonsai   25, 76–78
Bougainvillea   20, 22, 26, 29, 79–80
Bromeliad   21, 22, 80–82
bud   16–17, 24–25
budding   33–35

cambium   16, 33–35
Cactus   9, 16, 33, 66, 82–86
chlorosis   19
climate   1–3, 14
companion planting   143
compost   6–8
containers   20, 55–56, 62, 103
Croton   40, 58, 86–87
cuttings   16, 30–33, 53, 79

day length   23
design   44, 47–48, 58, 61, 64, 65–66
diseases
  bacteria   104, 135
  fungus   43, 104, 127, 130, 135–137, 139
  mycoplasma   127, 128, 137, 139
  virus   101, 137–138, 139

dormancy   17, 21, 93–94
drainage   9–10, 45, 49
drip irrigation   11
dry gardens   65–67
drought tolerance   9, 12, 46, 58, 82–85, 117

ethylene   21–22
Euphorbia   87–88

Ferns   14, 41, 51, 64, 88–91
fertilizer   7, 17–21, 39, 49, 53, 54, 62, 103
flower arrangement   67–68
flowering   22–24, 26
flowering shrubs   26, 58–59, 79–80, 87–88, 115–17
flowering trees   56–58, 120–121
foliar fertilizer   21
fragrance   47, 84
fruit   18, 20, 22, 127–129
fungicide   136

Gingers   16, 30, 90–95
grafting   33–35
Grass   16, 50–51, 66, 95–97
ground cover   50–51, 66

hedges   51–54, 113, 116, 122
Heliconia   16, 40, 98
herbicide   134
herbicide alternatives   134–135
Herbs and Spices   124, 130–131
Hibiscus   22, 99–100
hormones   21–22
housing   14
hydraulic ram   12

insecticides   43, 138–139, 141–143
irrigation   10–12, 45

Ixora   100

landscaping   44–67
lawns   18, 20, 49–50, 96, 140
leaves   16, 17, 32, 47, 56, 58
lighting   64
light and shade   14, 17, 46, 101–102
liming   4, 19

marcotting   see air layering
meristem   16, 33
mist propagation   29, 31
mulch   8–9, 135

nematodes   13, 99, 128, 140–141
nematicides   99

Orchids   14, 16, 29, 41–42, 100–106, 137

Palms   16, 22, 36, 54–58, 106–113
  for containers   55, 107–109
  for hedging   58, 113
  for shade   109–110
  for sun   110–112
  for wet areas   112–113
paths   44, 48, 76
perennials   22, 74–76
pesticides and alternatives   141–142
pesticide resistance   142
pests
  insects   13, 43, 49, 75, 89, 104, 138–140
  slugs   43, 104, 140
  snails   43, 140
  mites   13, 140
pollination   75, 80, 87, 126

172